Mary B. Ke[illegible]
323 Nottingham

Man, the Unknown

Man
The Unknown

BY

ALEXIS CARREL

Published by arrangement with Harper & Brothers

HALCYON HOUSE · NEW YORK

MAN, THE UNKNOWN

HALCYON HOUSE EDITION, OCTOBER, 1938
FIFTY-NINTH EDITION, OCTOBER, 1938
SIXTIETH EDITION, OCTOBER, 1938

HALCYON HOUSE *editions are published and distributed by Blue Ribbon Books, Inc., 386 Fourth Avenue, New York City*

PRINTED AND BOUND BY THE CORNWALL PRESS, INC., FOR
BLUE RIBBON BOOKS, INC., 386 FOURTH AVENUE, NEW YORK CITY

To My Friends

FREDERIC R. COUDERT

CORNELIUS CLIFFORD

and

BORIS A. BAKHMETEFF

this book is

dedicated

*

Contents

Preface

THE AUTHOR of this book is not a philosopher. He is only a man of science. He spends a large part of his time in a laboratory studying living matter. And another part in the world, watching human beings and trying to understand them. He does not pretend to deal with things that lie outside the field of scientific observation.

In this book he has endeavored to describe the known, and to separate it clearly from the plausible. Also to recognize the existence of the unknown and the unknowable. He has considered man as the sum of the observations and experiences of all times and of all countries. But what he describes he has either seen with his own eyes or learned directly from those with whom he associates. It is his good fortune to be in a position to study, without making any effort or deserving any credit, the phenomena of life in their bewildering complexity. He has observed practically every form of human activity. He is acquainted with the poor and the rich, the sound and the diseased, the learned and the ignorant, the weak-minded, the insane, the shrewd, the criminal, etc. He knows farmers, proletarians, clerks, shopkeepers, financiers, manufacturers, politicians, statesmen, soldiers, professors, school-teachers, clergymen, peasants, bourgeois, and aristocrats. The circumstances of his life have led him across the path of philosophers, artists, poets, and scientists. And also of geniuses, heroes, and saints. At the same time, he has studied the hidden mechanisms which, in the depth of the tissues and in the immensity of the brain, are the substratum of organic and mental phenomena.

He is indebted to the techniques of modern civilization for the possibility of witnessing such a gigantic spectacle. These techniques have enabled him simultaneously to give his attention to several subjects. He lives in the New World, and also in the Old. He has the privilege of spending most of his time in the Rockefeller Institute for Medical Research, as one of the scientists brought together in that Institute by Simon Flexner. There he has contemplated the phenomena of life while they were analyzed by incomparable experts such as Meltzer, Jacques Loeb, Noguchi, and many others. Owing to the genius of Flexner, the study of living things has been undertaken with a broadness of vision so far unequaled. Matter is investigated in those laboratories at every level of its organization, of its ascension toward the making of man. With the help of X-rays, physicists are unveiling the architectonic of the molecules of the simpler substances of our tissues—that is, the spatial relations of the atoms constituting those molecules. Chemists and physical chemists devote themselves to the analysis of the more complex substances encountered within the body, such as the hemoglobin of the blood, the proteins of the tissues and the humors, and the ferments responsible for the unceasing splitting and building up of those enormous aggregates of atoms. Instead of directing their attention to the molecular edifices themselves, other chemists consider the relations of those edifices with one another when they enter the fluids of the body. In short, the physicochemical equilibria that maintain constant the composition of blood serum in spite of the perpetual changes of the tissues. Thus are brought to light the chemical aspects of physiological phenomena. Several groups of physiologists, with the aid of the most varied techniques, are studying the larger structures resulting from the aggregation and organization of molecules, the cells of the tissues and of the blood—that is, living matter itself. They examine those cells, their ways of association, and the laws governing their relations with their surroundings; the whole made up of the organs and humors; the influence of the cosmic environment on this whole; and the effects of chemical substances on tissues and consciousness. Other specialists devote themselves to the investigation of those small beings, the viruses and bacteria, whose presence in our tissues is responsible for infectious diseases; of the marvelous methods used by the organism in its fight against them; of the degenerative diseases, such as cancer, heart lesions, nephritis. Finally, the momentous problem of individuality and of its chemical basis is being successfully attacked. The writer has had the exceptional opportunity of listening to great men specialized in these researches, and of following the results of their experiments. Thus, the effort of inert matter toward organization, the properties of living beings, and the harmony of our body and our mind appeared to him in their beauty. In addition, he himself has studied the most diverse subjects, from surgery to cell physiology and to metapsychics. This was made possible by facilities which, for the first time, were put at the disposal of science for the performance of its task. It seems that the subtle inspiration of Welch and the practical idealism of Frederick T. Gates caused new conceptions of biology and new formulas for research to spring from Flexner's mind. To the pure spirit of science Flexner gave the help of new methods designed to save the workers' time, to facilitate their free coöperation, and to create better experimental techniques. Owing to these innovations, one can not only undertake extensive researches of one's own, but also acquire a first-hand knowledge of subjects whose mastery in former days necessitated the whole lifetime of several scientists.

We now possess such a large amount of information on human beings that its very immensity prevents us from using it properly. In order to be of service, our knowledge must be synthetic and concise. This book, therefore, was not intended to be a treatise on Man. For such a treatise would run into dozens of volumes. The author's intention was merely to build up an intelligible synthesis of the data which we possess about ourselves. He has attempted to describe a large number of fundamental facts in a very simple manner, and still not to be elementary. Not to indulge in scientific popularization or to offer to the public a weak and childish aspect of reality. He has written for the scholar as well as for the layman.

He fully understands the difficulties inherent in the temerity of his undertaking. He has tried to confine all knowledge of man within the pages of a small book. Of course, he has not succeeded. He will not satisfy the specialists, because they know far more than he does, and they will regard him as superficial. Neither will he please the general public, for this volume contains too many technical details. However, in order to acquire a synthetic knowledge of ourselves, it was indispensable to summarize the data of several sciences, and also to depict with bold and rapid strokes the physical, chemical, and physiological mechanisms hidden under the harmony of our acts and our thoughts.

We must realize that an attempt, however awkward and though partly a failure, is better than no attempt at all.

The necessity of compressing a large amount of information into a short space has important drawbacks. It gives a dogmatic appearance to propositions which are nothing but conclusions of observations and experiments. Subjects that have engrossed physiologists, hygienists, physicians, educators, economists, sociologists for years have often had to be described in a few lines or a few words. Almost every sentence of this book is the expression of the long labor of a scientist, of his patient researches, sometimes of his entire lifetime spent in the study of a single problem. For the sake of conciseness, the writer has been obliged briefly to summarize gigantic masses of observations. Thus, descriptions of facts have been given the form of assertions. To a similar cause may be attributed a seeming lack of accuracy. Most organic and mental phenomena have been treated in a diagrammatic manner. Therefore, things that markedly differ appear to be grouped together. As, at a distance, houses, rocks, and trees are not distinguishable from one another. It must not be forgotten that in this book the expression of reality is only approximately accurate. A brief description of an immense subject involves inevitable defects. But the sketch of a landscape should not be expected to contain all the details of a photograph.

Before beginning this work the author realized its difficulty, its almost impossibility. He undertook it merely because somebody had to undertake it. Because men cannot follow modern civilization along its present course, because they are degenerating. They have been fascinated by the beauty of the sciences of inert matter. They have not understood that their body and consciousness are subjected to natural laws, more obscure than, but as inexorable as, the laws of the sidereal world. Neither have they understood that they cannot transgress these laws without being punished. They must, therefore, learn the necessary relations of the cosmic universe, of their fellow men, and of their inner selves, and also those of their tissues and their mind. Indeed, man stands above all things. Should he degenerate, the beauty of civilization, and even the grandeur of the physical universe, would vanish. For these reasons this book was written. It was not written in the peace of the country, but in the confusion, the noise, and the weariness of New York. The author has been urged to carry out this work by his friends, philosophers, scientists, jurists, economists, with whom he has for years discussed the great problems of our time. From Frederic R. Coudert, whose penetrating vision reaches, beyond the horizons of America, those of Europe, came the impulse responsible for this book. Indeed, the majority of the nations follow the lead of North America. Those countries that have blindly adopted the spirit and the techniques of industrial civilization, Russia as well as England, France, and Germany, are exposed to the same dangers as the United States. Humanity's attention must turn from the machines and the world of inanimate matter to the body and the soul of man, to the organic and mental processes which have created the machines and the universe of Newton and Einstein.

The only claim of this book is to put at everyone's disposal an ensemble of scientific data concerning the human beings of our time. We are beginning to realize the weakness of our civilization. Many want to shake off the dogmas imposed upon them by modern society. This book has been written for them, and also for those who are bold enough to understand the necessity, not only of mental, political, and social changes, but of the overthrow of industrial civilization and of the advent of another conception of human progress. This book is, therefore, dedicated to all whose everyday task is the rearing of children, the formation or the guidance of the individual. To school-teachers, hygienists, physicians, clergymen, social workers, professors, judges, army officers, engineers, economists, politicians, industrial leaders, etc. Also to those who are interested in the mere knowledge of our body and our mind. In short, to every man and every woman. It is offered to all as a simple account of facts revealed about human beings by scientific observation.

Man, the Unknown

Chapter I

THE NEED OF A BETTER KNOWLEDGE OF MAN

1. The sciences of life have progressed more slowly than those of inert matter. Our ignorance of ourselves. 2. This ignorance is due to our ancestors' mode of existence, to the complexity of man, and to the structure of our mind. 3. How mechanical, physical, and chemical sciences have modified our environment. 4. The results of such a change. 5. This change is harmful, having been made without due consideration of our nature. 6. Need of a more complete knowledge of ourselves.

I

THERE is a strange disparity between the sciences of inert matter and those of life. Astronomy, mechanics, and physics are based on concepts which can be expressed, tersely and elegantly, in mathematical language. They have built up a universe as harmonious as the monuments of ancient Greece. They weave about it a magnificent texture of calculations and hypotheses. They search for reality beyond the realm of common thought up to unutterable abstractions consisting only of equations of symbols. Such is not the position of biological sciences. Those who investigate the phenomena of life are as if lost in an inextricable jungle, in the midst of a magic forest, whose countless trees unceasingly change their place and their shape. They are crushed under a mass of facts, which they can describe but are incapable of defining in algebraic equations. From the things encountered in the material world, whether atoms or stars, rocks or clouds, steel or water, certain qualities, such as weight and spatial dimensions, have been abstracted. These abstractions, and not the concrete facts, are the matter of scientific reasoning. The observation of objects constitutes only a lower form of science, the descriptive form. Descriptive science classifies phenomena. But the unchanging relations between variable quantities—that is, the natural laws, only appear when science becomes more abstract. It is because physics and chemistry are abstract and quantitative that they had such great and rapid success. Although they do not pretend to unveil the ultimate nature of things, they give us the power to predict future events, and often to determine at will their occurrence. In learning the secret of the constitution and of the properties of matter, we have gained the mastery of almost everything which exists on the surface of the earth, excepting ourselves.

The science of the living beings in general, and especially of the human individual, has not made such great progress. It still remains in the descriptive state. Man is an indivisible whole of extreme complexity. No simple representation of him can be obtained. There is no method capable of apprehending him simultaneously in his entirety, his parts, and his relations with the outer world. In order to analyze ourselves, we are obliged to seek the help of various techniques and, therefore, to utilize several sciences. Naturally, all these sciences arrive at a different conception of their common object. They abstract only from man what is attainable by their special methods. And those abstractions, after they have been added together, are still less rich than the concrete fact. They leave behind them a residue, too important to be neglected. Anatomy, chemistry, physiology, psychology, pedagogy, history, sociology, political economy do not exhaust their subject. Man, as known to the specialists, is far from being the concrete man, the real man. He is nothing but a schema, consisting of other schemata built up by the techniques of each science. He is, at the same time, the corpse dissected by the anatomists, the consciousness observed by the psychologists and the great teachers of the spiritual life, and the personality which introspection shows to everyone as lying in the depth of himself. He is the chemical substances constituting the tissues and humors of the body. He is the amazing community of cells and nutrient fluids whose organic laws are studied by the physiologists. He is the compound of tissues and consciousness that hygienists and educators endeavor to lead to its optimum development while it extends into time. He is the *homo œconomicus* who must ceaselessly consume manufactured products in order that the machines, of which he is made a slave, may be kept at work. But he is also the poet, the hero, and the saint. He is not only the prodigiously complex being analyzed by our scientific techniques, but also the tendencies, the conjectures, the aspirations of humanity. Our conceptions of him are imbued with metaphysics. They are founded on so many and such imprecise data that the temptation is great to choose among them those which please us. Therefore, our idea of man varies according to our feelings and our beliefs. A materialist and a spiritualist accept the same definition of a crystal of sodium chloride. But they do not agree with one another upon that of the human being. A mechanistic physiologist and a vitalistic physiologist do not consider the organism in the same light. The living being of Jacques Loeb differs profoundly from that of Hans Driesch. Indeed, mankind has made a gigantic effort to know itself. Although we possess the treasure of the observations accumulated by the scientists, the philosophers, the poets, and the great mystics of all times, we have grasped only certain aspects of ourselves. We do not apprehend man as a whole. We know him as composed of distinct parts. And even these parts are created by our methods. Each one of us is made up of a procession of phantoms, in the midst of which strides an unknowable reality.

In fact, our ignorance is profound. Most of the questions put to themselves by those who study human beings remain without answer. Immense regions of our inner world are still unknown. How do the molecules of chemical substances associate in order to form the complex and temporary organs of the cell? How do the genes contained in the nucleus of a fertilized ovum determine the characteristics of the individual deriving from that ovum? How do cells organize themselves by their own efforts into societies, such as the tissues and the organs? Like the ants and the bees, they have advance knowledge of the part they are destined to play in the life of the community. And hidden mechanisms enable them to build up an organism both complex and simple. What is the nature of our duration, of psychological time, and of physiological time? We know that we are a compound of tissues, organs, fluids, and consciousness. But the relations between consciousness and cerebrum are still a mystery. We lack almost entirely a knowledge of the physiology of nervous cells. To what extent does will power modify the organism? How is the mind influenced by the state of the organs? In what manner can the organic and mental characteristics, which each individual inherits, be changed by the mode of life, the chemical substances contained in food, the climate, and the physiological and moral disciplines?

We are very far from knowing what relations exist between skeleton, muscles, and organs, and mental and spiritual activities. We are ignorant of the factors that bring about nervous equilibrium and resistance to fatigue and to diseases. We do not know how moral sense, judgment, and audacity could be augmented. What is the relative importance of intellectual, moral, and mystical activities? What is the significance of esthetic and religious sense? What form of energy is responsible for telepathic communications? Without any doubt, certain physiological and mental factors determine happiness or misery, success or failure. But we do not know what they are. We cannot artificially give to any individual the aptitude for happiness. As yet, we do not know what environment is the most favorable for the optimum development of civilized man. Is it possible to suppress struggle, effort, and suffering from our physiological and spiritual formation? How can we prevent the degeneracy of man in modern civilization? Many other questions could be asked on subjects which are to us of the utmost interest. They would also remain unanswered. It is quite evident that the accomplishments of all the sciences having man as an object remain insufficient, and that our knowledge of ourselves is still most rudimentary.

2

Our ignorance may be attributed, at the same time, to the mode of existence of our ancestors, to the complexity of our nature, and to the structure of our mind. Before all, man had to live. And that need demanded the conquest of the outer world. It was imperative to secure food and shelter, to fight wild animals and other men. For immense periods, our forefathers had neither the leisure nor the inclination to study themselves. They employed their intelligence in other ways, such as manufacturing weapons and tools, discovering fire, training cattle and horses, inventing the wheel, the culture of cereals, etc., etc. Long before becoming interested in the constitution of their body and their mind, they meditated on the sun, the moon, the stars, the tides, and the passing of the seasons. Astronomy was already far advanced at an epoch when physiology was totally unknown. Galileo reduced the earth, center of the world, to the rank of a humble satellite of the sun, while his contemporaries had not even the most elementary notion of the structure and the functions of brain, liver, or thyroid gland. As, under the natural conditions of life, the human organism works satisfactorily and needs no attention, science progressed in the direction in which it was led by human curiosity—that is, toward the outer world.

From time to time, among the billions of human beings who have successively inhabited the earth, a few were born endowed with rare and marvelous powers, the intuition of unknown things, the imagination that creates new worlds, and the faculty of discovering the hidden relations existing between certain phenomena. These men explored the physical universe. This universe is of a simple constitution. Therefore, it rapidly gave in to the attack of the scientists and yielded the secret of certain of its laws. And the knowledge of these laws enabled us to utilize the world of matter for our own profit. The practical applications of scientific discoveries are lucrative for those who promote them. They facilitate the existence of all. They please the public, whose comfort they augment. Everyone became, of course, much more interested in the inventions that lessen human effort, lighten the burden of the toiler, accelerate the rapidity of communications, and soften the harshness of life, than in the discoveries that throw some light on the intricate problems relating to the constitution of our body and of our consciousness. The conquest of the material world, which has ceaselessly absorbed the attention and the will of men, caused the organic and the spiritual world to fall into almost complete oblivion. In fact, the knowledge of our surroundings was indispensable, but that of our own nature appeared to be much less immediately useful. However, disease, pain, death, and more or less obscure aspirations toward a hidden power transcending the visible universe, drew the attention of men, in some measure, to the inner world of their body and their mind. At first, medicine contented itself with the practical problem of relieving the sick by empiric recipes. It realized only in recent times that the most effective method of preventing or curing illness is to acquire a complete understanding of the normal and diseased body—that is, to construct the sciences that are called anatomy, biological chemistry, physiology, and pathology. However, the mystery of our existence, the moral sufferings, the craving for the unknown, and the metapsychical phenomena appeared to our ancestors as more important than bodily pain and diseases. The study of spiritual life and of philosophy attracted greater men than the study of medicine. The laws of mysticity became known before those of physiology. But such laws were brought to light only when mankind had acquired sufficient leisure to turn a little of his attention to other things than the conquest of the outer world.

There is another reason for the slow progress of the knowledge of ourselves. Our mind is so constructed as to delight in contemplating simple facts. We feel a kind of repugnance in attacking such a complex problem as that of the constitution of living beings and of man. The intellect, as Bergson wrote, is characterized by a natural inability to comprehend life. On the contrary, we love to discover in the cosmos the geometrical forms that exist in the depths of our consciousness. The exactitude of the proportions of our monuments and the precision of our machines express a fundamental character of our mind. Geometry does not exist in the earthly world. It has originated in ourselves. The methods of nature are never so precise as those of man. We do not find in the universe the clearness and accuracy of our thought. We attempt, therefore, to abstract from the complexity of phenomena some simple systems whose components bear to one another certain relations susceptible of being described mathematically. This power of abstraction of the human intellect is responsible for the amazing progress of physics and chemistry. A similar success has rewarded the physicochemical study of living beings. The laws of chemistry and of physics are identical in the world of living things and in that of inanimate matter, as Claude Bernard thought long ago. This fact explains why modern physiology has discovered, for example, that the constancy of the alkalinity of the blood and of the water of the ocean is expressed by identical laws, that the energy spent by the contracting muscle is supplied by the fermentation of sugar, etc. The physicochemical aspects of human beings are almost as easy to investigate as those of the other objects of the terrestrial world. Such is the task which general physiology succeeds in accomplishing.

The study of the truly physiological phenomena—that is, of those resulting from the organization of living matter—meets with more important obstacles. On account of the extreme smallness of the things to be analyzed, it is impossible to use the ordinary techniques of physics and of chemistry. What method could bring to light the chemical constitution of the nucleus of the sexual cells, of its chromosomes, and of the genes that compose these chromosomes? Nevertheless, those very minute aggregates of chemicals are of capital importance, because they contain the future of the individual and of the race. The fragility of certain tissues, such as the nervous substance, is so great that to study them in the living state is almost impossible. We do not possess any technique capable of penetrating the mysteries of the brain, and of the harmonious association of its cells. Our mind, which loves the simple beauty of mathematical formulas, is bewildered when it contemplates the stupendous mass of cells, humors, and consciousness which make up the individual. We try, therefore, to apply to this compound the concepts that have proved useful in the realm of physics, chemistry, and mechanics, and in the philosophical and religious disciplines. Such an attempt does not meet with much success, because we can be reduced neither to a physicochemical system nor to a spiritual entity. Of course, the science of man has to use the concepts of all the other sciences. But it must also develop its own. For it is as fundamental as the sciences of the molecules, the atoms, and the electrons.

In short, the slow progress of the knowledge of the human being, as compared with the splendid ascension of physics, astronomy, chemistry, and mechanics, is due to our ancestors' lack of leisure, to the complexity of the subject, and to the structure of our mind. Those obstacles are fundamental. There is no hope of eliminating them. They will always have to be overcome at the cost of strenuous effort. The knowledge of ourselves will never attain the elegant simplicity, the abstractness, and the beauty of physics. The factors that have retarded its development are not likely to vanish. We must realize clearly that the science of man is the most difficult of all sciences.

3

The environment which has molded the body and the soul of our ancestors during many millenniums has now been replaced by another. This silent revolution has taken place almost without our noticing it. We have not realized its importance. Nevertheless, it is one of the most dramatic events in the history of humanity. For any modification in their surroundings inevitably and profoundly disturbs all living beings. We must, therefore, ascertain the extent of the transformations imposed by science upon the ancestral mode of life, and consequently upon ourselves.

Since the advent of industry, a large part of the population has been compelled to live in restricted areas. The workmen are herded together, either in the suburbs of the large cities or in villages built for them. They are occupied in the factories during fixed hours, doing easy, monotonous, and well-paid work. The cities are also inhabited by office workers, employees of stores, banks, and public administrations, physicians, lawyers, school-teachers, and the multitude of those who, directly or indirectly, draw their livelihood from commerce and industry. Factories and offices are large, well lighted, clean. Their temperature is uniform. Modern heating and refrigerating apparatuses raise the temperature during the winter and lower it during the summer. The skyscrapers of the great cities have transformed the streets into gloomy canyons. But inside of the buildings, the light of the sun is replaced by electric bulbs rich in ultra-violet rays. Instead of the air of the street, polluted by gasoline fumes, the offices and workshops receive pure air drawn in from the upper atmosphere by ventilators on the roof. The dwellers of the modern city are protected against all inclemencies of the weather. But they are no longer able to live as did our ancestors, near their workshops, their stores, or their offices. The wealthier inhabit the gigantic buildings of the main avenues. At the top of dizzy towers, the kings of the business world possess delightful homes, surrounded by trees, grass, and flowers. They live there, as sheltered from noise, dust, and all disturbances, as if they dwelt on the summit of a mountain. They are more completely isolated from the common herd than were the feudal lords behind the walls and the moats of their fortified castles. The less wealthy, even those with quite modest means, lodge in apartments whose comfort surpasses that which surrounded Louis XIV or Frederick the Great. Many have their residence far from the city. Each evening, express trains transport innumerable crowds to suburbs, where broad roads running between green strips of grass and rows of trees are bordered with pretty and comfortable houses. The workmen and the humblest employees live in dwellings better appointed than those of the rich of former times. The heating apparatuses that automatically regulate the temperature of the houses, the bathrooms, the refrigerators, the electric stoves, the domestic machinery for preparing food and cleaning rooms, and the garages for the automobiles, give to the abode of everybody, not only in the city and the suburbs, but also in the country, a degree of comfort which previously was found only in that of very few privileged individuals.

Simultaneously with the habitat, the mode of life has been transformed. This transformation is due chiefly to the increase in the rapidity of communications. Indeed, it is evident that modern trains and steamers, airplanes, automobiles, telegraph, telephone, and wireless have modified the relations of men and of nations all over the world. Each individual does a great many more things than formerly. He takes part in a much larger number of events. Every day he comes into contact with more people. Quiet and unemployed moments are exceptional in his existence. The narrow groups of the family and of the parish have been dissolved. Intimacy no longer exists. For the life of the small group has been substituted that of the herd. Solitude is looked upon as a punishment or as a rare luxury. The frequent attendance at cinema, theatrical, or athletic performances, the clubs, the meetings of all sorts, the gigantic universities, factories, department stores, and hotels have engendered in all the habit of living in common. The telephone, the radio, and the gramophone records carry unceasingly the vulgarity of the crowd, as well as its pleasures and its psychology, into everyone's house, even in the most isolated and remote villages. Each individual is always in direct or indirect communication with other human beings, and keeps himself constantly informed about the small or important events taking place in his town, or his city, or at the other end of the world. One hears the chimes of Westminster in the most retired houses of the French countryside. Any farmer in Vermont, if it pleases him to do so, may listen to orators speaking in Berlin, London, or Paris.

Everywhere, in the cities, as well as in the country, in private houses as in factories, in the workshop, on the roads, in the fields, and on the farms, machines have decreased the intensity of human effort. Today, it is not necessary to walk. Elevators have replaced stairs. Everybody rides in buses, motors, or street cars, even when the distance to be covered is very short. Natural bodily exercises, such as walking and running over rough ground, mountain-climbing, tilling the land by hand, clearing forests with the ax, working while exposed to rain, sun, wind, cold, or heat, have given place to well-regulated sports that involve almost no risk, and to machines that abolish muscular effort. Everywhere there are tennis-courts, golf-links, artificial skating-rinks, heated swimming-pools, and sheltered arenas where athletes train and fight while protected against the inclemencies of the weather. In this manner all can develop their muscles without being subjected to the fatigue and the hardships involved in the exercises pertaining to a more primitive form of life.

The aliments of our ancestors, which consisted chiefly of coarse flour, meat, and alcoholic drinks, have been replaced by much more delicate and varied food. Beef and mutton are no longer the staple foods. The principal elements of modern diet are milk, cream, butter, cereals refined by the elimination of the shells of the grain, fruits of tropical as well as of temperate countries, fresh or canned vegetables, salads, large quantities of sugar in the form of pies, candies, and puddings. Alcohol alone has kept its place. The food of children has undergone a profound change. It is now very artificial and abundant. The same may be said of the diet of adults. The regularity of the working-hours in offices and factories has entailed that of the meals. Owing to the wealth which was general until a few years ago, and to the decline in the religious spirit and in the observance of ritualistic fasts, human beings have never been fed so punctually and uninterruptedly.

It is also to the wealth of the post-war period that the enormous diffusion of education is due. Everywhere, schools, colleges, and universities have been erected, and immediately invaded by vast crowds of students. Youth has understood the rôle of science in the modern world. "Knowledge is power," wrote Bacon. All institutions of learning are devoted to the intellectual development of children and young people. At the same time, they give great attention to their physical condition. It is obvious that the main interest of these educational establishments consists in the promotion of mental and muscular strength. Science has demonstrated its usefulness in such an evident manner that it has obtained the first place in the curriculum. A great many young men and women submit themselves to its disciplines. Scientific institutions, universities, and industrial corporations have built so many laboratories that every scientific worker has a chance to make use of his particular knowledge.

The mode of life of modern men is profoundly influenced

by hygiene and medicine and the principles resulting from the discoveries of Pasteur. The promulgation of the Pastorian doctrines has been an event of the highest importance to humanity. Their application rapidly led to the suppression of the great infectious diseases which periodically ravaged the civilized world, and of those endemic in each country. The necessity for cleanliness was demonstrated. Infantile mortality at once decreased. The average duration of life has augmented to an amazing extent and has reached fifty-nine years in the United States, and sixty-five years in New Zealand. People do not live longer, but more people live to be old. Hygiene has considerably increased the quantity of human beings. At the same time, medicine, by a better conception of the nature of diseases and a judicious application of surgical techniques, has extended its beneficent influence to the weak, the defective, those predisposed to microbial infections, to all who formerly could not endure the conditions of a rougher life. It has permitted civilization to multiply its human capital enormously. It has also given to each individual much greater security against pain and disease.

The intellectual and moral surroundings in which we are immersed have equally been molded by science. There is a profound difference between the world that permeates the mind of modern men and the world wherein our ancestors lived. Before the intellectual victories that have brought us wealth and comfort, moral values have naturally given ground. Reason has swept away religious beliefs. The knowledge of the natural laws, and the power given us by this knowledge over the material world, and also over human beings, alone are of importance. Banks, universities, laboratories, medical schools, hospitals, have become as beautiful as the Greek temples, the Gothic cathedrals, and the palaces of the Popes. Until the recent economic crisis, bank or railroad presidents were the ideals of youth. The president of a great university still occupies a very high place in the esteem of the public because he dispenses science. And science is the mother of wealth, comfort, and health. However, the intellectual atmosphere, in which modern men live, rapidly changes. Financial magnates, professors, scientists, and economic experts are losing their hold over the public. The people of today are sufficiently educated to read newspapers and magazines, to listen to the speeches broadcasted by politicians, business men, charlatans, and apostles. They are saturated with commercial, political, or social propaganda, whose techniques are becoming more and more perfect. At the same time they read articles and books wherein science and philosophy are popularized. Our universe, through the great discoveries of physics and astronomy, has acquired a marvelous grandeur. Each individual is able, if it so pleases him, to hear about the theories of Einstein, or to read the books of Eddington and of Jeans, the articles of Shapley and of Millikan. The public is as interested in the cosmic rays as in cinema stars and baseball-players. Everyone is aware that space is curved, that the world is composed of blind and unknown forces, that we are nothing but infinitely small particles on the surface of a grain of dust lost in the immensity of the cosmos, and that this cosmos is totally deprived of life and consciousness. Our universe is exclusively mechanical. It cannot be otherwise, since it has been created from an unknown substratum by the techniques of physics and astronomy. Just as are all the surroundings of modern men, it is the expression of the amazing development of the sciences of inert matter.

4

The profound changes imposed on the habits of men by the applications of science have occurred recently. In fact, we are still in the midst of the industrial revolution. It is difficult, therefore, to know exactly how the substitution of an artificial mode of existence for the natural one and a complete modification of their environment have acted upon civilized human beings. There is, however, no doubt that such an action has taken place. For every living thing depends intimately on its surroundings, and adapts itself to any modification of these surroundings by an appropriate change. We must, therefore, ascertain in what manner we have been influenced by the mode of life, the customs, the diet, the education, and the intellectual and moral habits imposed on us by modern civilization. Have we benefited by such progress? This momentous question can be answered only after a careful examination of the state of the nations which were the first to profit by the application of scientific discoveries.

It is evident that men have joyfully welcomed modern civilization. They have abandoned the countryside and flocked to the cities and the factories. They eagerly adopt the mode of life and the ways of acting and of thinking of the new era. They lay aside their old habits without hesitation, because these habits demand a greater effort. It is less fatiguing to work in a factory or an office than on a farm. But even in the country, new techniques have relieved the harshness of existence. Modern houses make life easier for everybody. By their comfort, their warmth, and their pleasant lighting, they give their inmates a feeling of rest and contentment. Their up-to-date appointments considerably decrease the labor that, in bygone days, housekeeping demanded from women. Besides the lessening of muscular effort and the possession of comfort, human beings have accepted cheerfully the privilege of never being alone, of enjoying the innumerable distractions of the city, of living among huge crowds, of never thinking. They also appreciate being released, through a purely intellectual education, from the moral restraint imposed upon them by Puritan discipline and religious principles. In truth, modern life has set them free. It incites them to acquire wealth by any and every possible means, provided that these means do not lead them to jail. It opens to them all the countries of the earth. It has liberated them from all superstitions. It allows them the frequent excitation and the easy satisfaction of their sexual appetites. It does away with constraint, discipline, effort, everything that is inconvenient and laborious. The people, especially those belonging to the lower classes, are happier from a material standpoint than in former times. However, some of them progressively cease to appreciate the distractions and the vulgar pleasures of modern life. Occasionally, their health does not permit them to continue indefinitely the alimentary, alcoholic, and sexual excesses to which they are led by the suppression of all discipline. Besides, they are haunted by the fear of losing their employment, their means of subsistence, their savings, their fortune. They are unable to satisfy the need for security that exists in the depth of each of us. In spite of social insurances, they feel uneasy about their future. Those who are capable of thinking become discontented.

It is certain, nevertheless, that health is improving. Not only has mortality decreased, but each individual is handsomer, larger, and stronger. Today, children are much taller than their parents. An abundance of good food and physical exercises have augmented the size of the body and its muscular strength. Often the best athletes at the international games come from the United States. In the athletic teams of the American universities, there are many individuals who are really magnificent specimens of human beings. Under the present educational conditions, bones and muscles develop perfectly. America has succeeded in reproducing the most admirable forms of ancient beauty. However, the longevity of the men proficient in all kinds of sports and enjoying every advantage of modern life is not greater than that of their ancestors. It may even be less. Their resistance to fatigue and worry seems to have decreased. It appears that the individuals accustomed to natural bodily exercise, to hardships, and to the inclemencies of the weather, as were their fathers, are capable of harder and more sustained efforts than our athletes. We know that the products of modern education need much sleep, good food, and regular habits. Their nervous system is delicate. They do not endure the mode of existence in the large cities, the confinement in offices, the worries of business, and even the everyday difficulties and sufferings of life. They easily break down. Perhaps the triumphs of hygiene, medicine, and modern education are not so advantageous as we are led to believe.

We should also ask ourselves whether there are no inconveniences attached to the great decrease in the death rate during infancy and youth. In fact, the weak are saved as well as the strong. Natural selection no longer plays its part. No one knows what will be the future of a race so well protected by medical sciences. But we are confronted with much graver problems, which demand immediate solution. While infantile diarrhea, tuberculosis, diphtheria, typhoid fever, etc., are being eliminated, they are replaced by degenerative diseases. There are also a large number of affections of the nervous system and of the mind. In certain states the multitude of the insane confined in the asylums exceeds that of the patients kept in all other hospitals. Like insanity, nervous disorders and intellectual weakness seem to have become more frequent. They are the most active factors of individual misery and of the destruction of families. Mental deterioration is more dangerous for civilization than the infectious diseases to which hygienists and physicians have so far exclusively devoted their attention.

In spite of the immense sums of money expended on the education of the children and the young people of the United States, the intellectual élite does not seem to have increased. The average man and woman are, without any doubt, better educated and, superficially at least, more refined. The taste for reading is greater. More reviews and books are bought by the public than in former times. The number of people who are interested in science, letters, and art has grown. But most of them are chiefly attracted by the lowest form of literature and by the imitations of science and of art. It seems that the excellent hygienic conditions in which children are reared, and the care lavished upon them in school, have not raised their intellectual and moral standards. There may possibly be some antagonism between their physical development and their mental size. After all, we do not know whether a larger stature in a given race expresses a state of progress, as is assumed today, or of degeneracy. There is no doubt that children are much happier in the schools where compulsion has been suppressed, where they are allowed exclusively to study the subjects in which they are interested, where intellectual effort and voluntary attention are not exacted. What are the results of such an education? In modern civilization, the individual is characterized chiefly by a fairly great activity, entirely directed toward the practical side of life, by much ignorance, by a certain shrewdness, and by a kind of mental weakness which leaves him under the influence of the environment wherein he happens to be placed. It appears that intelligence itself gives way when character weakens. For this reason, perhaps, this quality, characteristic of France in former times, has so markedly failed in that country. In the United States, the intellectual standard remains low, in spite of the increasing number of schools and universities.

Modern civilization seems to be incapable of producing people endowed with imagination, intelligence, and courage. In practically every country there is a decrease in the intellectual and moral caliber of those who carry the responsibility of public affairs. The financial, industrial, and commercial organizations have reached a gigantic size. They are influenced not only by the conditions of the country where they are established, but also by the state of the neighboring countries and of the entire world. In all nations, economic and social conditions undergo extremely rapid changes. Nearly everywhere the existing form of government is again under discussion. The great democracies find themselves face to face with formidable problems—problems concerning their very existence and demanding an immediate solution. And we realize that, despite the immense hopes which humanity has placed in modern civilization, such a civilization has failed in developing men of sufficient intelligence and audacity to guide it along the dangerous road on which it is stumbling. Human beings have not grown so rapidly as the institutions sprung from their brains. It is chiefly the intellectual and moral deficiencies of the political leaders, and their ignorance, which endanger modern nations.

Finally, we must ascertain how the new mode of life will influence the future of the race. The response of the women to the modifications brought about in the ancestral habits by industrial civilization has been immediate and decisive. The birth rate has at once fallen. This event has been felt most precociously and seriously in the social classes and in the nations which were the first to benefit from the progress brought about, directly or indirectly, by the applications of scientific discoveries. Voluntary sterility is not a new thing in the history of the world. It has already been observed in a certain period of past civilizations. It is a classical symptom. We know its significance.

It is evident, then, that the changes produced in our environment by technology have influenced us profoundly. Their effects assume an unexpected character. They are strikingly different from those which were hoped for and which could legitimately be expected from the improvements of all kinds brought to the habitat, the mode of life, the diet, the education, and the intellectual atmosphere of human beings. How has such a paradoxical result been obtained?

5

A simple answer could be given to this question. Modern civilization finds itself in a difficult position because it does not suit us. It has been erected without any knowledge of our real nature. It was born from the whims of scientific discoveries, from the appetites of men, their illusions, their theories, and their desires. Although constructed by our efforts, it is not adjusted to our size and shape.

Obviously, science follows no plan. It develops at random. Its progress depends on fortuitous conditions, such as the birth of men of genius, the form of their mind, the direction taken by their curiosity. It is not at all actuated by a desire to improve the state of human beings. The discoveries responsible for industrial civilization were brought forth at the fancy of the scientists' intuitions and of the more or less casual circumstances of their careers. If Galileo, Newton, or Lavoisier had applied their intellectual powers to the study of body and consciousness, our world probably would be different today. Men of science do not know where they are going. They are guided by chance, by subtle reasoning, by a sort of clairvoyance. Each one of them is a world apart, governed by his own laws. From time to time, things obscure to others become clear to him. In general, discoveries are developed without any prevision of their consequences. These consequences, however, have revolutionized the world and made our civilization what it is.

From the wealth of science we have selected certain parts.

And our choice has in no way been influenced by a consideration of the higher interests of humanity. It has simply followed the direction of our natural tendencies. The principles of the greatest convenience and of the least effort, the pleasure procured by speed, change, and comfort, and also the need of escaping from ourselves, are the determining factors in the success of new inventions. But no one has ever asked himself how we would stand the enormous acceleration of the rhythm of life resulting from rapid transportation, telegraph, telephone, modern business methods, machines that write and calculate, and those that do all the housekeeping drudgery of former times. The tendency responsible for the universal adoption of the airplane, the automobile, the cinema, the telephone, the radio, and, in the near future, of television, is as natural as that which, in the night of the ages, led our ancestors to drink alcohol. Steam-heated houses, electric lighting, elevators, biological morals, and chemical adulteration of foodstuffs have been accepted solely because those innovations were agreeable and convenient. But no account whatever has been taken of their probable effect on human beings.

In the organization of industrial life the influence of the factory upon the physiological and mental state of the workers has been completely neglected. Modern industry is based on the conception of the maximum production at lowest cost, in order that an individual or a group of individuals may earn as much money as possible. It has expanded without any idea of the true nature of the human beings who run the machines, and without giving any consideration to the effects produced on the individuals and on their descendants by the artificial mode of existence imposed by the factory. The great cities have been built with no regard for us. The shape and dimensions of the skyscrapers depend entirely on the necessity of obtaining the maximum income per square foot of ground, and of offering to the tenants offices and apartments that please them. This caused the construction of gigantic buildings where too large masses of human beings are crowded together. Civilized men like such a way of living. While they enjoy the comfort and banal luxury of their dwelling, they do not realize that they are deprived of the necessities of life. The modern city consists of monstrous edifices and of dark, narrow streets full of gasoline fumes, coal dust, and toxic gases, torn by the noise of the taxicabs, trucks, and trolleys, and thronged ceaselessly by great crowds. Obviously, it has not been planned for the good of its inhabitants.

Our life is influenced in a large measure by commercial advertising. Such publicity is undertaken only in the interest of the advertisers and not of the consumers. For example, the public has been made to believe that white bread is better than brown. Then, flour has been bolted more and more thoroughly and thus deprived of its most useful components. Such treatment permits its preservation for longer periods and facilitates the making of bread. The millers and the bakers earn more money. The consumers eat an inferior product, believing it to be a superior one. And in the countries where bread is the principal food, the population degenerates. Enormous amounts of money are spent for publicity. As a result, large quantities of alimentary and pharmaceutical products, at the least useless, and often harmful, have become a necessity for civilized men. In this manner the greediness of individuals, sufficiently shrewd to create a popular demand for the goods that they have for sale, plays a leading part in the modern world.

However, the propaganda that directs our ways of living is not always inspired by selfish motives. Instead of being prompted by the financial interests of individuals or of groups of individuals, it often aims at the common good. But its effect may also be harmful when it emanates from people having a false or incomplete conception of the human being. For example, should physicians, by prescribing special foods, as most of them do, accelerate the growth of young children? In such an instance, their action is based on an incomplete knowledge of the subject. Are larger and heavier children better than smaller ones? Intelligence, alertness, audacity, and resistance to disease do not depend on the same factors as the weight of the body. The education dispensed by schools and universities consists chiefly in a training of the memory and of the muscles, in certain social manners, in a worship of athletics. Are such disciplines really suitable for modern men who need, above all other things, mental equilibrium, nervous stability, sound judgment, audacity, moral courage, and endurance? Why do hygienists behave as though human beings were exclusively liable to infectious diseases, while they are also exposed to the attacks of nervous and mental disorders, and to the weakening of the mind? Although physicians, educators, and hygienists most generously lavish their efforts for the benefit of mankind, they do not attain their goal. For they deal with schemata containing only a part of the reality. The same may be said of all those who substitute their desires, their dreams, or their doctrines for the concrete human being. These theorists build up civilizations which, although designed by them for man, fit only an incomplete or monstrous image of man. The systems of government, entirely constructed in the minds of doctrinaires, are valueless. The principles of the French Revolution, the visions of Marx and Lenin, apply only to abstract men. It must be clearly realized that the laws of human relations are still unknown. Sociology and economics are conjectural sciences—that is, pseudo-sciences.

Thus, it appears that the environment, which science and technology have succeeded in developing for man, does not suit him, because it has been constructed at random, without regard for his true self.

6

To summarize. The sciences of inert matter have made immense progress, while those of living beings remain in a rudimentary state. The slow advance of biology is due to the conditions of human existence, to the intricacy of the phenomena of life, and to the form of our intelligence, which delights in mechanical constructions and mathematical abstractions. The applications of scientific discoveries have transformed the material and mental worlds. These transformations exert on us a profound influence. Their unfortunate effect comes from the fact that they have been made without consideration for our nature. Our ignorance of ourselves has given to mechanics, physics, and chemistry the power to modify at random the ancestral forms of life.

Man should be the measure of all. On the contrary, he is a stranger in the world that he has created. He has been incapable of organizing this world for himself, because he did not possess a practical knowledge of his own nature. Thus, the enormous advance gained by the sciences of inanimate matter over those of living things is one of the greatest catastrophes ever suffered by humanity. The environment born of our intelligence and our inventions is adjusted neither to our stature nor to our shape. We are unhappy. We degenerate morally and mentally. The groups and the nations in which industrial civilization has attained its highest development are precisely those which are becoming weaker. And whose return to barbarism is the most rapid. But they do not realize it. They are without protection against the hostile surroundings that science has built about them. In truth, our civilization, like those preceding it, has created certain conditions of existence which, for reasons still obscure, render life itself impossible. The anxiety and the woes of the inhabitants of the modern city arise from their political, economic, and social institutions, but, above all, from their own weakness. We are the victims of the backwardness of the sciences of life over those of matter.

The only possible remedy for this evil is a much more profound knowledge of ourselves. Such a knowledge will enable us to understand by what mechanisms modern existence affects our consciousness and our body. We shall thus learn how to adapt ourselves to our surroundings, and how to change them, should a revolution become indispensable. In bringing to light our true nature, our potentialities, and the way to actualize them, this science will give us the explanation of our physiological weakening, and of our moral and intellectual diseases. We have no other means of learning the inexorable rules of our organic and spiritual activities, of distinguishing the prohibited from the lawful, of realizing that we are not free to modify, according to our fancy, our environment, and ourselves. Since the natural conditions of existence have been destroyed by modern civilization, the science of man has become the most necessary of all sciences.

Chapter II

THE SCIENCE OF MAN

1. Necessity of a choice among the heterogeneous data concerning man. The operational concept of Bridgman. Its application to living beings. Confusion of concepts. Rejection of philosophical and scientific systems. Function of conjectures. 2. The need of a complete survey. Every aspect of man to receive attention. No exaggerated importance to be given to any one part. Simple phenomena not to be preferred to complex ones. Unexplainable facts not to be ignored. Man in his entirety is within the jurisdiction of science. 3. The science of man is more important than all other sciences. Its analytic and synthetic character. 4. The analysis of man requires various techniques. Those techniques create body and soul, structure and functions, and divide the body into parts. The specialists. The need for non-specialized scientists. How to promote human biological research. 5. Technical difficulties encountered in the study of man. Utilization of animals of high intelligence. How experiments of long duration should be organized. 6. The character of a utilizable synthesis of our data about man.

I

Our ignorance of ourselves is of a peculiar nature. It does not arise from difficulty in procuring the necessary information, from its inaccuracy, or from its scarcity. On the contrary, it is due to the extreme abundance and confusion of the data accumulated about itself by humanity during the course of the ages. Also to the division of man into an almost infinite number of fragments by the sciences that have endeavored to study his body and his consciousness. This knowledge, to a large extent, has not been utilized. In fact, it is barely utilizable. Its sterility manifests itself in the meagerness of the classical abstractions, of the schemata that are the basis of medicine, hygiene, education, sociology, and political economy. There is, however, a living and rich reality buried in the enormous mass of definitions, observations, doctrines, desires, and dreams representing man's efforts toward a knowledge of himself. In addition to the systems and speculations of scientists and philosophers, we have the positive results of the experience of past generations, and also a multitude of observations carried out with the spirit and, occasionally, with the techniques of science. But we must make a judicious choice from these heterogeneous things.

Among the numerous concepts relating to the human being, some are mere logical constructs of our mind. We do not find in the outer world any being to whom they apply. The others are purely and simply the result of experience. They have been called by Bridgman operational concepts. An operational concept is equivalent to the operation or to the set of operations involved in its acquisition. Indeed, all positive knowledge demands the use of a certain technique, of certain physical or mental operations. When we say that an object is one meter long, we mean that it has the same length as a rod of wood or of metal, whose dimension is, in its turn, equal to that of the standard meter kept at the International Bureau of Weights and Measures in Paris. It is quite evident that the things we can observe are the only ones we really know. In the foregoing example, the concept of length is synonymous with the measurement of such length. According to Bridgman, concepts dealing with things situated outside the experimental field are meaningless. Thus, a question has no signification if it is not possible to discover the operations permitting us to answer it.

The precision of any concept whatsoever depends upon that of the operations by which it is acquired. If man is defined as a being composed of matter and consciousness, such a proposition is meaningless. For the relations between consciousness and bodily matter have not, so far, been brought into the experimental field. But an operational definition is given of man when we consider him as an organism capable of manifesting physicochemical, physiological, and psychological activities. In biology, as in physics, the concepts which will always remain real, and must be the basis of science, are linked to certain methods of observation. For example, our present idea of the cells of the cerebral cortex, their pyramidal body, their dendritic processes, and their smooth axon, results from the techniques invented by Ramon y Cajal. This is an operational concept. Such a concept will change only when new and more perfect techniques will be discovered. But to say that cerebral cells are the seat of mental processes is a worthless affirmation, for there is no possibility of observing the presence of mental processes in the body of cerebral cells. Operational concepts are the only solid foundation upon which we can build. From the immense fund of knowledge we possess about ourselves, we must select the data corresponding to what exists not only in our mind, but also in nature.

We know that among the concepts relating to man, some are specific of him, others belong to all living beings, and still others are those of chemistry, physics, and mechanics.

There are as many systems of concepts as of strata in the organization of living matter. At the level of the electronic, atomic, and molecular structures found in man's tissues, as well as in trees, stones, or clouds, the concepts of space-time continuum, energy, force, mass, entropy, should be used. And also those of osmotic tension, electric charge, ions, capillarity, permeability, diffusion. The concepts of micella, dispersion, adsorption, and flocculation appear at the level of the material aggregates larger than molecules. When the molecules and their combinations have erected tissue cells, and when these cells have associated together to form organs and organisms, the concepts of chromosome, gene, heredity, adaptation, physiological time, reflex, instinct, etc., must be added to those already mentioned. They are the very concepts of physiology. They exist simultaneously with the physicochemical concepts, but cannot be reduced to them. At the highest level of organization, in addition to electrons, atoms, molecules, cells, and tissues, we encounter a whole composed of organs, humors, and consciousness. Then, physicochemical and physiological concepts become insufficient. To them we must join the psychological concepts characteristic of man, such as intelligence, moral sense, esthetic sense, and social sense. The principles of minimum effort and of maximum production or of maximum pleasure, the quest for liberty, for equality, etc., have to be substituted for the thermodynamic laws and those of adaptation.

Each system of concepts can only be legitimately used in the domain of the science to which it belongs. The concepts of physics, chemistry, physiology, and psychology are applicable to the superposed levels of the bodily organization. But the concepts appropriate at one level should not be mingled indiscriminately with those specific of another. For example, the second law of thermodynamics, the law of dissipation of free energy, indispensable at the molecular level, is useless at the psychological level, where the principles of least effort and of maximum pleasure are applied. The concepts of capillarity and of osmotic tension do not throw any light on problems pertaining to consciousness. It is nothing but word play to explain a psychological phenomenon in terms of cell physiology, or of quantum mechanics. However, the mechanistic physiologists of the nineteenth century, and their disciples who still linger with us, have committed such an error in endeavoring to reduce man entirely to physical chemistry. This unjustified generalization of the results of sound experiments is due to overspecialization. Concepts should not be misused. They must be kept in their place in the hierarchy of sciences.

The confusion in our knowledge of ourselves comes chiefly from the presence, among the positive facts, of the remains of scientific, philosophic, and religious systems. If our mind adheres to any system whatsoever, the aspect and the significance of concrete phenomena are changed. At all times, humanity has contemplated itself through glasses colored by doctrines, beliefs, and illusions. These false or inexact ideas must be discarded. Long ago, Claude Bernard in his writings mentioned the necessity of getting rid of philosophical and scientific systems as one would break the chains of intellectual slavery. But such freedom has not yet been attained. Biologists and, above all, educators, economists, and sociologists, when facing extremely complex problems, have often yielded to the temptation to build up theories and afterwards to turn them into articles of faith. And their sciences have crystallized in formulas as rigid as the dogmas of a religion.

We meet with troublesome reminders of such mistakes in all the departments of knowledge. The quarrel of the vitalists and the mechanists, the futility of which astounds us today, arose from one of the most famous of these errors. The vitalists thought that the organism was a machine whose parts were integrated with one another by a factor that was not physicochemical. According to them, the processes responsible for the unity of the living being were governed by an independent spiritual principle, an entelechy, an idea analogous to that of an engineer who designs a machine. This autonomous factor was not a form of energy and did not produce energy. It was only concerned with the management of the organism. Evidently, entelechy is not an operational concept. It is purely a mental construct. In short, the vitalists considered the body as a machine, guided by an engineer, whom they called entelechy. And they did not realize that this engineer was nothing but the intelligence of the observer. As for the mechanists, they believed that all physiological and psychological activities could be explained by the laws of physics, chemistry, and mechanics. They thus built a machine, and, like the vitalists, they were the engineer of this machine. Then, as Woodger pointed out, they forgot the existence of that engineer. Such a concept is not operational. It is evident that mechanism and vitalism should be rejected for the same reason as all other systems. At the same time, we must free ourselves from the mass of illusions, errors, and badly observed facts, from the false problems investigated by the weak-minded of the realm of science, and from the pseudo-discoveries of charlatans and scientists extolled by the daily press. Also from the sadly useless investigations, the long studies of meaningless things, the inextricable jumble that has been standing mountain high ever since biological research became a profession like those of the school-teacher, the clergyman, and the bank clerk.

This elimination completed, the results of the patient labor of all sciences concerning themselves with man, the accumulated wealth of their experience, will remain as the unshakable basis of our knowledge. In the history of humanity, the expression of all our fundamental activities can be read at a single glance. In addition to positive observations, to sure facts, there are many things neither positive nor indubitable. They should not be rejected. Of course, operational concepts are the only foundation upon which science can be solidly built. But creative imagination alone is capable of inspiring conjectures and dreams pregnant with the worlds of the future. We must continue asking questions which, from the point of view of sound, scientific criticism, are meaningless. And even if we tried to prevent our mind from pursuing the impossible and the unknowable, such an effort would be vain. Curiosity is a necessity of our nature, a blind impulse that obeys no rule. Our mind turns around all external objects and penetrates within the depths of ourselves, as instinctively and as irresistibly as a raccoon explores, with its clever little paws, the slightest details of its narrow world. Curiosity impels us to discover the universe. It inexorably draws us in its train to unknown countries. And unclimbable mountains vanish before it like smoke before the wind.

2

A thorough examination of man is indispensable. The barrenness of classical schemata is due to the fact that, despite the great scope of our knowledge, we have never apprehended our whole being with a sufficiently penetrating effort. Thus, we must do more than consider the aspect of man at a certain period of his history, in certain conditions of his life. We must grasp him in all his activities, those that are ordinarily apparent as well as those that may remain potential. Such information can only be obtained by looking carefully in the present and in the past for all the manifestations of our organic and mental powers. Also by an examination, both analytic and synthetic, of our constitution and of our physical, chemical, and mental relations with our environment. We should follow the wise advice that Descartes, in his *Discourse on Method,* gave to those who seek the truth, and divide our subject into as many parts as are necessary in order to make a complete inventory of each one of them. But it should be clearly understood that such a division is only a methodological expedient, created by ourselves, and that man remains indivisible.

There is no privileged territory. In the abysses of our inner world everything has a meaning. We cannot choose only those things that please us, according to the dictates of our feelings, our imagination, the scientific and philosophical form of our mind. A difficult or obscure subject must not be neglected just because it is difficult and obscure. All methods should be employed. The qualitative is as true as the quantitative. The relations that can be expressed in mathematical terms do not possess greater reality than those that cannot be so expressed. Darwin, Claude Bernard, and Pasteur, whose discoveries could not be described in algebraic formulas, were as great scientists as Newton and Einstein. Reality is not necessarily clear and simple. It is not even sure that we are always able to understand it. In addition, it assumes infinitely varied aspects. A state of consciousness, the humeral bone, a wound, are equally real things. A phenomenon does not owe its importance to the facility with which scientific techniques can be applied to its study. It must be conceived in function, not of the observer and his method, but of the subject, the human being. The grief of the mother who has lost her child, the distress of the mystical soul plunged in the "dark night," the suffering of the patient tortured by cancer, are evident realities, although they are not measurable. The study of the phenomena of clairvoyance should not be neglected any more than that of the chronaxy of nerves, though clairvoyance can neither be produced at will nor measured, while it is possible to measure chronaxy exactly by a simple method. In making this inventory, we should utilize all possible means and be content with observing the phenomena that cannot be measured.

It often happens that undue importance is given to some part at the expense of the others. We are obliged to consider all the different aspects of man, physicochemical, anatomical, physiological, metapsychical, intellectual, moral, artistic, religious, economic, and social. Every specialist, owing to a well-known professional bias, believes that he understands the entire human being, while in reality he only grasps a tiny part of him. Fragmentary aspects are considered as representing the whole. And these aspects are taken at random, following the fashion of the moment, which in turn gives more importance to the individual or to society, to physiological appetites or to spiritual activities, to muscular development or to brain power, to beauty or to utility, etc. Man, therefore, appears with many different visages. We arbitrarily choose among them the one that pleases us, and forget the others.

Another mistake consists in suppressing a part of reality from the inventory. There are many reasons accounting for this. We prefer to study systems that can easily be isolated and approached by simple methods. We generally neglect the more complex. Our mind has a partiality for precise and definitive solutions and for the resulting intellectual security. We have an almost irresistible tendency to select the subjects of our investigations for their technical facility and clearness rather than for their importance. Thus, modern physiologists principally concern themselves with physicochemical phenomena taking place in living animals, and pay less attention to physiological and functional processes. The same thing happens with physicians when they specialize in subjects whose techniques are easy and already known, rather than in degenerative diseases, neuroses, and psychoses, whose study would require the use of imagination and the creation of new methods. Everyone realizes, however, that the discovery of some of the laws of the organization of living matter would be more important than, for example, that of the rhythm of the cilia of tracheal cells. Without any doubt, it would be much more useful to free humanity from cancer, tuberculosis, arteriosclerosis, syphilis, and the innumerable misfortunes caused by nervous and mental diseases, than to engross oneself in the minute study of physicochemical phenomena of secondary importance manifesting themselves in the course of diseases. On account of technical difficulties, certain matters are banished from the field of scientific research, and refused the right of making themselves known.

Important facts may be completely ignored. Our mind has a natural tendency to reject the things that do not fit into the frame of the scientific or philosophical beliefs of our time. After all, scientists are only men. They are saturated with the prejudices of their environment and of their epoch. They willingly believe that facts that cannot be explained by current theories do not exist. During the period when physiology was identified with physical chemistry, the period of Jacques Loeb and of Bayliss, the study of mental functions was neglected. No one was interested in psychology and in mind disorders. At the present time, scientists who are concerned solely in the physical, chemical, and physicochemical aspects of physiological processes still look upon telepathy and other metapsychical phenomena as illusions. Evident facts having an unorthodox appearance are suppressed. By reason of these difficulties, the inventory of the things which could lead us to a better understanding of the human being, has been left incomplete. We must, then, go back to a naïve observation of ourselves in all our aspects, reject nothing, and describe simply what we see.

At first glance, the scientific method seems not to be applicable to the analysis of all our activities. It is obvious that we, the observers, are unable to follow human personality into every region where it extends. Our techniques do not grasp things having neither dimensions nor weight. They only reach those situated in space and time. They are incapable of measuring vanity, hatred, love, beauty, or the dreams of the scientist, the inspiration of the poet, the elevation of the mystical soul toward God. But they easily record the physiological aspects and the material results of these psychological states. Mental and spiritual activities, when they play an important part in our life, express themselves by a certain behavior, certain acts, a certain attitude toward our fellow men. It is only in this manner that the moral, esthetic, and mystic functions can be explored by scientific methods. We also have at our disposal the statements of those who have traveled in these almost unknown regions. But the verbal expression of their experiences is, in general, disconcerting. Outside the domain of intelligence, nothing is clearly definable. Of course, the elusiveness of a thing does not signify its non-existence. When one sails in dense fog, the invisible rocks are none the less present. From time to time their menacing forms emerge from the white mist. And at once they are swallowed up again. To this phenomenon can be truthfully compared the evanescent visions of artists and, above all, of great mystics. Those things which our techniques are incapable of grasping nevertheless stamp the initiated with a visible mark. In such indirect ways does science know the spiritual world which, by definition, it is forbidden to enter. Man in his entirety is located within the jurisdiction of the scientific techniques.

3

The critical review of the data concerning man yields a large amount of positive information. We are thus enabled to make a complete inventory of human activities. Such an inventory will lead to the building up of new schemata, richer than the classical ones. But our knowledge will not, in this manner, progress very strikingly. We shall have to go farther and build up a real science of man. A science capable of undertaking, with the help of all known techniques, a more exhaustive examination of our inner world, and also of realizing that each part should be considered as a function of the whole. In order to develop such a science, we must, for some time, turn our attention away from mechanical inventions and even, in a certain measure, from classical hygiene and medicine, from the purely material aspects of our existence. Everybody is interested in things that increase wealth and comfort. But no one understands that the structural, functional, and mental quality of each individual has to be improved. The health of the intelligence and of the affective sense, moral discipline, and spiritual development are just as necessary as the health of the body and the prevention of infectious diseases.

No advantage is to be gained by increasing the number of mechanical inventions. It would perhaps be as well not to accord so much importance to discoveries of physics, astronomy, and chemistry. In truth, pure science never directly brings us any harm. But when its fascinating beauty dominates our mind and enslaves our thoughts in the realm of inanimate matter, it becomes dangerous. Man must now turn his attention to himself, and to the cause of his moral and intellectual disability. What is the good of increasing the comfort, the luxury, the beauty, the size, and the complications of our civilization, if our weakness prevents us from guiding it to our best advantage? It is really not worth while to go on elaborating a way of living that is bringing about the demoralization and the disappearance of the noblest elements of the great races. It would be far better to pay more attention to ourselves than to construct faster steamers, more comfortable automobiles, cheaper radios, or telescopes for examining the structure of remote nebulæ. What real progress will be accomplished when aircraft take us to Europe or to China in a few hours? Is it necessary to increase production unceasingly, so that men may consume larger and larger quantities of useless things? There is not the shadow of a doubt that mechanical, physical, and chemical sciences are incapable of giving us intelligence, moral discipline, health, nervous equilibrium, security, and peace.

Our curiosity must turn aside from its present path, and take another direction. It must leave the physical and physiological in order to follow the mental and the spiritual. So far, sciences concerning themselves with human beings have confined their activities to certain aspects of their subject. They have not succeeded in escaping from Cartesian dualism. They have been dominated by mechanism. In physiology, hygiene, and medicine, as well as in the study of education and of political and social economy, scientists have been chiefly absorbed by organic, humoral, and intellectual aspects of man. They have not paid any great attention to his affective and moral form, his inner life, his character, his esthetic and religious needs, the common substratum of organic and psychological activities, the intimate relations of the individual and of his mental and spiritual environment. A radical change is indispensable. This change requires both the work of specialists devoting their efforts to the particular knowledge related to our body and our mind, and of scientists capable of integrating the discoveries of the specialists in function of man as a whole. The new science must progress, by a double effort of analysis and synthesis, toward a conception of the human individual at once sufficiently complete and sufficiently simple to serve as a basis for our action.

4

Man cannot be separated into parts. He would cease to exist if his organs were isolated from one another. Although indivisible, he assumes different aspects. His aspects are the heterogeneous manifestations of his unity to our sense organs. He can be compared to an electric lamp whose presence is recorded in a different manner by a thermometer, a voltmeter, a photographic plate, or a selenium cell. We are incapable of directly apprehending him in his simplicity. We can only grasp him through our senses and our scientific instruments. According to our means of investigation, his activity appears to be physical, chemical, physiological, or psychological. The analysis of his manifoldness naturally demands the help of various techniques. As he manifests himself exclusively through the agency of these techniques, he necessarily takes on the appearance of being multiple.

The science of man makes use of all other sciences. This is one of the reasons for its slow progress and its difficulty. For example, in order to study the influence of a psychological factor on a sensitive individual, the methods of medicine, physiology, physics, and chemistry have to be employed. Let us suppose that our subject receives bad news. This psychological event may express itself simultaneously by moral suffering, nervous agitation, circulatory disturbances, lesions of the skin, physicochemical modifications of the blood, etc. When dealing with man we are obliged to employ the methods and concepts of several sciences, even for the simplest experiment. If we study the effects of a given food, either animal or vegetable, on a group of individuals, we must first learn the chemical composition of that food. And also the physiological and psychological states, and the ancestral characteristics of the individuals who are to be the subjects of the investigation. Then we have to record accurately the changes in weight, in height, in the form of the skeleton, in muscular strength, in susceptibility to diseases, in the physical, chemical, and anatomical characteristics of the blood, in nervous equilibrium, in intelligence, courage, fertility, longevity, which take place during the course of the experiment.

Obviously, no one scientist is capable of mastering all the techniques indispensable to the study of a single human problem. Therefore, progress in knowledge of ourselves requires the simultaneous efforts of various specialists. Each specialist confines himself to one part of the body, or consciousness, or of their relations with the environment. He is anatomist, physiologist, chemist, psychologist, physician, hygienist, educator, clergyman, sociologist, economist. Each speciality is divided into smaller and smaller parts. There are specialists in glandular physiology, in vitamines, in diseases of the rectum, in those of the nose, in education of small children or of adults, in hygiene of factories and of prisons, in psychology of all categories of individuals, in domestic economy, rural economy, etc. Such a division of the work has made possible the development of the particular sciences. Specialization is imperative. Scientists have to devote their attention to one department of knowledge. And it is impossible for a specialist, actively engaged in the pursuit of his own task, to understand the human being as a whole. Indeed, such a state of affairs is rendered necessary by the vast extent of the field of each science. But it presents a certain danger. For example, Calmette, who had specialized in bacteriology, wished to prevent the spread of tuberculosis among the French population. He, naturally, prescribed the use of the vaccine he had invented. If, in addition to being a bacteriologist, he had possessed a more general knowledge of hygiene and medicine, he would have advised also the adoption of measures with regard to dwellings, food, working conditions, and the way of living of the people. A similar occurrence took place in the United States in the organization of the elementary schools. John Dewey, who is a philosopher, undertook to improve the education of American children. But his methods were suited to the schema, the abstraction, which his professional bias made him take for the concrete child.

Still more harm is caused by the extreme specialization of the physicians. Medicine has separated the sick human being into small fragments, and each fragment has its specialist. When a specialist, from the beginning of his career, confines himself to a minute part of the body, his knowledge of the rest is so rudimentary that he is incapable of thoroughly understanding even that part in which he specializes. A similar thing happens to educators, clergymen, economists, and sociologists who, before limiting themselves entirely to their particular domain, have not taken the trouble to acquire a general knowledge of man. The more eminent the specialist, the more dangerous he is. Scientists who have strikingly distinguished themselves by great discoveries or useful inventions often come to believe that their knowledge of one subject extends to all others. Edison, for example, did not hesitate to impart to the public his views on philosophy and religion. And the public listened to his words with respect, imagining them to carry as much weight on these new subjects as on the former ones. Thus, great men, in speaking about things they do not thoroughly understand, hinder human progress in one of its fields, while having contributed to its advancement in another. The daily press often gives us the dubious benefit of the sociological, economic, and scientific opinions of manufacturers, bankers, lawyers, professors, physicians, whose highly specialized minds are incapable of apprehending in their breadth the momentous problems of our time. However, modern civilization absolutely needs specialists. Without them, science could not progress. But, before the result of their researches is applied to man, the scattered data of their analyses must be integrated in an intelligible synthesis.

Such a synthesis cannot be obtained by a simple round-table conference of the specialists. It requires the efforts of one man, not merely those of a group. A work of art has never been produced by a committee of artists, nor a great discovery made by a committee of scholars. The syntheses needed for the progress of our knowledge of man should be elaborated in a single brain. It is impossible to make use of the mass of information accumulated by the specialists. For no one has undertaken to coördinate the data already obtained, and to consider the human being in his entirety. Today there are many scientific workers, but very few real scientists. This peculiar situation is not due to lack of individuals capable of high intellectual achievements. Indeed, syntheses, as well as discoveries, demand exceptional mental power and physiological endurance. Broad and strong minds are rarer than precise and narrow ones. It is easy to become a good chemist, a good physicist, a good physiologist, a good psychologist, or a good sociologist. On the contrary, very few individuals are capable of acquiring and using knowledge of several different sciences. However, such men do exist. Some of those whom our scientific institutions and universities have forced to specialize narrowly could apprehend a complex subject both in its entirety and in its parts. So far, scientific workers devoting themselves, within a minute field, to prolonged study of a generally insignificant detail, have always been the most favored. An original piece of work, without any real importance, is considered of greater value than a thorough knowledge of an entire science. Presidents of universities and their advisers do not realize that synthetic minds are as indispensable as analytic ones. If the superiority of this kind of intellect were recognized, and its development encouraged, specialists would cease to be dangerous. For the significance of the parts in the organization of the whole could then be correctly estimated.

At the beginning of its history more than at its zenith a science needs superior minds. To become a great physician requires more imagination, judgment, and intelligence than to become a great chemist. At the present time our knowledge of man can only progress by attracting a powerful intellectual élite. Great mental capacities should be required from the young men who desire to devote themselves to biology. It seems that the increased number of scientific workers, their being split up into groups whose studies are limited to a small subject, and over-specialization have brought about a shrinking of intelligence. There is no doubt that the quality of any human group decreases when the number of the individuals composing this group increases beyond certain limits. The Supreme Court of the United States consists of nine men whose professional value and character are truly eminent. But if it were composed of nine hundred jurists instead of nine, the public would immediately lose, and rightly, its respect for the highest court of this country.

The best way to increase the intelligence of scientists would be to decrease their number. After all, the knowledge of man could be developed by a very small group of workers, provided that they were endowed with creative imagination and given powerful means for carrying out their researches. Great sums of money are wasted every year on scientific research, in America as well as in Europe, because those who are entrusted with this work do not generally possess the qualities necessary to the conquerors of new worlds. And also because the few individuals endowed with this exceptional power live under conditions precluding intellectual creation. Neither laboratories, nor apparatus, nor organization can give to scientists the surroundings indispensable to their success. Modern life is opposed to the life of the mind. However, men of science have to be mere units of a herd whose appetites are purely material and whose habits are entirely different from theirs. They vainly exhaust their strength and spend their time in the pursuit of the conditions demanded by the elaboration of thought. No one of them is wealthy enough to procure the isolation and the silence which in former times everybody could have for nothing, even in the largest cities. No attempt has so far been made to create, in the midst of the agitation of the new city, islands of solitude where meditation would be possible. Such an innovation, however, is an obvious necessity. The construction of vast syntheses is beyond the reach of minds unceasingly dispersed in the confusion of our present modes of existence. The development of the science of man, even more than that of the other sciences, depends on immense intellectual effort. The need of such an effort demands a revision, not only of our conception of the scientist, but also of the conditions under which scientific research is carried on.

5

Human beings are not good subjects for scientific investigation. One does not easily find people with identical characteristics. It is almost impossible to verify the results of an experiment by referring the subject to a sufficiently similar control. Let us suppose, for example, that we wish to compare two methods of education. For such a study we choose two groups of children, as nearly alike as possible. If these children, although of the same age and the same size, belong to different social classes, if their food is not the same, if they live in different psychological atmospheres, the results cannot be compared. In a like manner, the effects of two modes of life on children belonging to one family have little value. For, human races not being pure, there are often profound differences between the offspring of the same parents. On the contrary, the results will be conclusive when the children, whose behavior is compared under different conditions, are twins from a single ovum. We are generally obliged to be content with approximate information. This is one of the factors that have impeded the progress of the science of man.

In researches dealing with physics and chemistry, and also

with physiology, one always attempts to isolate relatively simple systems, and to determine their exact conditions. But when the human being has to be studied as an entirety, and in his relations with his environment, such a limitation of the subject is impossible. The observer must be endowed with sound judgment in order not to lose his way in the complexity of the facts. The difficulties become almost insurmountable in retrospective investigations. Such studies require a very experienced mind. Of course, we should as rarely as possible utilize the conjectural science which is called history. But there have been in the past certain events, revealing the existence in man of extraordinary potentialities. A knowledge of the genesis of these qualities would be of great importance. What factors caused, during the epoch of Pericles, the simultaneous appearance of so many geniuses? A similar event occurred at the time of the Renaissance. Whence sprang the immense expansion, not only of intelligence, scientific imagination, and esthetic intuition, but also of physical vigor, audacity, and the spirit of adventure in the men of this period? Why did they possess such mighty physiological and mental activities? One easily realizes how useful would be precise information regarding the mode of life, the food, the education, the intellectual, moral, esthetic, and religious surroundings of the people who lived during the time immediately preceding the appearance of a pleiad of great men.

Another cause of the difficulties in experimenting on human beings is the fact that the observer and his subject live at about the same rhythm. The effects of a certain diet, of an intellectual or moral discipline, of political or social changes, are felt but slowly. It is only after a lapse of thirty or forty years that the value of an educational method can be estimated. The influence of a given mode of living upon the physiological and mental activities of a human group does not manifest itself before a generation has passed. Inventors of new systems of diet, physical culture, hygiene, education, morals, social economy, are always too early in publishing the success of their own inventions. It is only now that the result of the Montessori system, or of the educational principles of John Dewey, could be profitably analyzed. We should wait another quarter of a century to know the significance of the intelligence tests which psychologists have made in the schools during these past years. The only way to ascertain the effect of a given factor on man is to follow a great number of individuals through the vicissitudes of their life right up to their death. And even then the knowledge thus obtained will be grossly approximate.

The progress of humanity appears to us to be very slow because we, the observers, are units of the herd. Each one of us can make but few observations. Our life is too short. Many experiments should be conducted for a century at the least. Institutions should be established in such a way that observations and experiments commenced by one scientist would not be interrupted by his death. Such organizations are still unknown in the realm of science. But they already exist in other lines of endeavor. In the monastery of Solesmes three successive generations of Benedictine monks have devoted themselves, over a period of about fifty-five years, to the reconstruction of Gregorian music. A similar method should be applied to the investigation of certain problems of human biology. Institutions, in some measure immortal, like religious orders, which would allow the uninterrupted continuation of an experiment as long as might be necessary, should compensate for the too short duration of the existence of individual observers.

Certain data, urgently needed, can be procured with the help of short-lived animals. For this purpose, mice and rats have been chiefly used. Colonies consisting of many thousands of these animals have been employed to study different diets, their influence on the rapidity of growth, on size, disease, longevity, etc. Unfortunately, rats and mice have only very remote analogies with man. It is dangerous, for example, to apply to children, whose constitution is so different, conclusions of researches made on these animals. Besides, the mental states accompanying anatomical and functional changes in bones, tissues, and humors under the influence of food and mode of life, cannot be properly investigated on such low types of animals. By observing more intelligent animals, such as monkeys and dogs, one would obtain more detailed and important information.

Monkeys, despite their cerebral development, are not good subjects for experimentation. Their pedigree is not available. They cannot be bred easily or in sufficiently large numbers. They are difficult to handle. On the contrary, intelligent dogs can be procured readily. Their ancestral characteristics are easily traced. Such animals propagate rapidly. They mature in a year. Generally, they do not live beyond fifteen years. Detailed psychological observations can be made without trouble, especially on shepherd dogs, which are sensitive, intelligent, alert, and attentive. With the aid of these animals of pure breed, and in sufficient number, the complex and important problem of the influence of environment on the individual could be elucidated. For example, we should ascertain whether the increase in stature, which is taking place in the population of the United States, is an advantage or a disadvantage. It is also imperative to know what effect modern life and food have on the nervous system of children, and on their intelligence, alertness, and audacity. An extensive experiment carried out on several hundred dogs over a period of twenty years would give some precise information on these subjects, which are of paramount importance to millions of people. It would indicate, more rapidly than the observation of human beings, in what direction the diet and mode of living of the population should be changed. Such study would effectively supplement the incomplete and brief experiments which now appear to satisfy nutrition specialists. However, the observation of even the highest type of animal cannot entirely replace that of man. In order to develop definitive knowledge, experiments on groups of human beings should be started under such conditions that they could be continued by several generations of scientists.

6

A better knowledge of ourselves cannot be acquired merely by selecting positive facts in the mass of information concerning man, and by making a complete inventory of his activities. Neither would the completion of these data by new observations and experiments, and the building up of a true science of man be sufficient. Above all, we need a synthesis that can be utilized. The purpose of this knowledge is not to satisfy our curiosity, but to rebuild ourselves and our surroundings. Such a purpose is essentially practical. The acquisition of a large quantity of new data, if these data remain scattered in the brains and in the books of specialists, is absolutely useless. A dictionary does not confer a literary or philosophical culture upon its owner. Our ideas must be assembled as a living whole, within the intelligence and the memory of a few superior individuals. Thus, the efforts which humanity has made, and is ceaselessly making, to attain a better knowledge of itself would become productive.

The science of man will be the task of the future. We must now be content with an initiation, both analytic and synthetic, into those characteristics of the human being which scientific criticism has demonstrated to be true. In the following pages man will appear to us as naïvely as to the observer and to his techniques. We shall view him in the form of fragments carved by these techniques. But as far as is possible, these fragments will be replaced in the whole. Such knowledge is, of course, most inadequate. But it is certain. It contains no metaphysical elements. It is also empirical, because no principle governs the choice and the order of the observations. We do not seek to prove or to disprove any theory. The different aspects of man are considered as simply as, when ascending a mountain, one considers the rocks, torrents, meadows, and pines, and even, above the shadows of the valley, the light of the peaks. In both cases, the observations are made as the chances of the way decide. These observations are, however, scientific. They constitute a more or less systematized body of knowledge. Naturally, they do not have the precision of those of astronomers and physicists. But they are as exact as is permitted by the techniques employed, and the nature of the object to which the techniques are applied. For instance, we know that men are endowed with memory and esthetic sense. Also that the pancreas secretes insulin, that certain mental diseases depend on lesions of the brain, that some individuals manifest phenomena of clairvoyance. Memory, and the activity of insulin can be measured. But not esthetic emotion or moral sense. The characteristics of telepathy, or the relations between mental diseases and the brain, lend themselves still less to exact study. Nevertheless, all these data, although approximate, are sure.

This knowledge may be reproached with being commonplace and incomplete. It is commonplace because body and consciousness, duration, adaptation, and individuality are well known to specialists in anatomy, physiology, psychology, metapsychics, hygiene, medicine, education, religion, and sociology. It is incomplete because a choice had to be made among an immense number of facts. And such a choice is bound to be arbitrary. It is limited to what appears to be most important. The rest is neglected, for a synthesis should be short and understandable at a single glance. Human intelligence is capable of retaining only a certain number of details. It would, then, seem that our knowledge of man, in order to be useful, must be incomplete. The likeness of a portrait is due to the selection of details, and not to their number. A drawing more forcibly expresses the character of an individual than a photograph does. We are going to trace only rough sketches of ourselves, similar to anatomical figures chalked on a blackboard. Our sketches will be true, in spite of the intentional suppression of details. They will be based on positive data and not on theories and dreams. They will ignore vitalism and mechanism, realism and nominalism, soul and body, mind and matter. But they will contain all that can be observed. Even the inexplicable facts left out by classical conceptions of man, those facts that stubbornly refuse to enter the frame of conventional thought, and therefore may lead to unknown realms. Thus, our inventory will include all actual and potential activities of the human being.

In this manner we shall become initiated into a knowledge of ourselves, which is only descriptive and still not far from the concrete. Such knowledge does not claim definitiveness or infallibility. It is empirical, approximative, commonplace, and incomplete. But also scientific and intelligible to everybody.

Chapter III

BODY AND PHYSIOLOGICAL ACTIVITIES

---

1. Man. His dual aspect. Human activities and their substratum. 2. The dimensions of the body. Its form. 3. Its outer and inner surfaces. 4. Its constitution. Cells and their societies. Their structure. Cell types. 5. Blood and organic medium. 6. Nutrition of tissues. Metabolism. 7. Circulatory apparatus, lungs, and kidneys. 8. Chemical relations of the body with its environment. Digestion. Nature of food. 9. Sexual functions. 10. Physical relations of the body with its environment. Voluntary nervous system. Skeletal and muscular systems. 11. Visceral nervous system. Sympathetic and parasympathetic. Automatism of the organs. 12. Complexity and simplicity of the body. Structural and functional limits of organs. Anatomical heterogeneity and physiological homogeneity. 13. Mode of organization of the body. Mechanical analogy. Antitheses and illusions. 14. Fragility and robustness of the body. Silence of the body during health. Factors which weaken the body. 15. The causes of disease. Infectious and degenerative diseases.

I

WE ARE conscious of existing, of possessing an activity of our own, a personality. We know that we are different from all other individuals. We believe that our will is free. We feel happy or unhappy. These intuitions constitute for each of us the ultimate reality.

Our states of consciousness glide through time as a river through a valley. Like the river, we are both change and permanence. We are independent of our environment, much more so than are the other animals. Our intelligence has set us free. Man is, above all, the inventor of tools, arms, and machines. With the aid of these inventions he was able to manifest his specific characteristics, and to distinguish himself from all other living beings. He has expressed his inner tendencies in an objective manner by erecting statues, temples, theaters, cathedrals, hospitals, universities, laboratories, and factories. He has, in this way, stamped the surface of the earth with the mark of his fundamental activities —that is, of his esthetic and religious feelings, his moral sense, his intelligence, and his scientific curiosity.

This focus of mighty activities can be observed from within or from without. Seen from within, it shows to the lone observer, who is our self, his own thoughts, tendencies, desires, joys, and sorrows. Seen from without, it appears as the human body, our own, and also that of all our fellow creatures. Thus, man assumes two totally different aspects. For this reason, he has been looked upon as being made up of two parts, the body and the soul. However, no one has ever observed a soul without a body, or a body without a soul. Only the outer surface of our body is visible to us. We perceive our functional activities as a vague sense of well-being. But we are not conscious of any of our organs. The body obeys mechanisms entirely hidden from us. It discloses its constitution only through the techniques of anatomy and physiology. Then, a stupendous complexity appears under its seeming simplicity. Man never allows himself to be observed simultaneously in his outer and public aspect, and in his inner and private one. Even if we penetrate the inextricable maze of the brain and the nervous functions, nowhere do we meet with consciousness. Soul and body are creations of our methods of observation. They are carved by those methods from an indivisible whole.

This whole consists of tissues, organic fluids, and consciousness. It extends simultaneously in space and in time. It fills the three dimensions of space, and that of time with its heterogeneous mass. However, it is not comprised fully within these four dimensions. For consciousness is located both within the cerebral matter and outside the physical continuum. The human being is too complex to be apprehended in his entirety. We have to divide him into small parts by our methods of observation. Technological necessity obliges us, therefore, to describe him as being composed of a corporal substratum and of various activities. And also to consider separately the temporal, adaptive, and individual aspects of these activities. At the same time we must avoid making the classical errors of reducing him to a body, or a consciousness, or an association of both, and of believing in the concrete existence of the parts abstracted from him by our mind.

2

The human body is placed, on the scale of magnitudes, halfway between the atom and the star. According to the size of the objects selected for comparison, it appears either large or small. Its length is equivalent to that of two hundred thousand tissue cells, or of two millions of ordinary microbes, or of two billions of albumin molecules, placed end to end. Man is gigantic in comparison with an electron, an atom, a molecule, or a microbe. But, when compared with a mountain, or with the earth, he is tiny. More than four thousand individuals would have to stand one upon the other in order to equal the height of Mount Everest. A terrestrial meridian is approximately equivalent to twenty millions of them placed end to end. Light, as is well known, travels about one hundred and fifty million times the length of our body in one second. The interstellar distances are such that they have to be measured in light years. Our stature, in relation to such a system of reference, becomes inconceivably small. For this reason, Eddington and Jeans, in their books of popular astronomy, always succeed in impressing their readers with the complete insignificance of man in the universe. In reality, our spatial greatness or smallness is without importance. For what is specific of man has no physical dimensions. The meaning of our presence in this world assuredly does not depend upon our size.

Our stature seems to be appropriate to the character of the tissue cells, and to the nature of the chemical exchanges, or metabolism, of the organism. As nerve impulses propagate in everybody at the same speed, men of a very much larger frame than ours would have too slow a perception of external things, and their muscular reactions would be too sluggish. At the same time the rate of their chemical exchanges would be profoundly modified. It is well known that the metabolism of large animals is lower than that of small ones. The horse, for instance, has a lesser metabolic activity than the mouse. A great increase in our stature would diminish the intensity of our exchanges. And probably deprive us of our agility and of the rapidity of our perceptions. Such an accident will not happen, because the size of human beings varies only within narrow limits. The dimensions of our body are determined simultaneously by heredity and developmental conditions.

In a given race, one observes tall and short individuals. These differences in the length of the skeleton come from the state of the endocrine glands and from the correlation of their activities in space and time. They are of profound significance. It is possible, by means of proper diet and mode of living, to augment or diminish the stature of the individuals composing a nation. Likewise, to modify the quality of their tissues and probably also of their mind. We must not blindly change the dimensions of the human body in order to give it more beauty and muscular strength. In fact, seemingly unimportant alterations of our size and form could cause profound modifications of our physiological and mental activities. There is no advantage in increasing man's stature by artificial means. Alertness, endurance, and audacity do not grow with the volume of the body. Men of genius are not tall. Mussolini is of medium size, and Napoleon was short.

Each man is characterized by his figure, his way of carrying himself, the aspect of his face. Our outward form expresses the qualities, the powers, of our body and our mind. In a given race, it varies according to the mode of life of the individuals. The man of the Renaissance, whose life was a constant fight, who was exposed continuously to dangers and to inclemencies, who was capable of as great an enthusiasm for the discoveries of Galileo as for the masterpieces of Leonardo da Vinci or Michelangelo, did not resemble modern man who lives in a steam-heated apartment, an air-conditioned office, a closed car, who contemplates absurd films, listens to his radio, and plays golf and bridge. Each epoch puts its seal on human beings. We begin to observe the new types created by motor-cars, cinemas, and athletics.

Some, more frequent in Latin countries, are characterized by an adipose aspect, flabby tissues, discolored skin, protruding abdomen, thin legs, awkward posture, unintelligent and brutal face. Others appear, especially among Anglo-Saxons, and show broad shoulders, narrow waist, and birdlike cranium. Our form is molded by our physiological habits, and even by our usual thoughts. Its characteristics are partly due to the muscles running under the skin or along the bones. The size of these muscles depends on the exercise to which they are submitted. The beauty of the body comes from the harmonious development of the muscles and the skeleton. It reached the height of perfection at the epoch of Pericles, in the Greek athletes whom Phidias and his disciples immortalized in their statues. The shape of the face, the mouth, the cheeks, the eyelids, and the lines of the visage are determined by the habitual condition of the flat muscles, which move in the adipose tissue underlying the skin. And the state of these muscles depends on that of our mind. Indeed, each individual can give his face the expression that he chooses. But he does not keep such a mask permanently. Unwittingly, our visage progressively models itself upon our states of consciousness. With the advance of age it becomes more and more pregnant with the feelings, the appetites, and the aspirations of the whole being. The beauty of youth comes from the natural harmony of the lineaments of the human face. That, so rare, of an old man, from his soul.

The visage expresses still deeper things than the hidden activities of consciousness. In this open book one can read not only the vices, the virtues, the intelligence, the stupidity, the feelings, the most carefully concealed habits, of an individual, but also the constitution of his body, and his tendencies to organic and mental diseases. In fact, the aspect of bones, muscles, fat, skin, and hair depends on the nutrition of tissues. And the nutrition of tissues is regulated by the composition of blood plasma, that is, by the activity of the glandular and digestive systems. The state of the organs is revealed by the aspect of the body. The surface of the skin reflects the functional conditions of the endocrine glands, the stomach, the intestines, and the nervous system. It points out the morbid tendencies of the individual. In fact, people who belong to different morphological classes—for instance, to the cerebral, digestive, muscular, or respiratory types—are not liable to the same organic or mental diseases. There are great functional disparities between tall and spare men, and broad and short ones. The tall type, either asthenic or athletic, is predisposed to tuberculosis and to dementia præcox. The short, pycnic type, to cyclic mania, diabetes, rheumatism, and gout. In the diagnosis and prognosis of diseases, ancient physicians, quite rightly, attributed great importance to temperament, idiosyncrasies, and diatheses. Each man bears on his face the description of his body and his soul.

3

The skin, which covers the outer surface of the body, is impermeable to water and to gases. It does not allow the microbes living on its surface to enter the organism. It is capable of destroying them with the aid of substances secreted by its glands. But it can be crossed by the minute and deadly beings, which we call viruses. Its external face is exposed to light, wind, humidity, dryness, heat, and cold. Its internal face is in contact with an aquatic world, warm and deprived of light, where cells live like marine animals. Despite its thinness, the skin effectively protects the organic fluids against the unceasing variations of cosmic surroundings. It is moist, supple, extensible, elastic, durable. Its durability is due to its mode of constitution, to its several layers of cells, which slowly and endlessly multiply. These cells die while remaining united to one another like the slates of a roof—like slates ceaselessly blown away by the wind and continually replaced by new slates. The skin, nevertheless, retains its moistness and suppleness, because small glands secrete on its surface both water and fatty substances. At the nostrils, mouth, anus, urethra, and vagina, it joins the mucosas, those membranes that cover the inner surface of the body. All its orifices, with the exception of the nostrils, are closed by elastic and contractile rings, the sphincters. Thus, it is the almost perfectly fortified frontier of a closed world.

Through its outer surface, the body enters into communication with all the things of the cosmic universe. In fact, the skin is the dwelling-place of an immense quantity of small receptor organs, each of which registers, according to its own structure, the changes taking place in the environment. Tactile corpuscles scattered all over its surface are sensitive to pressure, to pain, to heat, or to cold. Those situated in the mucosa of the tongue are affected by certain qualities of food, and also by temperature. Air vibrations act on the extremely complex apparatus of the internal ear by the medium of the tympanic membrane and the bones of the middle ear. The network of olfactory nerves, which extends into the nasal mucous membrane, is sensitive to odors. A strange phenomenon occurs in the embryo. The brain causes a part of itself, the optic nerve and the retina, to shoot out toward the surface of the body. The part of the skin overlying the young retina undergoes an astonishing modification. It becomes transparent, forms the cornea and the crystalline lens, and unites with other tissues to build up the prodigious optical system which we call the eye. The brain is, thus, enabled to record the electromagnetic waves comprised between red and violet.

Innumerable nerve fibers radiate from all these organs and connect them with the spinal cord and the brain. Through the agency of these nerves the central nervous system spreads like a web over the entire surface of the body where it enters into contact with the outer world. The aspect of the universe depends on the constitution of the sense organs, and on their degree of sensitiveness. For instance, should the retina record infra-red rays of great wave length, nature would take on a different visage. The color of water, rocks, and trees would vary with the seasons because of the changes in the temperature. July's clear days, when the smallest details of the landscape stand out sharply against dark shadows, would be obscured by a reddish haze. Heat rays, being visible, would conceal all objects. In winter, the atmosphere would become clear and the contours of things precise. The aspect of men, however, would remain very different. Their outline, vague. Their face, hidden by a red mist issuing from their mouth and nostrils. After violent exercise, the body would seem to increase in size, on account of the heat released by the skin and surrounding the figure with a larger aura. In a like manner, the cosmic world would assume another appearance if the retina became sensitive to ultra-violet rays and the skin to light rays. Or if the acuteness of all our sense organs were considerably augmented.

We ignore things which have no action on the nerve endings of the surface of the skin. Therefore, we do not perceive cosmic rays, although they pass right through our body. It seems that everything reaching the brain has to enter the sensory organs—that is, to influence the nervous layer enveloping our body. The unknown agent of telepathic communications is perhaps the only exception to this rule. In clairvoyance, it looks as though the subject directly grasps the external reality without the help of the usual nerve channels. But such phenomena are rare. As a rule, the senses are the gateway through which the physical and psychological universe penetrates our organism. Thus, the quality of an individual partly depends on that of his surface. For the brain is molded by the continual messages it receives from the outer world. Therefore, the state of our envelope should not be modified thoughtlessly by new habits of life. For instance, we are far from knowing completely what effect exposure to sun rays has upon the development of the entire body. Until the exact nature of this effect has been ascertained, nudism and exaggerated tanning of the skin by natural light, or by ultra-violet rays, should not be blindly accepted by the white races. The skin and its appendages play the part of a faithful keeper of our organs and our blood. They allow certain things to enter our inner world and exclude others. They are the ever open, though carefully watched, door to our central nervous system. They must be looked upon as being an essential part of ourselves.

Our internal frontier begins at the mouth and the nose, and ends at the anus. Through these openings the outside world penetrates into the respiratory and digestive systems. While the skin is impervious to water and to gas, the mucous membranes of the lungs and of the intestines allow these substances to pass. They are responsible for the chemical continuity of our body with its surroundings. Our inner surface is far larger than that of the skin. The area covered by the flat cells of the pulmonary alveoli is immense. It is approximately equal to five hundred square meters. The thin membrane formed by these cells is traversed by oxygen from the air and by carbon dioxide from the venous blood. It is easily affected by poisonous gases and by bacteria, and more particularly by pneumococci. Atmospheric air, before reaching the pulmonary alveoli, passes through the nose, the pharynx, the larynx, the trachea, and the bronchi, where it is moistened and freed from dust and microbes. But this natural protection is now insufficient because the air of cities has been polluted by coal dust, gasoline fumes, and bacteria set free by the multitude of human beings. Respiratory mucosa is much more delicate than skin. It is defenseless against strong irritants. Its fragility may cause entire populations to be exterminated by toxic gases in the great wars of the future.

From mouth to anus, the body is traversed by a stream of nutritive substances. The digestive membranes determine the nature of the chemical relations between the external world and the inner world of our tissues and organic fluids. But their functions are far more complex than those of the respiratory ones. They must profoundly transform the foodstuffs which reach their surface. They are not only a filter, but also a chemical factory. The ferments secreted by their glands collaborate with those of the pancreas in decomposing the aliments into substances capable of being absorbed by the intestinal cells. The digestive surface is extraordinarily vast. The mucosas secrete and absorb large quantities of fluids. Their cells allow the foodstuffs, when digested, to enter the body. But they resist the penetration of the bacteria that swarm in the digestive tract. These dangerous enemies are generally held in control by the thin intestinal membrane, and the leucocytes defending it. But they are always a menace. Viruses thrive in the pharynx and the nose. Streptococci, staphylococci, and microbes of diphtheria in the tonsils. The bacilli of typhoid fever and of dysentery multiply with ease in the intestines. The soundness of the respiratory and digestive membranes governs, in a large measure, the resistance of the organism to infectious diseases, its strength, its equilibrium, its effectivity, its intellectual attitude.

Thus, our body constitutes a closed universe, limited on one side by the skin, and on the other by the mucosas covering our inner surfaces. If these membranes are impaired at any point, the existence of the individual is endangered. Even a superficial burn, when extending over a large area of the skin, results in death. This covering separates our organs and humors from the cosmic environment, and yet allows most extensive physical and chemical communications between these two worlds. It accomplishes the miracle of being a barrier at once closed and open. For it does not protect our nervous system against our mental surroundings. We may be wounded, and even killed, by subtle enemies which, ignoring our anatomical frontiers, invade our consciousness, like aviators bombarding a city without taking any notice of its fortifications.

4

The inside of our body does not resemble the descriptions of classical anatomy. This science has constructed a schema of the human being that is purely structural and quite unreal. It is not merely by opening a corpse that one may learn how man is constituted. Of course, we can observe in this way his framework, the skeleton and the muscles, which are the scaffold of the organs. In a cage formed by the spinal column, the ribs, and the sternum, are suspended the heart and the lungs. The liver, spleen, kidneys, stomach, intestines, and sexual glands are attached, by the folds of the peritoneum, to the inner surface of a large cavity whose bottom is formed by the pelvis, the sides by the abdominal muscles, and the roof by the diaphragm. The most fragile of all the organs, the brain and the cord, are enclosed in osseous boxes, the cranium and the spine. They are protected against the hardness of the walls of their lodgings by a system of membranes and a cushion of liquid.

One cannot understand the living being by studying a dead body. For the tissues of a corpse have been deprived of their circulating blood and of their functions. In reality, an organ separated from its nutritive medium no longer exists. In the living body, blood is present everywhere. It pulsates in the arteries, glides through the veins, fills the capillary vessels, bathes all tissues in transparent lymph. In order to apprehend this inner world as it is, more delicate techniques than those of anatomy and of histology are indispensable. We must study organs of living animals and of men, as they are seen in the course of surgical operations, and not simply those of cadavers prepared for dissection. Their structure should be learned, both from microscopical sections of dead tissues more or less modified by fixatives and dyes, and from living tissues while functioning. Also from cinematographic films on which their movements have been recorded. We must not separate cells from medium and function from structure, as anatomy has done.

Within the body, the cells behave like small organisms plunged in an aerated and nutritive medium. This medium is analogous to sea water. However, it contains a smaller quantity of salts, and its composition is much richer and more varied. The leucocytes of the blood and the cells covering the walls of blood vessels and lymphatics are like fish swimming freely in the depth of the ocean or lying flat on the sandy bottom. But the cells forming the tissues do not float in a fluid. They are comparable, not to fish, but to amphibia inhabiting marshes or moist sand. All living cells depend absolutely on the medium in which they are immersed. They modify this medium unceasingly, and are modified by it. In fact, they are inseparable from it. As inseparable as their body is from its nucleus. Their structure and functions are entirely subordinated to the physical, physicochemical, and chemical conditions of the surrounding fluid. This fluid is the interstitial lymph which at once produces, and is produced by, blood plasma. Cells and medium, structure and function, cannot be separated from one another. The isolation of cells from their natural environment is altogether unwarranted. However, methodological necessity forces us to divide this ensemble into fragments, and to describe, on one side, the cells and tissues, and, on the other, the organic medium—that is, the blood and the humors.

The cells congregate in societies, which are called tissues and organs. But the analogy of these societies to human and insect communities is quite superficial. For the individuality of cells is much less definite than that of men and even of insects. The rules of these associations are merely the expression of the inherent properties of the individuals. The characteristics of human beings are more easily learned than those of their societies. Physiology is a science. Human sociology is not. On the contrary, cell sociology is more advanced than the science of the structure and functions of the cell as an individual. Anatomists and physiologists have long since known the characteristics of tissues and organs—that is, of cell societies. Only recently have they succeeded in analyzing the properties of the cells themselves, of the individuals making up the organic associations. Owing to the new procedures for the cultivation of tissues, it has been possible to study living cells in a flask as easily as bees in a hive. Those cells have revealed themselves as endowed with unsuspected powers, with astounding properties. Virtual in the normal conditions of life, these properties actualize under the influence of diseases, when the organic medium undergoes certain physicochemical changes. These functional characteristics, far more than their structure, give to tissues the power of building up the living body.

Despite its minuteness, each cell is a very complex organism. It does not in any way resemble the favorite abstraction of chemists, a drop of gelatin surrounded by a semi-permeable membrane. The substance, which biologists call protoplasm, is found neither in its nucleus nor in its body. Protoplasm is a concept deprived of objective meaning. Just as the concept anthropoplasm would be, if by such a concept one attempted to define the content of the human body. Cells can now be filmed and magnified to such an extent that, when thrown on the screen, they are larger than a man. All their organs are then visible. In the middle of their body floats a kind of ovoid, elastic-walled balloon, the nucleus, which appears to be full of an inert and transparent jelly. In this jelly are seen two nucleoli, which slowly and unceasingly change their shape. Around the nucleus there is a great agitation of small particles. The movements are particularly active around a cluster of vesicles, corresponding to the organ called by anatomists the apparatus of Golgi or of Renaut, and whose functions are connected with the nutrition of the cell. Small and indistinct granules form a kind of whirlpool in that same district. Larger globules endlessly zigzag through the cell, going as far as the extremities of its mobile and transitory arms. But the most remarkable organs are long filaments, the mitochondrias, which resemble snakes or, in certain cells, short bacteria..Vesicles, granulations, globules, and filaments glide, dance, and undulate perpetually in the free spaces of the cell body.

This structural complexity of the living cell is disconcerting, but its chemical constitution is still more intricate. The nucleus, which, with the exception of the nucleoli, appears to be completely empty, contains substances of a truly marvelous nature. The simplicity attributed by chemists to its constituent nucleoproteins is an illusion. In fact, the nuclear substance comprises the genes, those mysterious beings of which we know nothing except that they are the hereditary tendencies of cells and of men. Instead of being simple, the chemical composition of the nucleus must be of bewildering complexity. The genes are generally invisible. However, we know that they dwell in the chromosomes, those elongated bodies seen in the clear fluid of the nucleus when the cell is going to divide. At this moment the chromosomes form in a more or less distinct manner two groups. These groups move away from each other. At the same time, the entire cell shakes violently, tosses its contents in all directions, and divides into two parts. These parts, the daughter cells, withdraw from each other while still united by some elastic filaments. These filaments stretch and finally give way. Thus, two new elements of the organism have become individualized.

Cells, like animals, belong to many different races. These races, or types, are defined by both their structural and their functional characteristics. They spring from different fields, such as the thyroid gland, the spleen, the skin, the liver, etc. But, strange to say, cells originating from the same region may assume different types at successive periods of time. The organism is as heterogeneous in time as in space. The cell types that build up the body may be roughly divided into two classes. The fixed cells, whose associations form the tissues and the organs, and the mobile cells, which travel throughout the entire organism. The connective and epithelial types of cells belong to the fixed category. Epithelial cells are the noblest elements of the body. They constitute the brain, the skin, the endocrine glands, etc. Connective cells build up the framework of the organs. They are truly ubiquitous. Around them appear various substances, such as cartilage, calcium, fibrous tissue, elastic fibers, which give skeleton, muscles, blood vessels, and organs the solidity and elasticity indispensable to their functions. In addition, they metamorphose into contractile elements. These are the muscles of the heart, of the vessels, of the digestive apparatus, and also of the locomotive system. Although connective and epithelial cells seem to be immobile and are still called by their old name of fixed cells, nevertheless they move, as cinematography has shown. But their movements are slow. They glide in their medium like oil spreading over the surface of water. They drag with them their nucleus, suspended in the fluid mass of their body. They differ markedly from the mobile cells. Those cells include the different types of leucocytes of the blood and of the tissues. Their motion is rapid. The leucocytes, characterized by the presence of several nuclei, resemble amebas. The lymphocytes crawl more slowly, like small worms. The larger ones, the monocytes, have the appearance of an octopus. They extrude long tentacles from their substance, and also surround themselves with a thin, undulating membrane. After having enveloped dead cells and microbes in the folds of this membrane, they voraciously devour them.

When these different cell types are bred in flasks, their characteristics become just as apparent as those of the various kinds of microbes. Each type has its own inherent properties, which remain specific, even when several years have elapsed since its separation from the organism. Cell types are characterized by their mode of locomotion, their way of associating with one another, the aspect of their colonies, the rate of their growth, their response to various chemicals, the substances they secrete, the food they require, as well as by their shape and structure. This broader conception is taking the place of the purely morphological definitions of classical anatomy. The laws of organization of each cell community—that is, of each organ—derive from these elementary properties. Tissue cells, possessing only the characteristics ascribed to them by anatomy, would be incapable of building up a living organism. But they are endowed with much higher powers. They do not manifest all of them. Besides the activities which they usually display, they possess others, generally hidden, but capable of becoming actual in response to certain changes of the medium. They are thus enabled to deal with the unforeseeable events taking place in the course of normal life and during illnesses.

Cells unite in dense masses, the tissues and organs, whose architectonic depends on the structural and functional needs of the organism in its totality. The human body is a compact and mobile unit. And its harmony is assured by both the blood and the nerves which integrate all cell communities. The existence of tissues cannot be conceived without that of a fluid medium. The necessary relations of the anatomical elements and of the vessels carrying this nutritive medium determine the shape of the organs. Such shape also is influenced by the presence of the ducts through which glandular products are secreted. All spatial ordering of bodily structures is commanded by their food requirements. The architectural plan of each organ is inspired by the need of the cells to be immersed in a medium always rich in foodstuffs and never encumbered by waste products.

5

The organic medium is a part of the tissues. Should it be removed, the body would cease to exist. Every manifestation of the life of our organs and nervous centers, our thoughts, our affections, the cruelty, the ugliness, and the beauty of the universe, its very existence, depend on the physicochemical state of our humors. The organic medium is composed of blood, flowing in the vessels, and of fluids, plasma or lymph, which filter through the walls of the capillaries into the tissues. There is a general organic medium, the blood, and regional media, consisting of the interstitial lymph of each organ. An organ may be compared to a pond completely filled with aquatic plants and fed by a small brook. The almost stagnant water is polluted by waste products, dead fragments of plants, and chemical substances set free by them. The degree of stagnation and of pollution of the water depends on the rapidity and the volume of the brook. Such is the case with interstitial lymph. In short, the composition of the regional media inhabited by the various cells of the body rests, directly or indirectly, on blood.

The blood is a tissue, like all the other tissues. It is composed of about twenty-five or thirty thousand billions of red cells, and of fifty billions of white cells. But these cells are not, like those of the other tissues, immobilized in a framework. They are suspended in a viscous liquid, the plasma. Blood is a moving tissue, finding its way into all parts of the body. It carries to each cell the proper nourishment. Acting, at the same time, as a main sewer that takes away the waste products set free by living tissues. It also contains chemical substances and cells capable of repairing organs wherever necessary. These properties are indeed strange. When carrying out such astonishing duties, the blood stream behaves like a torrent which, with the help of the mud and the trees drifting in its stream, would set about repairing the houses situated on its banks.

Blood plasma is not exactly what chemists believe it to be. It is incomparably richer than the classical abstractions. Without any doubt, plasma really is the solution of bases, acids, salts, and proteins, whose physicochemical equilibria are expressed in the laws discovered by Van Slyke and Henderson. Owing to this particular composition, its ionic alkalinity is maintained near the neutral point, in spite of the acids ceaselessly liberated by the tissues. In this manner it supplies all the cells of the entire organism with an unvarying medium, neither too acid nor too alkaline. But it also contains proteins, polypeptides, amino acids, sugars, fats, enzymes, metals in infinitesimal quantities, and the secretions of all glands and tissues. The nature of the majority of these substances is still very imperfectly known. We are scarcely beginning to understand the immense complexity of their functions. Each cell type finds in the blood plasma the foodstuffs indispensable to its maintenance, and also substances accelerating or retarding its activity. Thus, certain fatty compounds linked to the proteins of serum are capable of curbing cellular proliferation, and even of preventing it completely. The serum also contains substances opposing the multiplication of bacteria, the antibodies. These antibodies appear when the tissues have to defend themselves against invading microbes. In addition, there is in blood plasma a protein, fibrinogen, father of fibrin, whose shreds spontaneously adhere to the wounds of blood vessels and stop hemorrhages.

Red and white corpuscles play an important part in the constitution of the organic medium. We know that blood plasma dissolves only a small amount of atmospheric oxygen. Without the help of the red corpuscles, it would, therefore, be incapable of supplying the immense population of body cells with the oxygen they require. These red corpuscles are not living cells. They are tiny sacks full of hemoglobin. During their passage through the lungs they take on a load of oxygen which, a few instants later, they hand over to the greedy tissue cells. When taking delivery of the oxygen, these cells simultaneously get rid of their carbon dioxide and other waste products by passing them on to the blood. The white corpuscles, on the contrary, are living organisms. Sometimes they float in the blood stream, sometimes they escape from the capillary vessels by slipping through their walls into the tissues, and creep on the surface of the cells of the mucous membranes, of the intestines, of the glands, and of all the organs. Owing to these microscopic elements, the blood acts as a mobile tissue, a repairing agent, a medium both solid and fluid, capable of going wherever its presence may be necessary. It can rapidly surround microbes attacking a region of the organism with a great mass of leucocytes, which fight the infection. It also brings to the surface of a wound of the skin or of any organ white corpuscles of the larger type, virtual material for the reconstruction of tissues. Such leucocytes have the power of transforming themselves into fixed cells. And those cells call connective fibers into being, and repair the injured tissues by means of a scar.

The fluids that escape from the capillary vessels constitute the local medium of tissues and organs. It is practically impossible to study the composition of this medium. However, when dyes, whose color changes with the ionic acidity of the tissues, are injected into the organism, as was done by Rous, the organs take on different hues. The diversity of the local media can be visualized. In reality, such diversity is much more profound than is shown by this procedure. But we are not able to detect all its characteristics. In the vast world of the human organism there are most varied countries. Although these countries are irrigated by branches of the same stream, the quality of the water in their lakes and their ponds also depends on the constitution of the soil and the nature of the vegetation. Each organ, each tissue, creates its own medium at the expense of blood plasma. On the reciprocal adjustment of the cells and their medium are based the health or disease, strength or weakness, happiness or misery, of each one of us.

6

Between the liquids composing the organic medium, and the world of tissues and organs, there are perpetual chemical exchanges. Nutritive activity is a mode of being of the cells, as fundamental as structure and form. As soon as their chemical exchanges, or metabolism, cease, the organs come into equilibrium with their medium and die. Nutrition is synonymous with existence. Living tissues crave oxygen and take it from blood. This means, in physicochemical terms, that they possess a high reducing potential, that a complex system of chemical substances and of ferments enables them to use atmospheric oxygen for energy-producing reactions. From the oxygen, hydrogen, and carbon supplied by sugars and fats, living cells procure the mechanical energy necessary for the maintenance of their structure and for their movements, the electrical energy manifesting itself in every change of the organic conditions, and the heat indispensable to chemical reactions and physiological processes. They also find in blood plasma the nitrogen, sulfur, phosphorus, etc., which they utilize for the construction of new cells, and in the processes of growth and repair. With the help of their ferments they divide the proteins, sugars, and fats contained in their medium into smaller and smaller fragments, and make use of the energy so liberated. They simultaneously build up, by means of energy-absorbing reactions, certain compounds, more complex and having a higher energy potential, and they incorporate them in their own substance.

The intensity of chemical exchanges in the cell communities, or in the entire being, expresses the intensity of organic life. Metabolism is measured by the quantity of oxygen absorbed and that of carbonic acid produced, when the body is in a state of complete repose. This is called basal metabolism. There is a great increase in the activity of the exchanges as soon as muscles contract and perform mechanical work. Metabolism is higher in a child than in an adult, in a mouse than in a dog. Any very large increase in the stature of human beings would, as mentioned heretofore, probably be followed by a decline of basal metabolism. Brain, liver, and endocrine glands need a great deal of chemical energy. But muscular exercise raises the intensity of the exchanges in the most marked manner. Nevertheless, all our activities cannot be expressed in chemical terms. Intellectual work, strange to say, does not increase metabolism. It seems to require no energy, or to consume a quantity of it too small to be detected by our present techniques. It is, indeed, an astonishing fact that human thought, which has transformed the surface of the earth, destroyed and built nations, discovered new universes in the immensity of the sidereal spaces, is elaborated without demanding a measurable amount of energy. The mightiest effort of our intelligence has incomparably less effect on metabolism than the contraction of the biceps when this muscle lifts a weight of a few grams. The ambition of Cæsar, the meditation of Newton, the inspiration of Beethoven, the passionate contemplation of Pasteur, did not modify the chemical exchanges of these great men as much as a few bacteria or a slight stimulation of the thyroid gland would easily have done.

Basal metabolism is remarkably constant. The organism maintains the normal activity of its chemical exchanges under the most adverse conditions. Exposure to intense cold does not decrease the rhythm of nutrition. The temperature of the body falls only on the approach of death. On the contrary, bears and raccoons lower their metabolism in winter, and fall into a state of slower life. Certain arthropodous animals, *Tardigrada,* completely stop their metabolism when they are dried. A condition of latent life is thus induced. After a lapse of several weeks, if one moistens these desiccated animals, they revive, and the rhythm of their life again becomes normal. We have not yet discovered the secret of producing such a suspension of nutrition in domestic animals and in man. It would be an evident advantage in cold countries if a state of latent life could be induced in sheep and cows for the duration of the winter. It might be possible, perhaps, to prolong life, cure certain diseases, and give higher opportunities to exceptionally gifted individuals, if human beings could be made to hibernate from time to time. But we are not capable of decreasing the rate of metabolism, except by the barbarous method that consists of removing the thyroid gland. And even that method is quite insufficient. As far as man is concerned, latent life, for the moment, is an impossible form of existence.

7

In the course of the chemical exchanges, waste products, or catabolites are set free by tissues and organs. They tend to accumulate in the regional medium and to render it uninhabitable for the cells. The phenomenon of nutrition, therefore, requires the existence of apparatuses capable of assuring, through a rapid circulation of lymph and blood, the replacement of the nutritive substances used by the tissues, and the elimination of waste products. The volume of the circulating fluids, compared with that of the organs, is very small. The weight of blood of a human being is hardly equal to one-tenth of his total weight. However, living tissues consume large amounts of oxygen and glucose. They also liberate into the inner medium considerable quantities of carbonic, lactic, hydrochloric, phosphoric acids, etc. A fragment of living tissue, cultivated in a flask, must be given a volume of liquid equal to two thousand times its own volume, in order not to be poisoned within a few days by its waste products. In addition, it requires a gaseous atmosphere at least ten times larger than its fluid medium. Consequently, a human body reduced to pulp and cultivated *in vitro* would demand about two hundred thousand liters of nutritive fluid. It is on account of the marvelous perfection of the apparatuses responsible for the circulation of the blood, its wealth of nutritive substances, and the constant elimination of the waste products, that our tissues can live in six or seven liters of fluid, instead of two hundred thousand.

The speed of circulation is sufficiently great to prevent the composition of blood from being modified by the catabolites of tissues. The acidity of plasma increases only after violent exercise. Each organ regulates the volume and the rapidity of its blood flow by means of vasomotor nerves. The interstitial lymph becomes acid as soon as circulation slackens or stops. The more or less injurious effects of such acid poisoning on the viscera depend on the type of their constituent cells. If we remove a dog's kidney, leave it on a table for an hour, and then replant it in the animal, the kidney is not disturbed by the temporary deprivation of blood, but resumes its functions and works indefinitely in a normal manner. Neither does the suspension of the circulation in a limb, for three or four hours, have any ill effects. The brain, however, is much more sensitive to lack of oxygen. When circulation is stopped and anemia complete in this organ for about twenty minutes, death always takes place. After only ten minutes, anemia produces serious and often irreparable disorders. Thus, it is impossible to bring back to normal life an individual whose brain has been completely deprived of circulation for a very short time. Lowering of the blood pressure is also dangerous. Brain and other organs demand a certain tension of the blood. Our conduct and the quality of our thoughts depend, in a large measure, on the state of our circulatory apparatus. All human activities are regulated by the physical and chemical conditions of the inner medium and, ultimately, by the heart and the arteries.

Blood maintains its composition constant by perpetually passing through apparatuses where it is purified and recuperates the nutritive substances removed by the tissues. When venous blood returns from the muscles and the organs, it is full of carbonic acid and waste products of nutrition. The pulsations of the heart then drive it into the immense network of the lung capillaries, where each red corpuscle comes into contact with atmospheric oxygen. This gas, in conformity with certain simple physicochemical laws, penetrates the blood and is taken up by the hemoglobin of the red cells. Carbon dioxide simultaneously escapes into the bronchi, whence it is expelled into the outside atmosphere by the respiratory movements. The more rapid the respiration, the more active are the chemical exchanges between air and blood. But during its passage through the lungs, blood gets rid of carbonic acid only. It still contains nonvolatile acids, and all other waste products of metabolism. Its purification is completed during its passage through the kidneys. The kidneys separate from the blood certain substances that are eliminated in the urine. They also regulate the quantity of salts indispensable to plasma in order that its osmotic tension may remain constant. The functioning of the kidneys and of the lungs is of a prodigious efficiency. It is the intense activity of these viscera that permits the fluid medium required by living tissues to be so limited, and the human body to possess such compactness and agility.

8

The nutritive material carried by the blood to the tissues derives from three sources. From atmospheric air by the agency of the lungs, from the intestinal surface, and, finally, from the endocrine glands. All substances used by the organism, with the exception of oxygen, are supplied by the intestines, either directly or indirectly. The food is successively treated by the saliva, the gastric juice, and the secretions of pancreas, liver, and intestinal mucosa. Digestive ferments divide the molecules of proteins, carbohydrates, and fats into smaller fragments. These fragments are capable of traversing the mucous membranes, which defend our inner frontier. They are then absorbed by the blood and lymph vessels of the intestinal mucosa, and penetrate the organic medium. Certain fats and sugars are the only substances to enter the body without previously undergoing modification. For this reason the consistency of adipose parts varies in conformity with the nature of the animal or vegetable fats included in the diet. By feeding a dog with fats of a high melting-point or with oils fluid at body temperature, we can render its adipose tissue either hard or soft. Proteins are broken up by digestive ferments into their constituent amino acids. They thus lose their individuality, their racial specificity. In this way, amino acids, and groups of amino acids derived from proteins of beef, mutton, wheat, etc., retain no evidence of their various origins. They build up in the body new proteins, specific for the human race and for the individual. The intestinal wall almost completely protects the organism from invasion by molecules belonging to the tissues of other beings, by opposing the penetration of animal or vegetal proteins into the blood. However, it sometimes allows such proteins to enter. So the body may silently become sensitive, or resistant, to many foreign substances. The barrier raised by the intestines against the outer world is not impassable.

The intestinal mucosa is not always capable of digesting or absorbing certain indispensable elements of the food. In such an instance, even if these substances are present in the intestinal lumen, they cannot enter our tissues. In fact, the chemical elements of the outer world act on each individual in different ways, according to the specific constitution of his intestinal mucosa. From these elements are built our tissues and our humors. Man is literally made from the dust of the earth. For this reason his physiological and mental activities are profoundly influenced by the geological constitution of the country where he lives, by the nature of the animals and plants on which he generally feeds. His structure and his functions depend also on the selection he makes of certain elements among the vegetal and animal foods at his disposal. The chiefs always had a diet quite different from that of their slaves. Those who fought, commanded, and conquered used chiefly meats and fermented drinks, whereas the peaceful, the weak, and the submissive were satisfied with milk, vegetables, fruits, and cereals. Our aptitudes and our destiny come, in some measure, from the nature of the chemical substances that construct our tissues. It seems as though human beings, like animals, could be artificially given certain bodily and mental characteristics if subjected from childhood to appropriate diets.

The third kind of nutritive substances contained in blood, in addition to atmospheric oxygen and to products of intestinal digestion, consists, as already mentioned, of the secretions of the endocrine glands. The organism has the peculiar property of being its own builder, of manufacturing new compounds from the chemical substances of the blood. These compounds serve to feed certain tissues and to stimulate certain functions. This sort of creation of itself by itself is analogous to the training of the will by an effort of the will. Glands, such as the thyroid, the suprarenal, the pancreas, etc., synthetize from the chemicals in solution in the organic medium a number of new compounds, thyroxin, adrenalin, insulin, etc. They are true chemical transformers. In this way, substances indispensable for the nutrition of cells and organs, and for physiological and mental activities, are produced. Such a phenomenon is as strange as if certain parts of a motor should create the oil used by other parts of the machine, the substances accelerating the combustion of the fuel, and even the thoughts of the engineer. Obviously, tissues are unable to feed exclusively on the compounds supplied by the diet after their passage through the intestinal mucosa. These compounds have to be remolded by the glands. To these glands is due the existence of the body with its manifold activities.

Man is, first of all, a nutritive process. He consists of a ceaseless motion of chemical substances. One can compare him to the flame of a candle, or to the fountains playing in the gardens of Versailles. Those beings, made of burning gases or of water, are both permanent and transitory. Their existence depends on a stream of gas or of liquid. Like ourselves, they change according to the quality and the quantity of the substances which animate them. As a large river coming from the external world and returning to it, matter perpetually flows through all the cells of the body. During its passing, it yields to tissues the energy they need, and also the chemicals which build the temporary and fragile structures of our organs and humors. The corporeal substratum of all human activities originates from the inanimate world and, sooner or later, goes back to it. Our organism is made from the same elements as lifeless things. Therefore, we should not be surprised, as some modern physiologists still are, to find at work within our own self the usual laws of physics and of chemistry as they exist in the cosmic world. Since we are parts of the material universe, the absence of those laws is unthinkable.

9

The sexual glands have other functions than that of impelling man to the gesture which, in primitive life, perpetuated the race. They also intensify all physiological, mental, and spiritual activities. No eunuch has ever become a great philosopher, a great scientist, or even a great criminal. Testicles and ovaries possess functions of overwhelming importance. They generate male or female cells. Simultaneously, they secrete into the blood certain substances, which impress the male or female characteristics on our tissues, humors, and consciousness, and give to all our functions their character of intensity. The testicle engenders audacity, violence, and brutality, the qualities distinguishing the fighting bull from the ox drawing the plow along the furrow. The ovary affects the organism of the woman in an analogous manner. But its action lasts only during a part of her life. At the menopause, the gland atrophies somewhat. The shorter life of the ovaries gives the aging woman great inferiority to man, whose testicles remain active until extreme old age.

The differences existing between man and woman do not come from the particular form of the sexual organs, the presence of the uterus, from gestation, or from the mode of education. They are of a more fundamental nature. They are caused by the very structure of the tissues and by the impregnation of the entire organism with specific chemical substances secreted by the ovary. Ignorance of these fundamental facts has led promoters of feminism to believe that both sexes should have the same education, the same powers, and the same responsibilities. In reality, woman differs profoundly from man. Every one of the cells of her body bears the mark of her sex. The same is true of her organs and, above all, of her nervous system. Physiological laws are as inexorable as those of the sidereal world. They cannot be replaced by human wishes. We are obliged to accept them just as they are. Women should develop their aptitudes in accordance with their own nature, without trying to imitate the males. Their part in the progress of civilization is higher than that of men. They should not abandon their specific functions.

With regard to the propagation of the race, the importance of the two sexes is unequal. Testicle cells unceasingly produce, during the entire course of life, animalcules endowed with very active movements, the spermatozoa. These spermatozoa swim in the mucus covering the vagina and uterus, and meet the ovum at the surface of the uterine mucosa. The ovum results from the slow ripening of the germinal cells of the ovary. In the ovary of a young woman there are about three hundred thousand ova. About four hundred of them reach maturity. Between two menstruations, the cyst containing the ovum bursts. Then, the ovum is projected upon the membrane of the Fallopian tube and is transported by the vibrating cilia of this membrane into the uterus. Its nucleus has already undergone an important change. It has ejected half of its substance—that is, half of each chromosome. A spermatozoon then penetrates its surface. And its chromosomes, which have also lost half of their substance, unite with those of the ovum. A human being is born. He is composed of a single cell, grafted on the uterine mucosa. This cell separates into two parts, and the development of the embryo begins.

The father and the mother contribute in equal proportions to the formation of the nucleus of the ovum, which engenders every cell of the new organism. But the mother gives also, in addition to half its nuclear substance, all the protoplasm surrounding the nucleus. She thus plays a more important part in the genesis of the embryo than the father does. Indeed, parental characteristics are transmitted to the offspring by the nucleus. But the remaining part of the cell also has some influence. The laws of heredity and the present theories of the geneticists do not entirely elucidate these complex phenomena. When discussing the relative importance of the father and the mother in reproduction, we should never forget the experiments of Bataillon and of Jacques Loeb. From an unfertilized egg, and without the intervention of the male element, a normal frog was obtained through an appropriate technique. The spermatozoon can be replaced by a chemical or physical agent. Only the female element is essential.

Man's part in reproduction is short. That of the woman lasts nine months. During this time the fetus is nourished by chemicals, which filter from the maternal blood through the membranes of the placenta. While the mother supplies her child with the elements from which its tissues are constructed, she receives certain substances secreted by the embryonic organs. Such substances may be beneficial or dangerous. The fetus, in fact, originates almost as much from the father as from the mother. Therefore, a being of partly foreign origin has taken up its abode in the woman's body. The latter is subjected to its influence during the entire pregnancy. In some instances she may be poisoned by her child. Her physiological and psychological conditions are always modified by it. But females, at any rate among mammals, seem only to attain their full development after one or more pregnancies. Women who have no children are not so well balanced and become more nervous than the others. In short, the presence of the fetus, whose tissues greatly differ from hers because they are young and are, in part, those of her husband, acts profoundly on the woman. The importance to her of the generative function has not been sufficiently recognized. Such function is indispensable to her optimum development. It is, therefore, absurd to turn women against maternity. The same intellectual and physical training, and the same ambitions, should not be given to young girls as to boys. Educators should pay very close attention to the organic and mental peculiarities of the male and the female, and to their natural functions. Between the two sexes there are irrevocable differences. And it is imperative to take them into account in constructing the civilized world.

10

Through his nervous system man records the stimuli impinging upon him from his environment. His organs and muscles supply the appropriate answer. He struggles for existence with his mind still more than with his body. In this ceaseless fight, his heart, lungs, liver, and endocrine glands are as indispensable as his muscles, hands, tools, machines, and weapons. Seemingly for this purpose he possesses two nervous systems. The central, or cerebrospinal system, conscious and voluntary, commands the muscles. The sympathetic system, autonomous and unconscious, controls the organs. The second system depends on the first. This double apparatus gives to the complexity of our body the simplicity required for its action on the outside world.

The central system consists of the brain, the cerebellum, and the spinal cord. It acts directly on the nerves of the muscles, and indirectly on those of the organs. It is composed of a soft, whitish, extremely fragile substance, filling the skull and the spinal column. This substance, by the agency of the sensitive nerves, receives the messages emanating from the surface of the body and from the sensory organs. In this way the nervous centers are in constant touch with the cosmic world. Simultaneously, they send their orders to all the muscles through the motor nerves, and to all the organs through the sympathetic system. An immense number of nervous fibers intersect the organism in every direction. Their microscopic endings creep between the cells of the skin, around the acini of the glands and their excretory ducts, in the coat of the arteries and the veins, into the contractile envelopes of the stomach and the intestines, on the surface of the muscular fibers, etc. They spread their delicate network through the whole body. They all originate from cells inhabiting the central nervous system, the double chain of the sympathetic ganglia, and the small ganglia disseminated through the organs.

These cells are the noblest and most elaborate of the epithelial cells. Owing to the techniques of Ramon y Cajal, they appear in all their structural beauty. They possess a large body which, in the varieties found on the surface of the brain, resembles a pyramid. And also most complex organs whose functions still remain unknown. They extend in the form of extremely slender filaments, the dendrites, and the axons. Certain axons cover the long distance separating the cerebral surface from the lower part of the cord. Axons, dendrites, and their mother cell constitute a distinct individual, the neuron. The fibrils of one cell never unite with those of another. Their extremities form a cluster of very tiny bulbs, which are in constant motion on their almost invisible stems, as is shown by cinematographic films. They articulate with the corresponding terminals of another cell by means of a membrane, known as the synaptic membrane. In each neuron the nervous influx always diffuses in the same direction in relation to the cellular body. This direction is centripetal for the dendrites, and centrifugal for the axons. It passes from one neuron to the other by crossing the synaptic membrane. Likewise, it penetrates muscular fibers from the bulbs in contact with their surface. But its passage is subject to a strange condition. The value of time, or chronaxy, must be identical in the contiguous neurons, or in the neuron and the muscular fiber. The propagation of nervous influx does not take place between two neurons having different time standards. Thus, a muscle and its nerve must be isochronic. If the chronaxy of the nerve or the muscle be modified by a poison, such as curare or strychnine, the influx no longer reaches the muscle. Paralysis occurs, although the muscle is normal. These temporal relations of nerve and muscle are as indispensable to normal function as is their spatial continuity. We do not yet know what takes place within the nerves during pain or voluntary motion. But we are aware that a variation of electric potential travels along the nerve during its activity. In fact, Adrian has shown, in isolated fibrils, the progress of negative waves, whose arrival in the brain is expressed by a sensation of pain.

Neurons articulate with each other in a system of relays, like electrical relays. They are divided into two groups. One group is composed of receptor and motor neurons, receiving stimuli from the outside world or from the organs, and controlling the voluntary muscles. The other group, of the neurons of association, whose vast number gives to our nervous centers their elaborate complexity. Our intelligence can no more realize the immensity of the brain than the extent of the sidereal universe. The cerebral substance contains more than twelve thousand millions of cells. These cells are connected with one another by fibrils, and each fibril possesses several branches. By means of these fibrils, they associate several trillions of times. And this prodigious crowd of tiny individuals and invisible fibrils, despite its undreamed-of complexity, works as if it were essentially one. To observers accustomed to the simplicity of the molecular and atomic worlds the brain appears as an unintelligible and marvelous phenomenon.

One of the principal functions of the nervous centers is to respond in an appropriate manner to stimuli coming from the environment, or, in other words, to produce reflex reactions. A beheaded frog is suspended with its legs hanging. If one of its toes is pinched, the leg moves, pulling away from the painful stimulus. This phenomenon is due to the presence of a reflex arc—that is, of two neurons, one sensitive and the other motive, articulated with one another within the cord. Generally, a reflex arc is not so simple and includes one or several associating neurons interposed between sensitive and motive neurons. The neuronic systems are responsible for reflexes such as respiration, swallowing, standing upright, walking, as well as for most of the acts of our every-day life. These movements are automatic. But some of them are influenced by consciousness. For example, when we think about our respiratory motion, its rhythm is at once modified. On the contrary, heart, stomach, and intestines are quite independent of our will. However, if we pay too much attention to them, their automatism may be disturbed. Although the muscles that permit standing, walking, and running receive their orders from the spinal cord, they depend for their coördination upon the cerebellum. Like the cord, the cerebellum does not concern itself with mental processes.

The cerebral surface, or cortex of the brain, is a mosaic of distinct nervous organs connected with the different parts of the body. For instance, the lateral part of the brain, known as region of Rolando, controls the movements of prehension and locomotion, and also articulate language. Farther back on the cortex are the visual centers. Wounds, tumors, and hemorrhages located in these different districts result in disturbances of the corresponding functions. Similar disorders appear when the lesions are situated in the fibers uniting the cerebral centers to the lower parts of the spinal cord. The reflexes called by Pavlov conditional reflexes take place in the cerebral cortex. A dog secretes saliva when food is placed in his mouth. This is an innate reflex. But he also secretes saliva when he sees the person who usually brings him his nourishment. This is an acquired, or conditional, reflex.

This property of the nervous system of animals and man renders education possible. If the surface of the brain is removed, the building up of new reflexes is quite impossible. Our knowledge of this intricate subject is still rudimentary. We do not know the relations between consciousness and nervous processes, between the mental and the cerebral. Neither do we know how events taking place in the pyramidal cells are influenced by previous or even future events, or how excitations are changed into inhibitions, and vice versa. We understand still less how unpredictable phenomena spring from the brain, how thought is born.

Brain and spinal cord, with nerves and muscles, constitute an indivisible system. Muscles, from a functional point of view, are only a part of the brain. It is with their help and that of the bones that human intelligence has put its mark on the world. Man has been given power over his environment by the shape of his skeleton. The limbs consist of articulated levers, composed of three segments. The upper limb is mounted upon a mobile plate, the shoulder blade, while the osseous girdle, the pelvis, to which the lower limb is jointed, is almost rigid and immobile. The motive muscles lie along the bones. Near the extremity of the arm, these muscles resolve into tendons, which move the fingers and the hand itself. The hand is a masterpiece. Simultaneously, it feels and it acts. It acts as if endowed with sight. Owing to the unique properties of its skin, its tactile nerves, its muscles, and its bones, the hand is capable of manufacturing arms and tools. We never would have acquired our mastery over matter without the aid of our fingers, those five small levers, each composed of three articulated segments, which are mounted upon the metacarpus and the bones of the wrist.

The hand adapts itself to the roughest work as well as to the most delicate. It has wielded with equal skill the flint knife of the primitive hunter, the blacksmith's hammer, the woodcutter's ax, the farmer's plow, the sword of the medieval knight, the controls of the modern aviator, the artist's brush, the journalist's pen, the threads of the silk-weaver. It is able to kill and to bless, to steal and to give, to sow grain on the surface of the fields and to throw grenades in the trenches. The elasticity, strength, and adaptiveness of the lower limbs, whose pendulum-like oscillations determine walking and running, have never been equaled by our machines, which only make use of the principle of the wheel. The three levers, articulated on the pelvis, adapt themselves with marvelous suppleness to all postures, efforts, and movements. They carry us on the polished floor of a ballroom and in the chaos of the ice-fields, upon the sidewalks of Park Avenue and on the slopes of the Rocky Mountains. They enable us to walk, to run, to fall, to climb, to swim, to wander all over the earth under all conditions.

There is another organic system composed of cerebral substance, nerves, muscles, and cartilages, which, to the same degree as the hand, has determined the superiority of man over all living beings. It consists of the tongue and the larynx, and their nervous apparatus. Owing to this system, we are capable of expressing our thoughts, of communicating with our fellow men by means of sounds. Were it not for language, civilization would not exist. The use of speech, like that of the hand, has greatly aided the development of the brain. The cerebral parts of the hand, the tongue, and the larynx extend over a large area of the brain surface. At the same time that the nervous centers control writing, speaking, and the grasping and handling of objects, they are, in return, stimulated by these acts. Simultaneously, they are determining and determined. It seems that the work of the mind is helped by the rhythmic contractions of the muscles. Certain exercises appear to stimulate thought. For this reason, perhaps, Aristotle and his disciples were in the habit of walking while discussing the fundamental problems of philosophy and science. No part of the nervous centers seems to act separately. Viscera, muscles, spinal cord, cerebrum, are functionally one. Skeletal muscles, for their coördinated action, depend on brain and spinal cord, and also on many organs. They receive their orders from the central nervous system, and their energy from the heart, the lungs, the endocrine glands, and the blood. To carry out the directions of the brain, they demand the help of the whole body.

II

The autonomous nervous system enables each viscus to coöperate with the entire organism in our dealings with the outside world. Organs such as the stomach, liver, heart, etc., are not subject to our will. We are incapable of decreasing or increasing the caliber of our arteries, the rhythm of our pulse or of the contractions of our intestines. The automatism of these functions is due to the presence of reflex arcs within the organs. These regional brains are made up of small clusters of nervous cells scattered in the tissues, under the skin, around the blood vessels, etc. There are numerous reflex centers, responsible for the independence of the viscera. For example, an intestinal loop, when removed from the organism and provided with artificial circulation, displays normal movements. A grafted kidney, although its nerves are cut, starts to work at once. Most organs are endowed with a certain freedom. They are thus able to function, even when isolated from the body. However, they are bound by innumerable nervous fibers to the double chain of sympathetic ganglia situated in front of the spinal column, and to other ganglia surrounding the abdominal vessels. These ganglia integrate all the organs and regulate their work. Moreover, through their relations with the spinal cord and the brain they coördinate the activity of the viscera with that of the muscles in the acts which demand an effort of the entire body.

The viscera, although dependent on the central nervous system, are, in some measure, independent of it. It is possible to remove, in a single mass, the lungs, heart, stomach, liver, pancreas, intestines, spleen, kidneys, and bladder, with their blood vessels and nerves, from the body of a cat or a dog, without the heart ceasing to beat, or the blood to circulate. If this visceral entity is placed in a warm bath and oxygen supplied to its lungs, life continues. The heart pulsates, the stomach and the intestines move and digest their food. The viscera can be effectively isolated from the central nervous system in a simpler way, as Cannon has done, by extirpating the double sympathetic chain from living cats. The animals which have undergone this operation continue to live in good health as long as they remain in their cage. But they are not capable of a free existence. In the struggle for life they can no longer call their heart, lungs, and glands to the help of their muscles, claws, and teeth.

The double chain of the sympathetic ganglia is connected with the cerebrospinal system by branches communicating with the cranial, dorsal, and pelvic regions of the nervous substance. The sympathetic or autonomous nerves of the cranial and pelvic regions are called parasympathetic. Those of the dorsal region are the sympathetic. In their action, the parasympathetic and the sympathetic are antagonistic to one another. Each organ receives its nerves simultaneously from these two systems. The parasympathetic slows the heart, and the sympathetic accelerates it. The latter dilates the pupil, while the former causes its contraction. The movements of the intestines are, on the contrary, decreased by the sympathetic and increased by the parasympathetic. According to the predominance of the one or the other of these systems, human beings are endowed with different temperaments. The circulation of each organ is regulated by these nerves. The sympathetic brings about constriction of the arteries and pallor of the face, such as are observed in emotion and certain diseases. Its section is followed by redness of the skin and contraction of the pupil. Some glands, such as the hypophysis and the suprarenals, are made up of both glandular and nervous cells. They enter into activity under the influence of the sympathetic. The chemical substances secreted by these cells have the same effect upon blood vessels as the stimulation of the nerve. They increase the power of the sympathetic. Like the sympathetic, adrenalin causes the vessels to contract. In fact, the autonomous nervous system, by means of its sympathetic and parasympathetic fibers, dominates the entire world of the viscera, and unifies their action. We shall describe later how the adaptive functions, those which enable the organism to endure, depend mostly on the sympathetic system.

The autonomous apparatus is linked, as we know, to the

central nervous system, supreme coördinator of all organic activities. It is represented by a center situated at the base of the brain. This center determines the manifestation of emotions. Wounds or tumors in this region bring about certain disorders of the affective functions. In fact, it is by the agency of the endocrine glands that our emotions express themselves. Shame, fear, and anger modify the cutaneous circulation. They cause pallor or flushing of the face, contraction or dilatation of the pupils, protrusion of the eye, discharge of adrenalin into the circulation, interruption of the gastric secretions, etc. Our states of consciousness have a marked effect upon the functions of the viscera. Many diseases of the stomach and of the heart originate in nervous troubles. The independence of the sympathetic system from the brain is not sufficient to protect our organs against the disturbances of our mind.

Organs are provided with sensitive nerves. They send frequent messages to the nervous centers and, more particularly, to the center of visceral consciousness. When, in the daily struggle for existence, our attention is attracted by the outside world, the stimuli coming from the organs do not pass the threshold of consciousness. However, they do give a certain color to our thoughts, our emotions, our actions, to all our life, though we do not clearly realize their hidden power. One sometimes experiences, without any reason, a feeling of imminent misfortune. Or an impression of joy, of unexplainable happiness. The state of our organic system obscurely acts on consciousness. A diseased viscus may, in this manner, sound an alarm. When a man, in either good or bad health, feels that he is in danger, that death approaches, such warning probably comes to him from the center of visceral consciousness. And visceral consciousness is rarely mistaken. Of course, in the inhabitants of the new city, sympathetic functions are often as ill balanced as mental activities. The autonomous system seems to become less capable of protecting the heart, stomach, intestines, and glands from the worries of existence. Against the dangers and brutality of primitive life it effectively defended the organs. But it is not strong enough to resist the constant shocks of modern life.

12

The body thus appears as an extremely complex thing, a stupendous association of different cell races, each race comprising billions of individuals. These individuals live immersed in humors made of chemical substances, which are manufactured by the organs, and of other substances derived from food. From one end of the body to the other, they communicate by chemical messengers—that is, by the agency of their secretions. Moreover, they are united by the nervous system. Their associations, as revealed by scientific techniques, are of an enormous complexity. Nevertheless, these immense crowds of individuals behave like a perfectly integrated being. Our acts are simple. For example, the act of accurately estimating a minute weight, or of selecting a given number of objects, without counting them and without making a mistake. However, such gestures appear to our mind to be composed of a multitude of elements. They require the harmonious functioning of muscular and tactile senses, of the retina, of the eye and hand muscles, of innumerable nervous and muscular cells. Their simplicity is probably real, their complexity, artificial—that is, created by our techniques of observation. No object seems to be simpler, more homogeneous, than the water of the ocean. But, if we could examine this water through a microscope having a magnifying power of about one million diameters, its simplicity would vanish. The clear drop would become a heterogeneous population of molecules of different dimensions and shapes, moving at various speeds in an inextricable chaos. Thus, the things of our world are simple or complex, according to the techniques that we select for studying them. In fact, functional simplicity always corresponds to a complex substratum. This is a primary datum of observation, which must be accepted just as it is.

Our tissues are of great structural heterogeneity. They are composed of many disparate elements. Liver, spleen, heart, kidneys are societies of specific cells. They are individuals definitely limited in space. For anatomists and surgeons, the organic heterogeneity of the body is unquestionable. Nevertheless, it may be more apparent than real. Functions are much less precisely located than organs. The skeleton, for example, is not merely the framework of the body. It also constitutes a part of the circulatory, respiratory, and nutritive systems, since, with the aid of the bone marrow, it manufactures leucocytes and red cells. The liver secretes bile, destroys poisons and microbes, stores glycogen, regulates sugar metabolism in the entire organism, and produces heparin. In a like manner, the pancreas, the suprarenals, the spleen, etc., do not confine themselves to one function. Each viscus possesses multiple activities and takes part in almost all the events of the body. Its structural frontiers are narrower than its functional ones. Its physiological individuality is far more comprehensive than its anatomical individuality. A cell community, by means of its manufactured products, penetrates all other communities. The vast cellular associations called viscera are placed, as we know, under the command of a single nervous center. This center sends its silent orders to every region of the organic world. In this way, heart, blood vessels, lungs, digestive apparatus, and endocrine glands become a functional whole in which all organic individualities blend.

The heterogeneity of the organism is, in fact, created by the fancy of the observer. Should an organ be defined by its histological elements or by the chemical substances it constantly fabricates? The kidneys appear to the anatomist as two distinct glands. From a physiological point of view, however, they are a single being. If one of them is removed, the size of the other at once increases. An organ is not limited by its surface. It reaches as far as the substances it secretes. In reality, its structural and functional condition depends on the rate of elimination of these substances or of their absorption by other organs. Each gland extends, by means of its internal secretions, over the whole organism. Let us suppose the substances set free in the blood by testicles to be blue. The entire body of the male would be blue. The testicles themselves would be more intensely colored. But their specific hue would be diffused in all tissues and organs Even in the cartilages at the extremity of the bones. The body would then appear to be formed of an immense testicle. The spatial and temporal dimensions of each gland are, in fact, equal to those of the entire organism. An organ consists of its inner medium as much as of its anatomical elements. It is constituted both by specific cells and specific fluid or medium. And this fluid, this inner medium, greatly transcends the anatomical frontier. When the concept of a gland is reduced to that of its fibrous framework, epithelial cells, blood vessels, and nerves, the existence of the living organism becomes incomprehensible. In short, the body is an anatomical heterogeneity and a physiological homogeneity. It acts as if it were simple. But it shows us a complex structure. Such an antithesis is created by our mind. We always delight in picturing man as being constructed like one of our machines.

13

Indeed, both a machine and our body are organisms. But the organization of our body is not similar to that of the machine. A machine is composed of many parts, originally separate. Once these parts are put together, its manifoldness becomes unity. Like the human individual, it is assembled for a specific purpose. Like him, it is both simple and complex. But it is primarily complex and secondarily simple. On the contrary, man is primarily simple and secondarily complex. He originates from a single cell. This cell divides into two others, which divide in their turn, and such division continues indefinitely. In the course of this process of structural elaboration, the embryo retains the functional simplicity of the egg. The cells seem to remember their original unity, even when they have become the elements of an innumerable multitude. They know spontaneously the functions attributed to them in the organized whole. If we cultivate epithelial cells over a period of several months, quite apart from the animal to which they belong, they arrange themselves in a mosaic, exactly as if to protect a surface. Yet the surface to be protected is lacking. Leucocytes, living in flasks, industriously devour microbes and red corpuscles, although there is no organism to be defended against the incursions of these enemies. The innate knowledge of the part they must play in the whole is a mode of being of all the elements of the body.

Isolated cells have the singular power of reproducing, without direction or purpose, the edifices characterizing each organ. If a few red corpuscles, impelled by gravity, flow from a drop of blood placed in liquid plasma and form a tiny stream, banks are soon built up. Then, these banks cover themselves with filaments of fibrin, and the stream becomes a pipe, through which the red cells glide just as in a blood vessel. Next, leucocytes come, adhere to the surface of the pipe, and surround it with their undulating membrane. The blood stream now assumes the appearance of a capillary vessel enveloped in a layer of contractile cells. Thus, isolated red and white corpuscles manage to construct a segment of circulatory apparatus, although there is neither heart, circulation, nor tissues to be irrigated. Cells are like bees erecting their geometrical alveoli, synthetizing honey, feeding their embryos, as though each one of them understood mathematics, chemistry, and biology, and unselfishly acted for the interests of the entire community. The spontaneous tendency toward formation of the organs by their constitutive cells, like the social aptitude of the insects, is a primary datum of observation. It cannot be explained in the light of our present concepts.

An organ builds itself by techniques very foreign to the human mind. It is not made of extraneous material, like a house. Neither is it a cellular construction, a mere assemblage of cells. It is, of course, composed of cells, as a house is of bricks. But it is born from a cell, as if the house originated from one brick, a magic brick that would set about manufacturing other bricks. Those bricks, without waiting for the architect's drawings or the coming of the bricklayers, would assemble themselves and form the walls. They would also metamorphose into windowpanes, roofing-slates, coal for heating, and water for the kitchen and the bathroom. An organ develops by means such as those attributed to fairies in the tales told to children in bygone times. It is engendered by cells which, to all appearances, have a knowledge of the future edifice, and synthetize from substances contained in blood plasma the building material and even the workers.

These methods used by the organism do not have the simplicity of ours. They appear strange to us. Our intelligence does not encounter itself in the intraorganic world. It is modeled on the simplicity of the cosmic universe, and not on the complexity of the inner mechanisms of living beings. For the moment, we cannot understand the mode of organization of our body and its nutritive, nervous, and mental activities. The laws of mechanics, physics, and chemistry are completely applicable to inert matter. Partly, to man. The illusions of the mechanicists of the nineteenth century, the dogmas of Jacques Loeb, the childish physicochemical conceptions of the human being, in which so many physiologists and physicians still believe, have to be definitely abandoned. We must also dismiss the philosophical and humanistic dreams of physicists and astronomers. Following many others, Jeans believes and teaches that God, creator of the sidereal universe, is a mathematician. If that is so, the material world, the living beings, and man have been created, obviously, by different Gods. How naïve our speculations! Our knowledge of the human body is, in truth, most rudimentary. It is impossible, for the present, to grasp its constitution. We must, then, be content with the scientific observation of our organic and mental activities. And, without any other guide, march forward into the unknown.

14

Our body is extremely robust. It adapts itself to all climates, arctic cold as well as tropical heat. It also resists starvation, weather inclemencies, fatigue, hardships, overwork. Man is the hardiest of all animals, and the white races, builders of our civilization, the hardiest of all races. However, our organs are fragile. They are damaged by the slightest shock. They disintegrate as soon as blood circulation stops. Such contrast between the strength and the fragility of the organism is, like most of the antitheses encountered in biology, an illusion of our mind. We always unconsciously compare our body with a machine. The strength of a machine depends on the metal used in its construction, and on the perfection of the assembling of its parts. But that of man is due to other causes. His endurance comes more especially from the elasticity of his tissues, their tenacity, their property of growing instead of wearing out, from the strange power displayed by the organism in meeting a new situation by adaptive changes. Resistance to disease, work, and worries, capacity for effort, and nervous equilibrium are the signs of the superiority of a man. Such qualities characterized the founders of our civilization in the United States as well as in Europe. The great white races owe their success to the perfection of their nervous system—nervous system which, although very delicate and excitable, can, however, be disciplined. To the exceptional qualities of their tissues and consciousness is due the predominance over the rest of the world of the peoples of western Europe, and of their swarms in the United States.

We are ignorant of the nature of this organic robustness, of this nervous and mental superiority. Must they be attributed to the structure of the cells, to the chemical substances they synthetize, to the mode of integration of the organs by the humors and nerves? We do not know. These qualities are hereditary. They have existed in our people for many centuries. But even in the greatest and richest nations they may disappear. The history of past civilizations shows that such a calamity is possible. But it does not explain clearly its genesis. Obviously, the resistance of the body and the mind must be conserved at all costs in a great nation. Mental and nervous strength is infinitely more important than muscular strength. The descendant of a great race, if he has not degenerated, is endowed with natural immunity to fatigue and to fear. He does not think about his health or his security. He is not interested in medicine, and ignores physicians. He does not believe that the Golden Age will arrive when physiological chemists have obtained in a pure state all vitamines and secretory products of endocrine glands. He looks upon himself as destined to fight, to love, to think, and to conquer. He knows that safety should not be first. His action on his environment is as essentially simple as the leap of a wild animal upon its prey. No more than the animal does he feel his structural complexity.

The sound body lives in silence. We do not hear, we do not feel, its working. The rhythms of our existence are expressed by cenesthesic impressions which, like the soft whirring of a sixteen-cylinder motor, fill the depths of our consciousness when we are in silence and meditation. The harmony of organic functions gives a feeling of peace. When an organ begins to deteriorate, this peace may be disturbed. Pain is a signal of distress. Many people, although they are not ill, are not in good health. Perhaps the quality of some of their tissues is defective. The secretions of such gland, or such mucosa, may be insufficient or too abundant. The excitability of their nervous system, exaggerated. Their organic functions, not exactly correlated in space or in time. Or their tissues, not as capable of resisting infections as they should be. Such individuals feel profoundly these organic deficiencies, which bring them much misery. The future discoverer of a method for inducing tissues and organs to develop harmoniously will be a greater benefactor of humanity than Pasteur himself. For he will present man with the most precious of all gifts, with an almost divine offering, the aptitude for happiness.

The weakening of the body has many causes. It is well known that the quality of tissues is lowered by too poor or too rich a diet, by alcoholism, syphilis, consanguineous unions, and also by prosperity and leisure. Wealth is as dangerous as ignorance and poverty. Civilized men degenerate in tropical climates. On the contrary, they thrive in temperate or cold countries. They need a way of life involving constant struggle, mental and muscular effort, physiological and moral discipline, and some privations. Such conditions inure the body to fatigue and to sorrows. They protect it against disease, and especially against nervous diseases. They irresistibly drive humanity to the conquest of the external world.

15

Disease consists of a functional and structural disorder. Its aspects are as numerous as our organic activities. There are diseases of the stomach, of the heart, of the nervous system, etc. But in illness the body preserves the same unity as in health. It is sick as a whole. No disturbance remains strictly confined to a single organ. Physicians have been led to consider each disease as a specialty by the old anatomical conception of the human being. Only those who know man both in his parts and in his entirety, simultaneously under his anatomical, physiological, and mental aspects, are capable of understanding him when he is sick.

There are two great classes of disease—infectious, or microbian, diseases, and degenerative diseases. The first are caused by viruses or bacteria penetrating into the body. Viruses are invisible beings, extremely small, hardly larger than a molecule of albumin. They live within the cells themselves. They are fond of the nervous substance, and also of the skin and the glands. They destroy those tissues in men and animals or modify their functions. They produce infantile paralysis, grippe, encephalitis lethargica, etc., as also measles, typhus, yellow fever, and perhaps cancer. They can transform inoffensive cells, the leucocytes of the hen, for instance, into ferocious beasts which invade muscles and organs and, in a few days, kill the animal affected with the disease. These formidable beings are unknown to us. Nobody has ever seen them. They only manifest themselves by their effects upon tissues. Before their onslaught, cells stand defenseless. They resist viruses no more than the leaves of a tree resist smoke. In comparison with viruses, bacteria are veritable giants. However, they easily penetrate into our body through the mucosas of the intestines, those of the nose, the eyes, the throat, or through the surface of a wound. They do not install themselves within the cells, but around them. They invade the loose tissues separating the organs. They multiply under the skin, between the muscles, in the abdominal cavity, in the membranes enveloping the brain and the cord. They secrete toxic substances in the interstitial lymph. They may also migrate into the blood. They throw into confusion all organic functions.

Degenerative diseases are often the consequence of bacterial infections, as in certain maladies of the heart and of the kidneys. They are also caused by the presence in the organism of toxic substances issuing from the tissues themselves. When the secretions of the thyroid gland become too abundant, or poisonous, the symptoms of exophthalmic goiter make their appearance. Certain disorders are due to lack of secretions indispensable to nutrition. The deficiency of endocrine glands, of thyroid, pancreas, liver, of gastric mucosa, brings on diseases such as myxedema, diabetes, pernicious anemia, etc. Other disorders are determined by the absence of elements required for the construction and maintenance of tissues, such as vitamines, mineral salts, iodine, metals. When the organs do not receive from the cosmic world through the intestine the building substances which they need, they lose their power of resistance to infection, develop structural lesions, manufacture poisons, etc. There are also diseases which have so far baffled all the scientists and the institutes for medical research of America, Europe, Africa, Asia, and Australia. Among them, cancer and a multitude of nervous and mental affections.

Great gains in health have been achieved since the beginning of this century. Tuberculosis is being vanquished. Deaths from infantile diarrhea, diphtheria, typhoid fever, etc., are being eliminated. All diseases of bacterial origin have decreased in a striking manner. The average length of life—that is, the expectation of life at birth—was only forty-nine years in 1900. Today it has gained more than eleven years. The chances of survival for each age up to maturity have notably augmented. Nevertheless, in spite of the triumphs of medical science, the problem of disease is very far from solved. Modern man is delicate. Eleven hundred thousand persons have to attend the medical needs of 120,000,000 other persons. Every year, among this population of the United States, there are about 100,000,000 illnesses, serious or slight. In the hospitals, 700,000 beds are occupied every day of the year. The care of these patients requires the efforts of 145,000 doctors, 280,000 nurses or student nurses, 60,000 dentists, and 150,000 pharmacists. It also necessitates 7,000 hospitals, 8,000 clinics, and 60,000 pharmacies. The public spends annually $715,000,000 in medicines. Medical care, under all its forms, costs about $3,500,000,000 yearly. Obviously, disease is still a heavy economic burden. Its importance in modern life is incalculable.

Medicine is far from having decreased human sufferings as much as it endeavors to make us believe. Indeed, the number of deaths from infectious diseases has greatly diminished. But we still must die, and we die in a much larger proportion from degenerative diseases. The years of life which we have gained by the suppression of diphtheria, smallpox, typhoid fever, etc., are paid for by the long sufferings and the lingering deaths caused by chronic affections, and especially by cancer, diabetes, and heart disease. In addition, man is liable, as he was in former times, to chronic nephritis, brain tumors, arterial sclerosis, syphilis, cerebral hemorrhages, hypertension, and also to the intellectual, moral, and physiological decay determined by these maladies. He is equally subject to the organic and functional disorders brought in their train by excess of food, insufficient physical exercise, and overwork. The lack of equilibrium and the neuroses of the visceral nervous system bring about many affections of the stomach and the intestines. Heart diseases become more frequent. And also diabetes. The maladies of the central nervous system are innumerable. In the course of his life, every individual suffers from some attack of neurasthenia, of nervous depression, engendered by constant agitation, noise, and worries. Although modern hygiene has made human existence far safer, longer, and more pleasant, diseases have not been mastered. They have simply changed in nature.

This change comes undoubtedly from the elimination of infections. But it may be due also to modifications in the constitution of tissues under the influence of the new modes of life. The organism seems to have become more susceptible to degenerative diseases. It is continually subjected to nervous and mental shocks, to toxic substances manufactured by disturbed organs, to those contained in food and air. It is also affected by the deficiencies of the essential physiological and mental functions. The staple foods may not contain the same nutritive substances as in former times. Mass production has modified the composition of wheat, eggs, milk, fruit, and butter, although these articles have retained their familiar appearance. Chemical fertilizers, by increasing the abundance of the crops without replacing all the exhausted elements of the soil, have indirectly contributed to change the nutritive value of cereal grains and of vegetables. Hens have been compelled, by artificial diet and mode of living, to enter the ranks of mass producers. Has not the quality of their eggs been modified? The same question may be asked about milk, because cows are now confined to the stable all the year round, and are fed on manufactured provender. Hygienists have not paid sufficient attention to the genesis of diseases. Their studies of conditions of life and diet, and of their effects on the physiological and mental state of modern man, are superficial, incomplete, and of too short duration. They have, thus, contributed to the weakening of our body and our soul. And they leave us without protection against the degenerative diseases, the diseases resulting from civilization. We cannot understand the characteristics of these affections before having considered the nature of our mental activities. In disease as in health, body and consciousness, although distinct, are inseparable.

Chapter IV

MENTAL ACTIVITIES

1. Operational concept of consciousness. Body and soul. Meaningless questions. Man consists of all his manifested activities. 2. Intellectual activities. Their measurement. Conditions of their development. Scientific certainty. Intuition. Logical and intuitive minds. Clairvoyance and telepathy. 3. Moral activities. Metabolism and emotion. Moral constitution. Moral beauty. 4. Esthetic activities. Popular art. Beauty and its practical importance. 5. Mystic activities. Asceticism and contemplation. Operational concept of mystic experience. 6. Correlation of the activities of consciousness. Intelligence and moral sense. Intelligence, esthetic, and mystic activities. 7. Effects of physiological on mental activities. 8. Effects of mental on organic activities. Meditation and Action. Prayer. Miracles. 9. Effects of social environment on mental activities. Atrophy of consciousness. 10. Mental diseases. Feeble-minded and insane. Organic basis of mental diseases. Feeble-mindedness in dogs. Social environment and mental diseases.

I

SIMULTANEOUSLY with physiological activities, the body manifests other activities, which are called mental. The organs express themselves by mechanical work, heat, electrical phenomena, and chemical transformations, measurable by the techniques of physics and chemistry. The existence of the mind, of consciousness, is detected by other procedures, such as those employed in introspection and in the study of human behavior. The concept of consciousness is equivalent to the analysis made by ourself of our own self, and of the expression of the self of our fellow men. It is convenient to divide the mental activities into intellectual, moral, esthetic, and religious, although such classification is nothing but an artefact. In reality, the body and the soul are views taken of the same object by different methods, abstractions obtained by our reason from the concrete unity of our being. The antithesis of matter and mind represents merely the opposition of two kinds of techniques. The error of Descartes was to believe in the reality of these abstractions and to consider the material and the mental as heterogeneous, as two different things. This dualism has weighed heavily upon the entire history of our knowledge of man. For it has engendered the false problem of the relations of the soul and the body.

There are no such relations. Neither the soul nor the body can be investigated separately. We observe merely a complex being, whose activities have been arbitrarily divided into physiological and mental. Of course, one will always continue to speak of the soul as an entity. Just as one speaks of the setting and the rising of the sun, although everybody knows, since Galileo's time, that the sun is relatively immobile. The soul is the aspect of ourselves that is specific of our nature and distinguishes man from all other animals. We are not capable of defining this familiar and profoundly mysterious entity. What is thought, that strange being, which lives in the depths of ourselves without consuming a measurable quantity of chemical energy? Is it related to the known forms of energy? Could it be a constituent of our universe, ignored by the physicists, but infinitely more important than light? The mind is hidden within the living matter, completely neglected by physiologists and economists, almost unnoticed by physicians. And yet it is the most colossal power of this world. Is it produced by the cerebral cells, like insulin by the pancreas and bile by the liver? From what substances is it elaborated? Does it come from a preexisting element, as glucose from glycogen, or fibrin from fibrinogen? Does it consist of a kind of energy differing from that studied by physics, expressing itself by other laws, and generated by the cells of the cerebral cortex? Or should it be considered as an immaterial being, located outside space and time, outside the dimensions of the cosmic universe, and inserting itself by an unknown procedure into our brain, which would be the indispensable condition of its manifestations and the determining agent of its characteristics?

At all times, and in all countries, great philosophers have devoted their lives to the investigation of these problems. They have not found their solution. We cannot refrain from asking the same questions. But those questions will remain unanswered until new methods for penetrating more deeply into consciousness are discovered. Meanwhile, we feel the urge to know, and not merely to speculate or to dream. If our understanding of this essential, specific aspect of the human being is to progress, we must make a careful study of the phenomena attainable by our present methods of observation, and of their relations with physiological activities. We must also have the courage to explore those regions of the self whose horizons, on every side, are shrouded in dense mist.

Man consists of all his actual and potential activities. The functions which, at certain epochs and in certain environments, remain virtual, are as real as those which constantly express themselves. The writings of Ruysbroeck the Admirable contain as many truths as those of Claude Bernard. *The Adornment of the Spiritual Marriage,* and the *Introduction to the Study of Experimental Medicine* describe two aspects, the former less frequent and the latter more usual, of the same being. The forms of human activity considered by Plato are more specific of our nature than hunger, thirst, sexual appetite, and greed. Since the Renaissance, a privileged position has arbitrarily been given to certain aspects of man. Matter has been separated from mind. To matter has been attributed a greater reality than to mind. Physiology and medicine have directed their attention to the chemical manifestations of the body's activities and to the organic disorders expressed by microscopical lesions of the tissues. Sociology has envisaged man almost uniquely from the point of view of his ability to run machines, of his output of work, of his capacity as a consumer, of his economic value. Hygiene has concerned itself with his health, the means of increasing the population, prevention of infectious diseases, and with every possible addition to our physiological welfare. Pedagogy has directed its efforts toward the intellectual and muscular development of the children. But these sciences have neglected the study of the various aspects of consciousness. They should have examined man in the converging light of physiology and psychology. They should have utilized equitably the data supplied by introspection and by the study of behavior. Both these techniques attain the same object. But one considers man from inside, and the other from outside. There is no reason to give to one a greater value than to the other.

2

The existence of intelligence is a primary datum of observation. This power of discerning the relations between things assumes a certain value and a certain form in each individual. Intelligence is measurable by appropriate techniques. These measurements deal only with a conventional aspect of the mind. They do not give an accurate idea of intellectual value. But they permit a rough classification of human beings. They are useful in selecting suitable men for unimportant positions, such as those open to factory hands and minor bank or store clerks. In addition, they have brought to light an important fact, the weakness of the mind of most individuals. There is, indeed, an enormous diversity in the quantity and the quality of the intelligence possessed by each one. In this respect certain men are giants, and many, dwarfs. Every human being is born with different intellectual capacities. But, great or small, these potentialities require, in order to be actualized, constant exercise and certain ill-defined environmental conditions. Intellectual power is augmented by the habit of precise reasoning, the study of logic, the use of mathematical language, mental discipline, and complete and deep observation of things. On the contrary, incomplete and superficial observations, a rapid succession of impressions, multiplicity of images, and lack of intellectual discipline hinder the development of mind. We know how unintelligent the children are who live in a crowded city, among multitudes of people and events, in trains and automobiles, in the confusion of the streets, among the absurdities of the cinemas, in schools where intellectual concentration is not required. There are other factors capable of facilitating or hampering the growth of intelligence. They consist of certain habits of living and of eating. But their effect is not clearly known. It seems that overabundance of food and excess of athletics prevent intellectual progress. Athletes are not, in general, very intelligent. In order to reach its highest development the mind probably demands an ensemble of conditions, which has occurred only at certain epochs and in certain countries. What were the mode of existence, the diet, and the education of the men of the great periods of the history of civilization? We are almost totally ignorant of the genesis of intelligence. And we believe that the mind of children can be developed by the mere training of their memory and by the exercises practiced in modern schools!

Intelligence alone is not capable of engendering science. But it is an indispensable factor in its creation. Science, in its turn, fortifies intelligence. It has brought to humanity a new intellectual attitude, the certainty given by observation, experimentation, and logical reasoning. Certainty derived from science is very different from that derived from faith. The latter is more profound. It cannot be shaken by arguments. It resembles the certainty given by clairvoyance. But, strange to say, it is not completely foreign to science. Obviously, great discoveries are not the product of intelligence alone. Men of genius, in addition to their powers of observation and comprehension, possess other qualities, such as intuition and creative imagination. Through intuition they learn things ignored by other men, they perceive relations between seemingly isolated phenomena, they unconsciously feel the presence of the unknown treasure. All great men are endowed with intuition. They know, without analysis, without reasoning, what is important for them to know. A true leader of men does not need psychological tests, or reference cards, when choosing his subordinates. A good judge, without going into the details of legal arguments, and even, according to Cardozo, starting from erroneous premises, is capable of rendering a just sentence. A great scientist instinctively takes the path leading to a discovery. This phenomenon, in former times, was called inspiration.

Men of science belong to two different types—the logical and the intuitive. Science owes its progress to both forms of minds. Mathematics, although a purely logical structure, nevertheless makes use of intuition. Among the mathematicians there are intuitives and logicians, analysts and geometricians. Hermitte and Weierstrass were intuitives. Riemann and Bertrand, logicians. The discoveries of intuition have always to be developed by logic. In ordinary life, as in science, intuition is a powerful but dangerous means of acquiring knowledge. Sometimes it can hardly be distinguished from illusion. Those who rely upon it entirely are liable to mistakes. It is far from being always trustworthy. But the great man, or the simple whose heart is pure, can be led by it to the summits of mental and spiritual life. It is a strange quality. To apprehend reality without the help of intelligence appears inexplicable. One of the aspects of intuition resembles a very rapid deduction from an instantaneous observation. The knowledge that great physicians sometimes possess concerning the present and the future state of their patients is of such a nature. A similar phenomenon occurs when one appraises in a flash a man's value, or senses his virtues and his vices. But under another aspect, intuition takes place quite independently of observation and reasoning. We may be led by it to our goal when we do not know how to attain this goal and even where it is located. This mode of knowledge is closely analogous to clairvoyance, to the sixth sense of Charles Richet.

Clairvoyance and telepathy are a primary datum of scientific observation.[1] Those endowed with this power grasp the secret thoughts of other individuals without using their sense organs. They also perceive events more or less remote in

[1] The existence of telepathic phenomena, as well as other metapsychic phenomena, is not accepted by most biologists and physicians. The attitude of these scientists should not be blamed. For these phenomena are exceptional and elusive. They cannot be reproduced at will. Besides, they are hidden in the enormous mass of the superstitions, lies, and illusions accumulated for centuries by mankind. Although they have been mentioned in every country and at every epoch, they have not been investigated scientifically. It is, nevertheless, a fact that they are a normal, although rare, activity of the human being. The author began their study when he was a young medical student. He was interested in this subject in the same manner as in physiology, chemistry, and pathology. He realized long ago the deficiencies of the methods used by the specialists of psychical research, of the séances where professional mediums often utilize the amateurism of the experimenters. He has made his own observations and experiments. He has used in this chapter the knowledge that he has acquired himself. And not the opinion of others. The study of metapsychics does not differ from that of psychology and physiology. Scientists should not be alarmed by its unorthodox appearance. Several attempts, as is well known, have already been made to apply scientific techniques to clairvoyance and telepathy, and have met with moderate success. The Society for Psychical Research was founded in London in 1882, under the presidency of Henry Sidgwick, Professor of Moral Philosophy at the University of Cambridge. In 1919, an International Institute of Metapsychics was established in Paris with the approval of the French Government, and under the auspices of the great physiologist, Richet, the discoverer of anaphylaxis, and of a learned physician, Joseph Teissier, Professor of Medicine at the University of Lyons. Among the members of its Committee of Administration are a professor at the Medical School of the University of Paris, and several physicians. Its president, Charles Richet, has written a treatise on Metapsychics. The Institute publishes the *Revue Métapsychique*. In the United States this branch of human psychology has hardly attracted the attention of the scientific institutions. However, the Department of Psychology of Duke University has undertaken some valuable metapsychical researches under the direction of Dr. J. B. Rhine.

space and time. This quality is exceptional. It develops in only a small number of human beings. But many possess it in a rudimentary state. They use it without effort and in a spontaneous fashion. Clairvoyance appears quite commonplace to those having it. It brings to them a knowledge which is more certain than that gained through the sense organs. A clairvoyant reads the thoughts of other people as easily as he examines the expression of their faces. But the words to see and to feel do not accurately express the phenomena taking place in his consciousness. He does not observe, he does not think. He knows. The reading of thoughts seems to be related simultaneously to scientific, esthetic, and religious inspiration, and to telepathy. Telepathic communications occur frequently. In many instances, at the time of death or of great danger, an individual is brought into a certain kind of relation with another. The dying man, or the victim of an accident, even when such accident is not followed by death, appears to a friend in his usual aspect. The phantom generally remains silent. Sometimes he speaks and announces his death. The clairvoyant may also perceive at a great distance a scene, an individual, a landscape, which he is capable of describing minutely and exactly. There are many forms of telepathy. A number of persons, although not endowed with the gift of clairvoyance, have received, once or twice in their lifetime, a telepathic communication.

Thus, knowledge of the external world may come to man through other channels than sense organs. It is certain that thought may be transmitted from one individual to another, even if they are separated by long distance. These facts, which belong to the new science of metapsychics, must be accepted just as they are. They constitute a part of the reality.

They express a rare and almost unknown aspect of ourselves. They are possibly responsible for the uncanny mental acuteness observed in certain individuals. What extraordinary penetration would result from the union of disciplined intelligence and of telepathic aptitude! Indeed, intelligence, which has given us mastery over the physical world, is not a simple thing. We know only one of its aspects. We endeavor to develop it in the schools and universities. This aspect is but a small part of a marvelous activity consisting of reason, judgment, voluntary attention, intuition, and perhaps clairvoyance. To such a function, man is indebted for his power to apprehend reality, and to understand his environment, his fellow creatures, and himself.

3

Intellectual activity is, at the same time, distinct and indistinct from the flowing mass of our other states of consciousness. It is a mode of our being and changes as we do. We may compare it to a cinematographic film, which would record the successive phases of a story on a surface varying in sensitiveness from one point to another. It is even more analogous to the valleys and the hills of the long billows of the ocean, which reflect in a different manner the clouds passing in the sky. Intelligence projects its visions on the perpetually changing screen of our affective states, of our sorrows or our joys, of our love or our hatred. To study this aspect of ourselves, we separate it artificially from an indivisible wholeness. In reality, the man who thinks, observes, and reasons is, at the same time, happy or unhappy, disturbed or serene, stimulated or depressed by his appetites, his aversions, and his desires. The world, therefore, assumes a different visage, according to the affective and physiological states, which are the moving background of consciousness during intellectual activity. Everyone knows that love, hate, anger, and fear are capable of bringing confusion even to logic. In order to manifest themselves, these states of consciousness require certain modifications of the chemical exchanges. The more intense the emotional disturbances, the more active become these exchanges. We know that, on the contrary, metabolism is not modified by intellectual work. Affective functions are very near the physiological. They give to each human being his temperament. Temperament changes from one individual to the other, from one race to the other. It is a mixture of mental, physiological, and structural characteristics. It is man himself. It is responsible for his narrowness, his mediocrity, or his strength. What factors bring about the weakening of temperament in certain social groups and in certain nations? It seems that the violence of the emotional moods diminishes when wealth increases, when education is generalized, when diet becomes more elaborate. At the same time, affective functions are observed to separate from intelligence, and to exaggerate unduly certain of their aspects. The forms of life, of education, or of food brought by modern civilization perhaps tend to give us the qualities of cattle, or to develop our emotional impulses inharmoniously.

Moral activity is equivalent to the aptitude possessed by man to impose upon himself a rule of conduct, to choose between several possible acts those which he considers to be good, to get rid of his own selfishness and maliciousness. It creates in him the feeling of obligation, of duty. This peculiar sense is observed only in a small number of individuals. In most of them it remains virtual. But the fact of its existence cannot be denied. If moral sense did not exist, Socrates would not have drunk the hemlock. Today it may be observed, even in a state of high development, in certain social groups and in certain countries. It has manifested itself at all epochs. In the course of the history of mankind its importance has been demonstrated to be fundamental. It is related both to intelligence and to esthetic and religious senses. It impels us to distinguish right from wrong, and to choose right in preference to wrong. In highly civilized beings, will and intelligence are one and the same function. From will and intelligence come all moral values.

Moral sense, like intellectual activity, apparently depends on certain structural and functional states of the body. These states result from the immanent constitution of our tissues and our minds, and also from factors which have acted upon us during our development. In his essay on the *Foundation of Ethics*, presented at the Royal Society of Sciences of Copenhagen, Schopenhauer expressed the opinion that the moral principle has its basis in our nature. In other terms, human beings possess innate tendencies to selfishness, meanness, or pity. These tendencies appear very early in life. They are obvious to any careful observer. There are, writes Gallavardin, the pure egoists, completely indifferent to the happiness or misery of their fellow men. There are the malicious, who take pleasure in witnessing the misfortunes or sufferings of others, and even in causing them. There are those who suffer themselves from the sufferings of any human being. This power of sympathy engenders kindness and charity, and the acts inspired by those virtues. The capacity of feeling the pain of others is the essential characteristic of the human being who endeavors to alleviate, among his brothers, the burden and the misery of existence. Each one, in a certain measure, is born good, mediocre, or bad. But, like intelligence, moral sense can be developed by education, discipline, and will power.

The definition of good and evil is based both on reason and on the immemorial experience of humanity. It is related to basic necessities of individual and social life. However, it is somewhat arbitrary. But at each epoch and in each country it should be very clearly defined and identical for all classes of individuals. The good is equivalent to justice, charity, beauty. The evil, to selfishness, meanness, ugliness. In modern civilization, the theoretical rules of conduct are based upon the remains of Christian morals. No one obeys them. Modern man has rejected all discipline of his appetites. However, biological and industrial morals have no practical value, because they are artificial and take into consideration only one aspect of the human being. They ignore some of our most essential activities. They do not give to man an armor strong enough to protect him against his own inherent vices.

In order to keep his mental and organic balance, man must impose upon himself an inner rule. The state can thrust legality upon people by force. But not morality. Everyone should realize the necessity of selecting the right and avoiding the wrong, of submitting himself to such necessity by an effort of his own will. The Roman Catholic Church, in its deep understanding of human psychology, has given to moral activities a far higher place than to intellectual ones. The men, honored by her above all others, are neither the leaders of nations, the men of science, nor the philosophers. They are the saints—that is, those who are virtuous in a heroic manner. When we watch the inhabitants of the new city, we fully understand the practical necessity of moral sense. Intelligence, will power, and morality are very closely related. But moral sense is more important than intelligence. When it disappears from a nation the whole social structure slowly commences to crumble away. In biological research, we have not given so far to moral activities the importance that they deserve. Moral sense must be studied in as positive a manner as intelligence. Such a study is certainly difficult. But the many aspects of this sense in individuals and groups of individuals can easily be discerned. It is also possible to analyze the physiological, psychological, and social effects of morals. Of course, such researches cannot be undertaken in a laboratory. Field work is indispensable. There are still today many human communities which show the various characteristics of moral sense, and the results of its absence or of its presence in different degrees. Without any doubt, moral activities are located within the domain of scientific observation.

In modern civilization individuals whose conduct is inspired by a moral ideal are very seldom encountered. However, such individuals still exist. We cannot help noticing their aspect when we meet them. Moral beauty is an exceptional and very striking phenomenon. He who has contemplated it but once never forgets its aspect. This form of beauty is far more impressive than the beauty of nature and of science. It gives to those who possess its divine gifts, a strange, an inexplicable power. It increases the strength of intellect. It establishes peace among men. Much more than science, art, and religious rites, moral beauty is the basis of civilization.

4

Esthetic sense exists in the most primitive human beings as in the most civilized. It even survives the disappearance of intelligence. For the idiot and the insane are capable of artistic productions. The creation of forms, or of series of sounds, capable of awakening an esthetic emotion, is an elementary need of our nature. Man has always contemplated with delight animals, flowers, trees, sky, ocean, and mountains. Before the dawn of civilization he used his rough tools to reproduce the profile of living beings on wood, ivory, and stone. Today, when his esthetic sense is not dulled by his education, his habits of life, and the stupidity of factory work, he takes pleasure in making objects after his own inspiration. He enjoys an esthetic feeling in concentrating on such work. In Europe, and especially in France, there are still cooks, butchers, stone-cutters, sabot-makers, carpenters, blacksmiths, cutlers, and mechanics who are artists. Those who make pastry of beautiful shape and delicate taste, who sculpture in lard houses, men, and animals, who forge majestic iron gates, who build handsome pieces of furniture, who carve a rough statue from stone or wood, who weave beautiful wool or silk materials, experience, as much as great sculptors, painters, musicians, or architects, the divine pleasure of creation.

Esthetic activity remains potential in most individuals because industrial civilization has surrounded them with coarse, vulgar, and ugly sights. Because we have been transformed into machines. The worker spends his life repeating the same gesture thousands of times each day. He manufactures only single parts. He never makes the complete object. He is not allowed to use his intelligence. He is the blind horse plodding round and round the whole day long to draw water from a well. Industrialism forbids man the very mental activities which could bring him every day some joy. In sacrificing mind to matter, modern civilization has perpetrated a momentous error. An error all the more dangerous because nobody revolts against it, because it is accepted as easily as the unhealthy life of great cities and the confinement in factories. However, those who experience even a rudimentary esthetic feeling in their work are far happier than those who produce merely in order to be able to consume. In its present form, industry has deprived the worker of originality and beauty. The vulgarity and the gloom of our civilization are due, at least partly, to the suppression from our daily life of the simpler forms of esthetic pleasure.

Esthetic activity manifests itself in both the creation and the contemplation of beauty. It is completely disinterested. In the joy of creation, consciousness escapes from itself and becomes absorbed in another being. Beauty is an inexhaustible source of happiness for those who discover its abode. It is hidden everywhere. It springs up from the hands which model or decorate homemade earthenware, which carve wood, which weave silk, which chisel marble, which open and repair human flesh. It animates the bloody art of the surgeons, as well as that of the painters, the musicians, and the poets. It is present also in the calculations of Galileo, in the visions of Dante, in the experiments of Pasteur, in the rising of the sun on the ocean, in the winter storms on the high mountains. It becomes still more poignant in the immensity of the sidereal and atomic worlds, in the prodigious harmony of the brain cells, or in the silent sacrifice of the man who gives his life for the salvation of others. Under its multiple forms it is always the noblest and most important guest of the human cerebrum, creator of our universe.

The sense of beauty does not develop spontaneously. It exists in our consciousness in a potential state. At certain epochs, in certain circumstances, it remains virtual. It may even vanish in nations which formerly were proud of their great artists and their masterpieces. Today, France despises the majestic remnants of her past and even destroys her natural beauties. The descendants of the men who conceived and erected the monastery of Mount Saint-Michel no longer understand its splendor. They cheerfully accept the indescribable ugliness of the modern houses in Normandy and Brittany, and especially in the Paris suburbs. Like Mount Saint-Michel and the majority of French cities and villages, Paris has been disgraced by a hideous commercialism. During the history of a civilization, the sense of beauty, like moral sense, grows, reaches its optimum, declines, and disappears.

5

In modern men, we seldom observe the manifestations of mystical activity, or religious sense.[1] The tendency to

[1] Although religious activity has played an important part in the history of humanity, one cannot acquire easily even a superficial knowledge of this form, now so rare, of our mental functions. Indeed, the literature concerning asceticism and mysticity is immense. The writings of the great

mysticity, even in its most rudimentary form, is exceptional. Much more exceptional than moral sense. Nevertheless, it remains one of the essential human activities. Humanity has been more thoroughly impregnated with religious inspiration than with philosophical thought. In the ancient city, religion was the basis of family and social life. The cathedrals and the ruins of the temples erected by our ancestors still cover the soil of Europe. Indeed, their meaning is today scarcely understood. To the majority of modern men the churches are only museums for dead religions. The attitude of the tourists visiting the cathedrals of Europe clearly shows how completely religious sense has been eliminated from modern life. Mystical activity has been banished from most religions. Even its meaning has been forgotten. Such ignorance is probably responsible for the decadence of the churches. The strength of a religion depends upon the focuses of mystical activity where its life constantly grows. However, religious sense remains today an indispensable activity of the consciousness of a number of individuals. It is again manifesting itself among people of high culture. And, strange to say, the monasteries of the

---

Christian mystics are at our disposal. One may meet also, even in the new city, men and women who are centers of true religious activity. Generally, however, the mystics are out of our reach in monasteries. Or they occupy humble positions and are completely ignored. The author became interested in asceticism and mysticity at the same time as in metapsychical phenomena. He has known a few genuine mystics and saints. He does not hesitate to mention mysticity in this book, because he has observed its manifestations. But he realizes that his description of this aspect of mental activity will please neither men of science nor men of religion. Scientists will consider such an attempt as puerile or insane. Ecclesiastics, as improper and aborted, because mystical phenomena belong only in an indirect way to the domain of science. Both these criticisms will be justified. Nevertheless, it is impossible not to count mysticism among fundamental human activities.

great religious orders are too small to receive all the young men and women who crave to enter the spiritual world through asceticism and mysticity.

Religious activity assumes various aspects, as does moral activity. In its more elementary state it consists of a vague aspiration toward a power transcending the material and mental forms of our world, a kind of unformulated prayer, a quest for more absolute beauty than that of art or science. It is akin to esthetic activity. The love of beauty leads to mysticism. In addition, religious rites are associated with various forms of art. Song easily becomes transformed into prayer. The beauty pursued by the mystic is still richer and more indefinable than the ideal of the artist. It has no form. It cannot be expressed in any language. It hides within the things of the visible world. It manifests itself rarely. It requires an elevation of the mind toward a being who is the source of all things, toward a power, a center of forces, whom the mystic calls God. At each period of history in each nation there have been individuals possessing to a high degree this particular sense. Christian mysticism constitutes the highest form of religious activity. It is more integrated with the other activities of consciousness than are Hindu and Tibetan mysticisms. Over Asiatic religions it has the advantage of having received, in its very infancy, the lessons of Greece and of Rome. Greece gave it intelligence, and Rome, order and measure.

Mysticism, in its highest state, comprises a very elaborate technique, a strict discipline. First, the practice of asceticism. It is as impossible to enter the realm of mysticity without ascetic preparation as to become an athlete without submitting to physical training. Initiation to asceticism is hard.

Therefore, very few men have the courage to venture upon the mystic way. He who wants to undertake this rough and difficult journey must renounce all the things of this world and, finally, himself. Then he may have to dwell for a long time in the shadows of spiritual night. While asking for the grace of God and deploring his degradation and undeservedness, he undergoes the purification of his senses. It is the first and dark stage of mystic life. He progressively weans himself from himself. His prayer becomes contemplation. He enters into illuminative life. He is not capable of describing his experiences. When he attempts to express what he feels, he sometimes borrows, as did St. John of the Cross, the language of carnal love. His mind escapes from space and time. He apprehends an ineffable being. He reaches the stage of unitive life. He is in God and acts with Him.

The life of all great mystics consists of the same steps. We must accept their experiences as described by them. Only those who themselves have led the life of prayer are capable of understanding its peculiarities. The search for God is, indeed, an entirely personal undertaking. By the exercise of the normal activities of his consciousness, man may endeavor to reach an invisible reality both immanent in and transcending the material world. Thus, he throws himself into the most audacious adventure that one can dare. He may be looked upon as a hero, or a lunatic. But nobody should ask whether mystical experience is true or false, whether it is autosuggestion, hallucination, or a journey of the soul beyond the dimensions of our world and its union with a higher reality. One must be content with having an operational concept of such an experience. Mysticism is splendidly generous. It brings to man the fulfillment of his highest desires. Inner strength, spiritual light, divine love, ineffable peace. Religious intuition is as real as esthetic inspiration. Through the contemplation of superhuman beauty, mystics and poets may reach the ultimate truth.

6

These fundamental activities are not distinct from one another. Their limits are convenient, but artificial. They may be compared to an ameba whose multiple and transitory limbs, the pseudopods, consist of a single substance. They are also analogous to the unrolling of superposed films, which remain undecipherable unless separated from one another. Everything happens as if the bodily substratum, while flowing in time, showed several simultaneous aspects of its unity. Aspects, which our techniques divide into physiological and mental. Under its mental aspect, human activity ceaselessly modifies its form, its quality, and its intensity. This essentially simple phenomenon is described as an association of different functions. The plurality of the manifestations of the mind is born from a methodological necessity. In order to describe consciousness we are obliged to separate it into parts. As the pseudopods of the ameba are the ameba itself, the aspects of consciousness are man himself, and blend in his oneness.

Intelligence is almost useless to those who possess nothing else. The pure intellectual is an incomplete human being. He is unhappy because he is not capable of entering the world that he understands. The ability to grasp the relations between phenomena remains sterile unless associated with other activities, such as moral sense, affectivity, will power, judgment, imagination, and some organic strength. It can only be utilized at the cost of an effort. Those who want to conquer real knowledge have to endure a long and hard preparation. They submit themselves to a kind of ascedicism. In the absence of concentration, intelligence is unproductive. Once disciplined, it becomes capable of pursuing truth. But to reach its goal it requires the help of moral sense. Great scientists always have profound intellectual honesty. They follow reality wherever led by it. They never seek to substitute their own desires for facts, or to hide these facts when they become troublesome. The man who longs for the contemplation of truth has to establish peace within him. His mind should be like the still water of a lake. Affective activities, however, are indispensable to the progress of intelligence. But they should consist only of enthusiasm, that passion which Pasteur called the inner god. Thought grows only within those who are capable of love and hate. It requires the aid of the whole body, besides that of the other mental functions. When intelligence ascends the highest summits and is illuminated by intuition and creative imagination, it still needs a moral and organic frame.

The exclusive development of the affective, esthetic, or mystic activities brings into being inferior individuals, idle dreamers, narrow, unsound minds. Such types are often encountered, although intellectual education is given nowadays to everybody. However, high culture is not necessary to fertilize esthetic and religious senses and to bring forth artists, poets, and mystics, all those who disinterestedly contemplate the various aspects of beauty. The same is true of moral sense and judgment. These activities are almost sufficient within themselves. They do not require to be associated with great intelligence to supply man with an aptitude for happiness. They seem to strengthen organic functions. Their development must be the supreme goal of education, because they give equilibrium to the individual. They make him a solid building-stone of the social edifice. To those who constitute the multitudes of industrial civilization, moral sense is far more necessary than intelligence.

The distribution of mental activities varies greatly in the different social groups. Most civilized men manifest only an elementary form of consciousness. They are capable of the easy work which, in modern society, insures the survival of the individual. They produce, they consume, they satisfy their physiological appetites. They also take pleasure in watching, among great crowds, athletic spectacles, in seeing childish and vulgar moving pictures, in being rapidly transported without effort, or in looking at swiftly moving objects. They are soft, sentimental, lascivious, and violent. They have no moral, esthetic, or religious sense. They are extremely numerous. They have engendered a vast herd of children whose intelligence remains rudimentary. They constitute a part of the population of the three million criminals living in freedom, of those inhabiting the jails, and of the feeble-minded, the morons, the insane, who overflow from asylums and specialized hospitals.

The majority of criminals, who are not in penitentiaries, belong to a higher class. They are marked, however, by the atrophy of certain activities of consciousness. The born criminal, invented by Lombroso, does not exist. But there are born defectives who become criminals. In reality, many criminals are normal. They are often more clever than policemen and judges. Sociologists and social workers do not meet them during their survey of prisons. The gangsters and crooks, heroes of the cinema and the daily papers, sometimes display normal and even high mental, affective, and esthetic activities. But their moral sense has not developed. This disharmony in the world of consciousness is a phenomenon characteristic of our time. We have succeeded in giving organic health to the inhabitants of the modern city. But, despite the immense sums spent on education, we have failed to develop completely their intellectual and moral activities. Even in the élite of the population, consciousness often lacks harmony and strength. The elementary functions are dispersed, of poor quality, and of low intensity. Some of them may be quite deficient. The mind of most people can be compared to a reservoir containing a small quantity of water of doubtful composition and under low pressure. And that of only a few individuals to a reservoir containing a large volume of pure water under high pressure.

The happiest and most useful men consist of a well-integrated whole of intellectual, moral, and organic activities. The quality of these activities, and their equilibrium, gives to such a type its superiority over the others. Their intensity determines the social level of a given individual. It makes of him a tradesman or a bank president, a little physician or a celebrated professor, a village mayor or a president of the United States. The development of complete human beings must be the aim of our efforts. It is only with such thoroughly developed individuals that a real civilization can be constructed. There is also a class of men who, although as disharmonious as the criminal and the insane, are indispensable to modern society. They are the men of genius. These are characterized by a monstrous growth of some of their psychological activities. A great artist, a great scientist, a great philosopher, is rarely a great man. He is generally a man of common type, with one side over-developed. Genius can be compared to a tumor growing upon a normal organism. These ill-balanced beings are often unhappy. But they give to the entire community the benefit of their mighty impulses. Their disharmony results in the progress of civilization. Humanity has never gained anything from the efforts of the crowd. It is driven onward by the passion of a few abnormal individuals, by the flame of their intelligence, by their ideal of science, of charity, and of beauty.

7

Mental activities evidently depend on physiological activities. Organic modifications are observed to correspond to the succession of the states of consciousness. Inversely, psychological phenomena are determined by certain functional states of the organs. The whole consisting of body and consciousness is modifiable by organic as well as by mental factors. Mind and organism commune in man, like form and marble in a statue. One cannot change the form without breaking the marble. The brain is supposed to be the seat of the psychological functions, because its lesions are followed by immediate and profound disorders of consciousness. It is probably by means of the cerebral cells that mind inserts itself in matter. Brain and intelligence develop simultaneously in children. When senile atrophy occurs, intelligence decreases. The presence of the spirochetes of syphilis around the pyramidal cells brings about delusions of grandeur. When the virus of lethargic encephalitis attacks the brain substance, profound disturbances of personality appear. Mental activity suffers temporary changes under the influence of alcohol carried by blood from the stomach to the nervous cells. The fall of blood pressure due to a hemorrhage suppresses all manifestations of consciousness. In short, mental life is observed to depend on the state of the cerebrum.

These observations do not suffice to demonstrate that the brain alone is the organ of consciousness. In fact, the cerebral centers are not composed exclusively of nervous matter. They also consist of fluids in which the cells are immersed and whose composition is regulated by blood serum. And blood serum contains the gland and tissue secretions that diffuse through the entire body. Every organ is present in the cerebral cortex by the agency of blood and lymph. Therefore, our states of consciousness are linked to the chemical constitution of the humors of the brain as much as to the structural state of its cells. When the organic medium is deprived of the secretions of the suprarenal glands, the patient falls into a profound depression. He resembles a cold-blooded animal. The functional disorders of the thyroid gland bring about either nervous and mental excitation or apathy. Moral idiots, feeble-minded, and criminals are found in families where lesions of this gland are hereditary. Everyone knows how human personality is modified by diseases of the liver, the stomach, and the intestines. Obviously, the cells of the organs discharge into the bodily fluids certain substances that react upon our mental and spiritual functions.

The testicle, more than any other gland, exerts a profound influence upon the strength and quality of the mind. In general, great poets, artists, and saints, as well as conquerors, are strongly sexed. The removal of the genital glands, even in adult individuals, produces some modifications of the mental state. After extirpation of the ovaries, women become apathetic and lose part of their intellectual activity or moral sense. The personality of men who have undergone castration is altered in a more or less marked way. The historical cowardice of Abélard in face of the passionate love and sacrifice of Héloïse was probably due to the brutal mutilation imposed upon him. Almost all great artists were great lovers. Inspiration seems to depend on a certain condition of the sexual glands. Love stimulates mind when it does not attain its object. If Beatrice had been the mistress of Dante, there would perhaps be no *Divine Comedy*. The great mystics often used the expressions of Solomon's Song. It seems that their unassuaged sexual appetites urged them more forcibly along the path of renouncement and complete sacrifice. A workman's wife can request the services of her husband every day. But the wife of an artist or of a philosopher has not the right to do so as often. It is well known that sexual excesses impede intellectual activity. In order to reach its full power, intelligence seems to require both the presence of well-developed sexual glands and the temporary repression of the sexual appetite. Freud has rightly emphasized the capital importance of sexual impulses in the activities of consciousness. However, his observations refer chiefly to sick people. His conclusions should not be generalized to include normal individuals, especially those who are endowed with a strong nervous system and mastery over themselves. While the weak, the nervous, and the unbalanced become more abnormal when their sexual appetites are repressed, the strong are rendered still stronger by practicing such a form of asceticism.

The dependence of mental activities and physiological functions does not agree with the classical conception that places the soul exclusively in the brain. In fact, the entire body appears to be the substratum of mental and spiritual energies. Thought is the offspring of the endocrine glands as well as of the cerebral cortex. The integrity of the organism is indispensable to the manifestations of consciousness. Man thinks, invents, loves, suffers, admires, and prays with his brain and all his organs.

8

Each state of consciousness probably has a corresponding organic expression. Emotions, as is well known, determine the dilatation or the contraction of the small arteries, through the vasomotor nerves. They are, therefore, accompanied by changes in the circulation of the blood in tissues and organs. Pleasure causes the skin of the face to flush. Anger and fear turn it white. In certain individuals, bad news may bring about a spasm of the coronary arteries, anemia of the heart, and sudden death. The affective states act on all the glands by increasing or decreasing their circulation. They stimulate or stop the secretions, or modify their chemical constitution. The desire for food causes salivation, even in the absence of any aliment. In Pavlov's dogs, salivation followed the sound of a bell, if the bell had previously rung while the animal was being fed. An emotion may set in activity complex mechanisms. When one induces a sentiment of fear in a cat, as Cannon did in a famous experiment, the vessels of the suprarenal glands become dilated, the glands secrete adrenalin, adrenalin increases the pressure of the blood and the rapidity of its circulation, and prepares the whole organism for attack or defense.

Thus, envy, hate, fear, when these sentiments are habitual, are capable of starting organic changes and genuine diseases. Moral suffering profoundly disturbs health. Business men who do not know how to fight worry die young. The old clinicians thought that protracted sorrows and constant anxiety prepare the way for the development of cancer. Emotions induce, in especially sensitive individuals, striking modifications of the tissues and humors. The hair of a Belgian woman condemned to death by the Germans became white during the night preceding the execution. On the arm of another woman, an eruption appeared during a bombardment. After the explosion of each shell, the eruption became redder and larger. Such phenomena are far from being exceptional. Joltrain has proved that a moral shock may cause marked changes in the blood. A patient, after having experienced great fright, showed a drop in arterial pressure, and a decrease in the number of the white corpuscles, and in the coagulation time of blood plasma. The French expression, *se faire du mauvais sang,* is literally true. Thought can generate organic lesions. The instability of modern life, the ceaseless agitation, and the lack of security create states of consciousness which bring about nervous and organic disorders of the stomach and of the intestines, defective nutrition, and passage of intestinal microbes into the circulatory apparatus. Colitis and the accompanying infections of the kidneys and of the bladder are the remote results of mental and moral unbalance. Such diseases are almost unknown in social groups where life is simpler and not so agitated, where anxiety is less constant. In a like manner, those who keep the peace of their inner self in the midst of the tumult of the modern city are immune from nervous and organic disorders.

Physiological activities must remain outside the field of consciousness. They are disturbed when we turn our attention toward them. Thus, psychoanalysis, in directing the mind of the patient upon himself, may aggravate his state of unbalance. Instead of indulging in self-analysis, it is better to escape from oneself through an effort that does not scatter the mind. When our activity is set toward a precise end, our mental and organic functions become completely harmonized. The unification of the desires, the application of the mind to a single purpose, produce a sort of inner peace. Man integrates himself by meditation, just as by action. But he should not be content with contemplating the beauty of the ocean, of the mountains, and of the clouds, the masterpieces of the artists and the poets, the majestic constructions of philosophical thought, the mathematical formulas which express natural laws. He must also be the soul which strives to attain a moral ideal, searches for light in the darkness of this world, marches forward along the mystic way, and renounces itself in order to apprehend the invisible substratum of the universe.

The unification of the activities of consciousness leads to greater harmony of organic and mental functions. In the communities where moral sense and intelligence are simultaneously developed, nervous and nutritive diseases, criminality, and insanity are rare. In such groups, the individual is happier. But when psychological activities become more intense and specialized, they may bring about certain disturbances of the health. Those who pursue moral, scientific, or religious ideals do not seek physiological security or longevity. To those ideals they sacrifice themselves. It seems also that certain states of consciousness determine true pathological changes. Most of the great mystics have endured physiological and mental suffering, at least during a part of their life. Moreover, contemplation may be accompanied by nervous phenomena resembling those of hysteria and clairvoyance. In the history of the saints, one reads descriptions of ecstasies, thought transmission, visions of events happening at a distance, and even of levitations. According to the testimony of their companions, several of the Christian mystics have manifested this strange phenomenon. The subject, absorbed in his prayer, totally unconscious of the outside world, gently rises above the ground. But it has not been possible so far to bring these extraordinary facts into the field of scientific observation.

Certain spiritual activities may cause anatomical as well as functional modifications of the tissues and the organs. These organic phenomena are observed in various circumstances, among them being the state of prayer. Prayer should be understood, not as a mere mechanical recitation of formulas, but as a mystical elevation, an absorption of consciousness in the contemplation of a principle both permeating and transcending our world. Such a psychological state is not intellectual. It is incomprehensible to philosophers and scientists, and inaccessible to them. But the simple seem to feel God as easily as the heat of the sun or the kindness of a friend. The prayer which is followed by organic effects is of a special nature. First, it is entirely disinterested. Man offers himself to God. He stands before Him like the canvas before the painter or the marble before the sculptor. At the same time, he asks for His grace, exposes his needs and those of his brothers in suffering. Generally, the patient who is cured is not praying for himself. But for another. Such a type of prayer demands complete renunciation—that is, a higher form of asceticism. The modest, the ignorant, and the poor are more capable of this self-denial than the rich and the intellectual. When it possesses such characteristics, prayer may set in motion a strange phenomenon, the miracle.

In all countries, at all times, people have believed in the existence of miracles, in the more or less rapid healing of the sick at places of pilgrimage, at certain sanctuaries.[1] But after the great impetus of science during the nineteenth cen-

[1] Miraculous cures seldom occur. Despite their small number, they prove the existence of organic and mental processes that we do not know. They show that certain mystic states, such as that of prayer, have definite effects. They are stubborn, irreducible facts, which must be taken into account. The author knows that miracles are as far from scientific orthodoxy as mysticity. The investigation of such phenomena is still more delicate than that of telepathy and clairvoyance. But science has to explore the entire field of reality. He has attempted to learn the characteristics of this mode of healing, as well as of the ordinary modes. He began this study in 1902, at a time when the documents were scarce, when it was difficult for a young doctor, and dangerous for his future career, to become interested in such a subject. Today, any physician can observe the patients brought to Lourdes, and examine the records kept in the Medical Bureau. Lourdes is the center of an International Medical Association, composed of many members. There is a slowly growing literature about miraculous healing. Physicians are becoming more interested in these extraordinary facts. Several cases have been reported at the Medical Society of Bordeaux by professors of the medical school of the university and other eminent physicians. The Committee on Medicine and Religion of the New York Academy of Medicine, presided over by Dr. F. Peterson, has recently sent to Lourdes one of its members in order to begin a study of this important subject.

tury, such belief completely disappeared. It was generally admitted, not only that miracles did not exist, but that they could not exist. As the laws of thermodynamics make perpetual motion impossible, physiological laws oppose miracles. Such is still the attitude of most physiologists and physicians. However, in view of the facts observed during the last fifty years this attitude cannot be sustained. The most important cases of miraculous healing have been recorded by the Medical Bureau of Lourdes. Our present conception of the influence of prayer upon pathological lesions is based upon the observation of patients who have been cured almost instantaneously of various affections, such as peritoneal tuberculosis, cold abscesses, osteitis, suppurating wounds, lupus, cancer, etc. The process of healing changes little from one individual to another. Often, an acute pain. Then a sudden sensation of being cured. In a few seconds, a few minutes, at the most a few hours, wounds are cicatrized, pathological symptoms disappear, appetite returns. Sometimes functional disorders vanish before the anatomical lesions are repaired. The skeletal deformations of Pott's disease, the cancerous glands, may still persist two or three days after the healing of the main lesions. The miracle is chiefly characterized by an extreme acceleration of the processes of organic repair. There is no doubt that the rate of cicatrization of the anatomical defects is much greater than the normal one. The only condition indispensable to the occurrence of the phenomenon is prayer. But there is no need for the patient himself to pray, or even to have any religious faith. It is sufficient that some one around him be in a state of prayer. Such facts are of profound significance. They show the reality of certain relations, of still unknown nature, between psychological and organic processes. They prove the objective importance of the spiritual activities, which hygienists, physicians, educators, and sociologists have almost always neglected to study. They open to man a new world.

9

Mental activities are influenced by social environment as profoundly as by the fluids of the body. Like physiological activities, they improve with exercise. Driven by the ordinary necessities of life, organs, bones, and muscles work without interruption. Thus, they are compelled to develop. But, according to the mode of existence of the individual, they become more or less harmonious and strong. The constitution of an Alpine guide is much superior to that of an inhabitant of New York. Nevertheless, the organs and muscles of the latter suffice for sedentary life. Mind, on the contrary, does not unfold spontaneously. The son of a scholar inherits no knowledge from his father. If left alone on a desert island, he would be no better than Cro-Magnon men. The powers of the mind remain virtual in the absence of education and of an environment bearing the stamp of the intellectual, moral, esthetic, and religious accomplishments of our ancestors. The psychological state of the social group determines, in a large measure, the number, the quality, and the intensity of the manifestations of individual consciousness. If the social environment is mediocre, intelligence and moral sense fail to develop. These activities may become thoroughly vitiated by bad surroundings. We are immersed in the habits of our epoch, like tissue cells in the organic fluids. Like these cells, we are incapable of defending ourselves against the influence of the community. The body more effectively resists the cosmic than the psychological world. It is guarded against the incursions of its physical and chemical enemies by the skin, and the digestive and respiratory mucosas. On the contrary, the frontiers of the mind are entirely open. Consciousness is thus exposed to the attacks of its intellectual and spiritual surroundings. According to the nature of these attacks, it develops in a normal or defective manner.

Intelligence depends largely on education and environment. Also, on inner discipline, on the current ideas of one's time and one's group. It has to be molded by the habit of logical thinking, by that of mathematical language, and by a methodical study of humanities and sciences. Schoolteachers and university professors, as well as libraries, laboratories, books, and reviews, are adequate means for developing the mind. Even in the absence of professors, books could suffice for this task. One may live in an unintelligent social environment and yet acquire a high culture. The education of the intelligence is relatively easy. But the formation of the moral, esthetic, and religious activities is very difficult. The influence of environment on these aspects of consciousness is much more subtle. No one can learn to distinguish right from wrong, and beauty from vulgarity, by taking a course of lectures. Morality, art, and religion are not taught like grammar, mathematics, and history. To feel and to know are two profoundly different mental states. Formal teaching reaches intelligence alone. Moral sense, beauty, and mysticity are learned only when present in our surroundings and part of our daily life. We have mentioned that the growth of intelligence is obtained by training and exercise, whereas the other activities of consciousness demand a group with whose existence they are identified.

Civilization has not succeeded, so far, in creating an environment suitable to mental activities. The low intellectual and spiritual value of most human beings is due largely to deficiencies of their psychological atmosphere. The supremacy of matter and the dogmas of industrial religion have destroyed culture, beauty, and morals, as they were understood by the Christian civilization, mother of modern science. The small social groups, possessing their own individuality and traditions, have also been broken up by the changes in their habits. The intellectual classes have been debased by the immense spread of newspapers, cheap literature, radios, and cinemas. Unintelligence is becoming more and more general, in spite of the excellence of the courses given in schools, colleges, and universities. Strange to say, it often exists with advanced scientific knowledge. School children and students form their minds on the silly programs of public entertainments. Social environment, instead of favoring the growth of intelligence, opposes it with all its might. However, it is more propitious to the development of the appreciation of beauty. America has imported the greatest musicians of Europe. Its museums are organized with a magnificence so far unequaled. Industrial art is growing rapidly. Architecture has entered into a period of triumph. Buildings of extraordinary splendor have transformed the aspect of large cities. Each individual, if he wishes, may cultivate his esthetic sense in a certain measure.

Moral sense is almost completely ignored by modern society. We have, in fact, suppressed its manifestations. All are imbued with irresponsibility. Those who discern good and evil, who are industrious and provident, remain poor and are looked upon as morons. The woman who has several children, who devotes herself to their education, instead of to her own career, is considered weak-minded. If a man saves a little money for his wife and the education of his children, this money is stolen from him by enterprising financiers. Or taken by the government and distributed to those who have been reduced to want by their own improvidence and the short-sightedness of manufacturers, bankers, and economists. Artists and men of science supply the community with beauty, health, and wealth. They live and die in poverty. Robbers enjoy prosperity in peace. Gangsters are protected by politicians and respected by judges. They are the heroes whom children admire at the cinema and imitate in their games. A rich man has every right. He may discard his aging wife, abandon his old mother to penury, rob those who have entrusted their money to him, without losing the consideration of his friends. Homosexuality flourishes. Sexual morals have been cast aside. Psychoanalysts supervise men and women in their conjugal relations. There is no difference between wrong and right, just and unjust. Criminals thrive at liberty among the rest of the population. No one makes any objection to their presence. Ministers have rationalized religion. They have destroyed its mystical basis. But they do not succeed in attracting modern men. In their half-empty churches they vainly preach a weak morality. They are content with the part of policemen, helping in the interest of the wealthy to preserve the framework of present society. Or, like politicians, they flatter the appetites of the crowd.

Man is powerless against such psychological attacks. He necessarily yields to the influence of his group. If one lives in the company of criminals or fools, one becomes a criminal or a fool. Isolation is the only hope of salvation. But where will the inhabitants of the new city find solitude? "Thou canst retire within thyself when thou wouldst," said Marcus Aurelius. "No retreat is more peaceful or less troubled than that encountered by man in his own soul." But we are not capable of such an effort. We cannot fight our social surroundings victoriously.

10

The mind is not as robust as the body. It is remarkable that mental diseases by themselves are more numerous than all the other diseases put together. Hospitals for the insane are full to overflowing, and unable to receive all those who should be restrained. In the State of New York, according to an article in the *Psychiatric Quarterly* by Mr. Benjamin Malzberg and Dr. H. M. Pollock, one person out of every twenty-two has to be placed in an asylum at some time or other. In the whole of the United States, the hospitals care for almost eight times more feeble-minded or lunatics than consumptives. Each year, about sixty-eight thousand new cases are admitted to insane asylums and similar institutions. If the admissions continue at such a rate, about one million of the children and young people who are today attending schools and colleges will, sooner or later, be confined in asylums. In the state hospitals there were, in 1932, 340,000 insane. There were also in special institutions 81,580 feeble-minded and epileptics, and 10,930 on parole. These statistics do not include the mental cases treated in private hospitals. In the whole country, besides the insane, there are 500,000 feeble-minded. And in addition, surveys made under the auspices of the National Committee for Mental Hygiene have revealed that at least 400,000 children are so unintelligent that they cannot profitably follow the courses of the public schools. In fact, the individuals who are mentally deranged are far more numerous. It is estimated that several hundred thousand persons, not mentioned in any statistics, are affected with psychoneuroses. These figures show how great is the fragility of the consciousness of civilized men, and how important for modern society is the problem of mental health. The diseases of the mind are a serious menace. They are more dangerous than tuberculosis, cancer, heart and kidney diseases, and even typhus, plague, and cholera. They are to be feared, not only because they increase the number of criminals, but chiefly because they profoundly weaken the dominant white races. It should be realized that there are not many more feeble-minded and insane among the criminals than in the rest of the nation. Indeed, a large number of defectives are found in the prisons. But we must not forget that most intelligent criminals are at large. The frequency of neurosis and psychosis is doubtless the expression of a very grave defect of modern civilization. The new habits of existence have certainly not improved our mental health.

Modern medicine has failed in its endeavor to assure to everyone the possession of the activities which are truly specific of the human being. Physicians are utterly incapable of protecting consciousness against its unknown enemies. The symptoms of mental diseases and the different types of feeble-mindedness have been well classified. But we are completely ignorant of the nature of these disorders. We have not ascertained whether they are due to structural lesions of the brain or to changes in the composition of blood-plasma, or to both these causes. It is probable that our nervous and psychological activities depend simultaneously on the anatomical conditions of the cerebral cells, on the substances set free in the blood by endocrine glands and other tissues, and on our mental states themselves. Functional disorders of the glands, as well as structural lesions of the brain, may be responsible for neuroses and psychoses. Even a complete knowledge of these phenomena would not bring about great progress. The pathology of the mind depends on psychology, as the pathology of the organs on physiology. But physiology is a science, while psychology is not. Psychology awaits its Claude Bernard or its Pasteur. It is in the state of surgery when surgeons were barbers, of chemistry before Lavoisier, at the epoch of the alchemists. However, it would be unjust to incriminate modern psychologists and their methods for the rudimentary condition of their science. The extreme complexity of the subject is the main cause of their ignorance. There are no techniques permitting the exploration of the unknown world of the nervous cells, of their association and projection fibers, and of the cerebral and mental processes.

It has not been possible to bring to light any precise relations between schizophrenic manifestations, for example, and structural alterations of the cerebral cortex. The hopes of Kraepelin, the famous pioneer in the maladies of the mind, have not materialized. The anatomical study of these diseases has not thrown much light on their nature. Mental disorders are perhaps not localized in space. Some symptoms can be attributed to a lack of harmony in the temporal succession of nervous phenomena, to changes in the value of time for cells constituting a functional system. We know also that the lesions produced in certain regions of the cerebrum, either by the spirochetes of syphilis or by the mysterious agent of encephalitis lethargica, bring about definite modifications of the personality. This knowledge is vague, uncertain, in process of formation. However, it is imperative not to wait for a complete understanding of the nature of insanity before developing a truly effective hygiene of the mind.

The discovery of the causes of mental diseases would be more important than that of their nature. Such knowledge could lead to the prevention of these maladies. Feeble-mindedness and insanity are perhaps the price of industrial civilization, and of the resulting changes in our ways of life. However, these affections are often part of the inheritance received from his parents by each individual. They manifest themselves among people whose nervous system is already unbalanced. In the families which have already produced neurotic, queer, oversensitive individuals, the insane and the feeble-minded suddenly appear. However, they also spring up from lineages which have so far been free from mental disorders. There are certainly other causes of insanity than hereditary factors. We must, therefore, ascertain how modern life acts upon consciousness.

In successive generations of pure-bred dogs, nervousness is often observed to increase. We find among these animals individuals closely resembling the feeble-minded and the insane. This phenomenon occurs in subjects brought up under artificial conditions, living in comfortable kennels, and provided with choice food quite different from that of their ancestors, the shepherds, which fought and defeated the wolves. It seems that the new conditions of existence, imposed upon dogs, as well as upon men, tend to modify the nervous system unfavorably. But experiments of long duration are necessary in order to obtain a precise knowledge of the mechanism of this degeneration. The factors promoting the development of idiocy and insanity are of great complexity. Dementia præcox and circular insanity manifest themselves more especially in the social groups where life is restless and disordered, food too elaborate or too poor, and syphilis frequent. And also when the nervous system is hereditarily unstable, when moral discipline has been suppressed, when selfishness, irresponsibility, and dispersion are customary. There are probably some relations between these factors and the genesis of psychoses. The modern habits of living hide a fundamental defect. In the environment created by technology, our most specific functions develop incompletely. Despite the marvels of scientific civilization, human personality tends to dissolve.

Chapter V

INWARD TIME

1. Duration. Its measurement by a clock. Extension of things in space and time. Mathematical, or abstract, time. Operational concept of concrete, or physical, time. 2. Definition of inward time. Physiological and psychological times. Measurement of physiological time. Growth index of blood plasma. Its variations according to chronological age. 3. Characteristics of physiological time. Recording of the past by tissues and humors. Irregularity and irreversibility of physiological time. 4. Substratum of physiological time. Reciprocal alterations of tissues and their medium. Progressive changes of blood plasma in the course of life. 5. Longevity. The span of life has not increased. Causes of this phenomenon. Possibility of increasing the span of life. Should it be done? 6. Artificial rejuvenation. Is rejuvenation possible? 7. Operational concept of inward time. The true value of physical time during youth and old age. 8. Utilization of the concept of inward time. Respective durations of man and civilization. Physiological time and society. Physiological time and the individual. 9. Rhythm of physiological time and artificial molding of man.

I

THE duration of man, just as his size, varies according to the unit used for its measurement. It is long when related to that of mice or butterflies. Short in comparison with the life of an oak. Insignificant, if placed in the frame of the earth's history. We measure it by the motion of the hands of a clock around the dial. We liken it to the passage of those hands over equal intervals, the seconds, the minutes, the hours. The time of a clock corresponds to certain rhythmic events, such as the earth's rotation on its axis and around the sun. Our duration is, then, expressed in units of solar time and consists of about twenty-five thousand days. For the clock which measures it, a child's day is equal to that of its parents. In reality, those twenty-four hours represent a very small part of the child's future life, and a much larger fraction of that of its parents. But they may also be looked upon as a minute fragment of an old man's past existence and a far more important part of that of a nursling. Thus, the value of physical time seems to differ according to whether we look back to the past or forward to the future.

We have to refer our duration to a clock because we are immersed in the physical continuum. And the clock measures one of the dimensions of this continuum. On the surface of our planet, those dimensions are discerned through particular characteristics. The vertical is identified by the phenomenon of gravity. We are unable to make any distinction between the two horizontal dimensions. We could, however, separate them from each other if our nervous system were endowed with the properties of a magnetic needle. As for the fourth dimension, or time, it takes on a strange aspect. While the other three dimensions of things are short and almost motionless, it appears as ceaselessly extending and very long. We travel quite easily over the two horizontal dimensions. But in order to move in the vertical one, we must use a staircase or an elevator, an aircraft or a balloon, for we have to contend with gravity. To travel in time is absolutely impossible. Wells has not divulged the secrets of construction of the machine which enabled one of his heroes to leave his room by the fourth dimension and to escape into the future. For concrete man, time is very different from space. But the four dimensions would seem identical to an abstract man inhabiting the sidereal spaces. Although distinct from space, time is inseparable from it, at the surface of the earth as in the rest of the universe, when considered by the biologist as well as by the physicist.

In nature, time is always found united to space. It is a necessary aspect of material beings. No concrete thing has only three spatial dimensions. A rock, a tree, an animal cannot be instantaneous. Indeed, we are capable of building up in our minds beings entirely described within three dimensions. But all concrete objects have four. And man extends both in time and in space. To an observer living far more slowly than we do he would appear as something narrow and elongated, analogous to the incandescent trail of a meteor. Besides, he possesses another aspect, impossible to define clearly. For he is not wholly comprised within the physical continuum. Thought is not confined within time and space. Moral, esthetic, and religious activities do not inhabit the physical continuum exclusively. Moreover, we know that clairvoyants may detect hidden things at great distances. Some of them perceive events which have already happened or which will take place in the future. It should be noted that they apprehend the future in the same way as the past. They are sometimes incapable of distinguishing the one from the other. For example, they may speak, at two different epochs, of the same fact, without suspecting that the first vision relates to the future, and the second to the past. Certain activities of consciousness seem to travel over space and time.

The nature of time varies according to the objects considered by our mind. The time that we observe in nature has no separate existence. It is only a mode of being of concrete objects. We ourselves create mathematical time. It is a mental construct, an abstraction indispensable to the building up of science. We conveniently compare it to a straight line, each successive instant being represented by a point. Since Galileo's day this abstraction has been substituted for the concrete data resulting from the direct observation of things. The philosophers of the Middle Ages considered time as an agent concretizing abstractions. Such a conception resembled more closely that of Minkowski than that of Galileo. To them, as to Minkowski, to Einstein, and to modern physicists, time, in nature, appeared as completely inseparable from space. In reducing objects to their primary qualities—that is, to what can be measured and is susceptible of mathematical treatment—Galileo deprived them of their secondary qualities, and of duration. This arbitrary simplification made possible the development of physics. At the same time, it led to an unwarrantably schematic conception of the world, especially of the biological world. We must listen to Bergson and attribute to time a reality of its own. And give back their secondary qualities and duration to inanimate and living beings.

The concept of time is equivalent to the operation required to estimate duration in the objects of our universe. Duration consists of the superposition of the different aspects of an identity. It is a kind of intrinsic movement of things. The earth revolves on its axis and, without losing its primary qualities, shows a surface which is sometimes lighted and sometimes darkened. Mountains may progressively change their shape under the action of snow, rain, and erosion, although they remain themselves. A tree grows, and does not lose its identity. The human individual retains his personality throughout the flux of the organic and mental processes that make up his life. Each inanimate or living being comprises an inner motion, a succession of states, a rhythm, which is his very own. Such motion is inherent time. It can be measured by reference to the motion of another being. Thus, we measure our duration by comparing it with solar time. As we inhabit the surface of the earth, we find it convenient to place in its frame the spatial and temporal dimensions of everything found thereon. We estimate our height with the aid of the meter, which is approximately the forty-millionth part of the meridian of our planet. In a like manner, the rotation of the earth, or the number of hours ticked off by a clock, is the standard to which we refer our temporal dimensions or the flow of our time. It is natural for human beings to use the intervals separating the rising of the sun from its setting as the means to measure their duration and organize their lives. However, the moon could serve the same purpose. In fact, to fishermen dwelling on shores where the tides are very high, lunar time is more important than solar time. Their way of living, and the hours reserved for sleeping and eating, are determined by the rhythm of the tides. In such circumstances, human duration is fitted into the frame of the daily variations of the sea-level. In short, time is a specific character of things. Its nature varies according to the constitution of each object. Human beings have acquired the habit of identifying their duration, and that of all other beings, with the time shown by clocks. Nevertheless, our inner time is as distinct from, and independent of, this extrinsic time, as our body is, in space, distinct from, and independent of, the earth and the sun.

2

Inner time is the expression of the changes of the body and its activities during the course of life. It is equivalent to the uninterrupted succession of the structural, humoral, physiological, and mental states which constitute our personality. It is truly a dimension of ourselves. Imaginary slices carved from our body and soul through such dimension would be as heterogeneous as the sections made by anatomists perpendicularly to the three spatial axes. As Wells says in the *Time Traveller*, a man's portraits at eight years, fifteen years, seventeen years, twenty-three years, and so on, are sections, or rather images, in three dimensions of a being of four dimensions, who is a fixed and unalterable thing. The differences between these sections express changes progressively occurring in the constitution of the individual. These changes are organic and mental. Thus, inward time has to be divided into physiological and psychological times.

Physiological time is a fixed dimension, consisting of the series of all organic changes undergone by a human being from the beginning of his embryonic life to his death. It may also be considered as a movement, as the successive states which build up our fourth dimension under the eyes of the observer. Some of these states are rhythmic and reversible, such as the pulsations of the heart, the contractions of the muscles, the movements of the stomach and those of the intestines, the secretions of the glands of the digestive apparatus, and the phenomena of menstruation. Others are progressive and irreversible, such as the loss of the skin's elasticity, the increase in the quantity of the red blood cells, the sclerosis of the tissues and the arteries. But the rhythmic and reversible movements are likewise altered during the course of life. They themselves also undergo a progressive and irreversible change. Simultaneously, the constitution of the tissues and the humors becomes modified. This complex movement is physiological time.

The other aspect of inner time is psychological time. Consciousness, under the influence of the stimuli coming from the outside world, records its own motion, the series of its states. Time, according to Bergson, is the very stuff of psychological life. "Duration is not one instant replacing another. . . . Duration is the continuous progress of the past which gnaws into the future and which swells as it advances. . . . The piling up of the past upon the past goes on without relaxation. In reality, the past is preserved by itself, automatically. In its entirety, probably, it follows us at every instant. . . . Doubtless we think with only a small part of our past, but it is with our entire past, including the original bent of our soul, that we desire, will and act."[1] We are a history. And the length of that history, rather than the number of our years, expresses the wealth of our inner life. We obscurely feel that we are not today identical with what we were yesterday. The days seem to fly more and more rapidly. But none of these changes is sufficiently precise or constant to be measured. The intrinsic motion of our consciousness is indefinable. Certain of our psychological activities are not

[1] Bergson, Henri. *Creative Evolution,* 4-5. Translation by Arthur Mitchell. New York, Henry Holt and Company, Inc.

modified by duration. They deteriorate only when the brain succumbs to illness or to senility.

Inward time cannot be properly measured in units of solar time. However, it is generally expressed in days and years because these units are convenient and applicable to the classification of terrestrial events. But such a procedure gives no information about the rhythm of the inner processes constituting our intrinsic time. Obviously, chronological age does not correspond to physiological age. Puberty occurs at different epochs in different individuals. It is the same with menopause. True age is an organic and functional state. It has to be measured by the rhythm of the changes of this state. Such rhythm varies according to individuals. Some remain young for many years. On the contrary, the organs of others wear out early in life. The value of physical time in a Norwegian, whose life is long, is far from being identical with that in an Eskimo, whose life is short. To estimate true, or physiological, age, we must discover, either in the tissues or in the humors, a measurable phenomenon, which progresses without interruption during the whole lifetime.

Man is constituted, in his fourth dimension, by a series of forms following, and blending into, each other. He is egg, embryo, infant, adolescent, adult, mature and old man. These morphological aspects are the expression of chemical, organic, and psychological events. Most of these variations cannot be measured. When measurable, they are generally found to take place only during a certain period of the existence of the individual. But physiological duration is equivalent to our fourth dimension in its entire length. The progressive slackening of growth during infancy and youth, the phenomena of puberty and of menopause, the diminution of basal metabolism, the whitening of the hair, etc., are the manifestations of different stages of our duration. The rate at which tissues grow also declines with age. Such growth activity may be roughly estimated in fragments of tissues extirpated from the body and cultivated in flasks. But, as far as the age of the organism itself is concerned, the information thus obtained is far from being reliable. Indeed, some tissues grow more active, others less active, at certain periods of physiological life. Each organ changes at its own rhythm, which differs from that of the body as a whole. Certain phenomena, however, express a general modification of the organism. For example, the rate of healing of a superficial wound varies in function of the age of the patient. It is well known that the progress of cicatrization can be calculated with two equations set up by Lecomte du Noüy. The first of these equations gives a coefficient, called index of cicatrization, which depends on the surface and the age of the wound. By introducing this index in a second equation, one may, from two measurements of the wound taken at an interval of several days, predict the future progress of repair. The smaller the wound and the younger the man, the greater is the index. With the help of this index, Lecomte du Noüy has discovered a constant that expresses the regenerative activity characteristic of a given age. This constant is equal to the product of the index by the square root of the surface of the wound. The curve of its variations shows that a twenty-year-old patient heals twice as quickly as a forty-year-old one. Through these equations, the physiological age of a man can be deduced from the rate of healing of a wound. From ten to about forty-five years, the information thus obtained is very definite. But later, the variations of the index of cicatrization are so small that they lose all significance.

Blood plasma alone displays, throughout the entire lifetime, progressive modifications characterizing the senescence of the body as a whole. We know that it contains the secretions of all tissues and organs. Plasma and tissues being a closed system, any alteration in the tissues reacts on the plasma, and vice versa. During the course of life, this system undergoes continuous changes. Some of these changes may be detected both by chemical analysis and by physiological reactions. The plasma or the serum of an aging animal has been found to increase its restraining effect on the growth of cell colonies. The ratio of the area of a colony living in serum, to that of an identical colony living in a saline solution and acting as a control, is called the growth index. The older the animal to which the serum belongs, the smaller is this index. Thus, the rhythm of physiological time can be measured. During the first days of life, blood serum does not inhibit the growth of cell colonies any more than does the control solution. At this moment the value of the index approaches unity. As the animal becomes older, its serum restrains cell multiplication more effectively. And the index decreases. During the last years of life, it is generally equal to zero.

Although very imperfect, this method gives some precise information on the rhythm of physiological time at the beginning of life, when aging is rapid. But in the final period of maturity, when aging is slow, it becomes quite insufficient. By the variations of the growth index the life of a dog can be divided into ten units of physiological time. The duration of this animal may roughly be expressed in these units instead of in years. Thus, it has become possible to compare physiological time with solar time. And their rhythms appear to be very different. The curve showing the decrease of the index value in function of chronological age falls sharply during the first year. During the second and third years, its slope becomes less and less pronounced. The segment of the curve corresponding to the mature years has a tendency to become a straight line. And the portion representing old age does not deviate from the horizontal. Obviously, aging progresses much more rapidly at the beginning than at the end of life. When infancy and old age are expressed in solar years, infancy appears to be very short and old age very long. On the contrary, measured in units of physiological time, infancy is very long and old age very short.

3

We have mentioned that physiological time is quite different from physical time. If all the clocks accelerated or retarded their motion, and if the earth correspondingly modified the rhythm of its rotation, our duration would remain unchanged. But it would seem to decrease or to increase. In this manner, the alteration undergone by solar time would become apparent. While we are swept onward upon the stream of physical time, we move at the rhythm of the inner processes constituting physiological duration. Indeed, we are not mere grains of dust floating on a river. But also drops of oil spreading out over the surface of the water with a motion of their own, while being borne along by the current. Physical time is foreign to us, whereas inner time is ourself. Our present does not drop into nothingness as does the present of a pendulum. It is recorded simultaneously in mind, tissues, and blood. We keep within ourselves the organic, humoral, and psychological marks of all the events of our life. Like a nation, like an old country, like the cities, the factories, the farms, the cultivated fields, the Gothic cathedrals, the feudal castles, the Roman monuments of Europe, we are the result of a history. Our personality is enriched by each new experience of our organs, humors, and consciousness. Each thought, each action, each illness, has definitive consequences, inasmuch as we never separate ourselves from our past. We may completely recover from a disease, or from a wrong deed. But we bear forever the scar of those events.

Solar time flows at a uniform rate. It consists of equal intervals. Its pace never changes. On the contrary, physiological time differs from one man to another. In the races enjoying long life, it is slower, and more rapid in those whose life is short. It also varies within a single individual at the different periods of his life. A year is richer in physiological and mental events during infancy than during old age. The rhythm of these events decreases rapidly at first, and later on much more slowly. The number of units of physical time corresponding to a unit of physiological time becomes progressively greater. In short, the body is an ensemble of organic movements, whose rhythm is very fast during infancy, much less rapid during youth, and very slow in maturity and old age. It is when our physiological activities begin to weaken that our mind attains the summit of its development.

Physiological time is far from having the precision of a

clock. Organic processes undergo certain fluctuations. Their rhythm is not constant. Their slackening in the course of life is expressed by an irregular curve. These irregularities are due to accidents in the concatenation of the physiological phenomena constituting our duration. At some moments, the progress of age seems to cease. At other periods, it accelerates. There are also phases in which personality concentrates and grows, and phases in which it dissipates. As stated above, inner time and its organic and psychological substratum do not possess the regularity of solar time. A sort of rejuvenation may be brought about by a happy event, or a better equilibrium of the physiological and psychological functions. Possibly, certain states of mental and bodily well-being are accompanied by modifications of the humors characteristic of a true rejuvenation. Moral suffering, business worries, infectious and degenerative diseases accelerate organic decay. The appearance of senescence may be induced in a dog by injections of sterile pus. The animal grows thin, becomes tired and depressed. At the same time, his blood and tissues display physiological reactions analogous to those of old age. But those reactions are reversible and, later, the organic functions reëstablish their normal rhythm. An old man's aspect changes but slightly from one year to another. In the absence of disease, senescence is a very slow process. When it becomes rapid, the intervention of factors other than physiological ones are to be suspected. In general, such a phenomenon may be accounted for by anxiety and sorrow, by substances deriving from bacterial infections, by a degenerating organ, or by cancer. The speeding up of senescence always expresses the presence of an organic or moral lesion in the aging body.

Like physical time, physiological time is irreversible. In fact, it is as irreversible as the processes responsible for its existence. In the higher animals, duration never changes its direction. However, in hibernating mammals, it becomes partly suspended. In a dried rotifer, its flow comes to a complete standstill. The organic rhythm of cold-blooded animals accelerates when their environment becomes warmer. The flies kept by Jacques Loeb at an abnormally high temperature aged much more rapidly and died sooner. Likewise, the value of the physiological time of an alligator changes if the surrounding temperature goes up from 20° to 40° C. In this instance, the index of cicatrization of a superficial wound rises and falls with the temperature. But, in using such simple procedures, it is not possible to induce in men any profound change of the tissues. The rhythm of physiological time is not modifiable except by interference with certain fundamental processes and their mode of association. We cannot retard senescence, or reverse its direction, unless we know the nature of the mechanisms which are the substratum of duration.

4

Physiological duration owes its existence and its characteristics to a certain type of organization of animate matter. It appears as soon as a portion of space containing living cells becomes relatively isolated from the cosmic world. At all levels of organization, in the body of a cell or in that of a man, physiological time depends on modifications of the medium produced by nutrition, and on the response of the cells to those modifications. A cell colony begins to record time as soon as its waste products are allowed to stagnate, and thus to alter its surroundings. The simplest system, where the phenomenon of senescence is observed, consists of a group of tissue cells cultivated in a small volume of nutritive medium. In such a system, the medium is progressively modified by the products of nutrition and, in its turn, modifies the cells. Then appear senescence and death. The rhythm of physiological time depends on the relations between the tissues and their medium. It varies according to the volume, the metabolic activity, the nature of the cell colony, and the quantity and the chemical composition of the fluid and gaseous media. The technique used in the preparation of a culture accounts for the rhythm of life of such culture. For example, a fragment of heart fed with a single drop of plasma in the confined atmosphere of a hollow slide, and another one immersed in a flask containing a large volume of nutritive fluids and gases, have quite different fates. The rate of accumulation of the waste products in the medium, and the nature of these products, determine the characteristics of the duration of the tissues. When the composition of the medium is maintained constant, the cell colonies remain indefinitely in the same state of activity. They record time by quantitative, and not by qualitative, changes. If, by an appropriate technique, their volume is prevented from increasing, they never grow old. Colonies obtained from a heart fragment removed in January, 1912, from a chick embryo, are growing as actively today as twenty-three years ago. In fact, they are immortal.

Within the body, the relations of the tissues and of their medium are incomparably more complex than in the artificial system represented by a culture of cells. Although the lymph and the blood, which constitute the organic medium, are continually modified by the waste products of cell nutrition, their composition is maintained constant by the lungs, kidneys, liver, etc. However, in spite of these regulatory mechanisms, very slow changes do take place in humors and tissues. They are detected by variations in the growth index of plasma, and in the constant that expresses the regenerative activity of skin. They correspond to successive states in the chemical composition of the humors. The proteins of blood serum become more abundant and their characters are modified. It is chiefly the fats which give to serum the property of acting upon certain cell types and of diminishing the rapidity of their multiplication. These fats increase in quantity and change in nature during life. The modifications of serum are not the result of a progressive accumulation, of a sort of retention of fats and proteins in the organic medium. It is quite easy to remove from a dog the greater part of its blood, to separate the plasma from the corpuscles, and to replace it by a saline solution. The blood cells, thus freed from the proteins and fatty substances of plasma, are reinjected into the animal. In less than a fortnight, plasma is observed to be regenerated by the tissues, without any change in its composition. Its state is, therefore, due to the condition of the tissues, and not to an accumulation of harmful substances. And this state is specific of each age. Even if blood serum is removed several times, it always regenerates with the characteristics corresponding to the age of the animal. The state of the humors during senescence thus appears to be determined by substances contained in the organs as in almost inexhaustible reservoirs.

In the course of life, the tissues undergo important alterations. They lose much water. They are encumbered with non-living elements and connective fibers, which are neither elastic nor extensible. The organs acquire more rigidity. Arteries become hard. Circulation is less active. Profound modifications take place in the structure of the glands. Epithelial cells lose their qualities little by little. They regenerate more slowly, or not at all. Their secretions are less rich. Such changes occur at various rates, according to the organs. Certain organs grow old more rapidly than others. But we do not know as yet the reason for this phenomenon. Such regional senescence may attack the arteries, the heart, the brain, the kidneys, or any other organ. The aging of a single system of tissues is dangerous. Longevity is much greater when the elements of the body grow old in a uniform way. If the skeletal muscles remain active when the heart and the vessels are already worn out, they become a danger to the entire body. Abnormally vigorous organs in a senile organism are almost as harmful as senile organs in a young organism. The youthful functioning of any anatomical system, either sexual glands, digestive apparatus, or muscles, is very dangerous for old men. Obviously, the value of time is not the same for all tissues. This heterochronism shortens the duration of life. If excessive work is imposed on any part of the body, even in individuals whose tissues are isochronic, aging is also accelerated. An organ which is submitted to overactivity, toxic influences, and abnormal stimulations, wears out more quickly than the others. And its premature senility brings on the death of the organism.

We know that physiological time, like physical time, is not an entity. Physical time depends on the constitution of the clocks and of the solar system. Physiological time, on that of tissues and humors, and on their reciprocal relations. The characteristics of duration are those of the structural and functional processes specific of a certain type of organization. The length of life is conditioned by the very mechanisms that make man independent of the cosmic environment and give him his spatial mobility. By the small volume of the blood. By the activity of the systems responsible for the purification of the humors. These systems do not succeed in preventing certain progressive modifications of the serum and the tissues from occurring. Perhaps the tissues are not completely freed of waste products by the blood stream. Perhaps they are insufficiently fed. If the volume of the organic medium were much greater, and the elimination of waste products more complete, human life might last longer. But our body would be far larger, softer, less compact. It would resemble the gigantic prehistoric animals. We certainly would be deprived of the agility, the speed, and the skill that we now possess.

Like physiological time, psychological time is only an aspect of ourselves. Its nature, as that of memory, is unknown. Memory is responsible for our awareness of the passage of time. However, psychological duration is composed of other elements. Personality is partly made up of recollections. But it also comes from the impression left upon all our organs by every physical, chemical, physiological, or psychological event of our life. We obscurely feel the passing of duration. We are capable of estimating such duration, in a grossly approximative manner, in terms of physical time. We perceive its flux as, perhaps, do muscular or nervous elements. Each cell type records physical time in its own way. The value of time for nerves and muscles is expressed, as already mentioned, in chronaxies. All anatomical elements are far from having the same chronaxy. The isochronism and heterochronism of cells play a capital part in their work. This estimation of time by the tissues may possibly reach the threshold of consciousness, and be responsible for the indefinable feeling in the depths of our self of silently flowing waters, on which float our states of consciousness, like the spots of a searchlight on the dark surface of an immense river. We realize that we change, that we are not identical with our former self. But that we are the same being. The distance from which we look back upon the small child, who was ourself, is precisely the dimension of our organism and of our consciousness which we compare to a spatial dimension. Of this aspect of inward time we know nothing, except that it is both dependent and independent of the rhythm of organic life, and moves more and more rapidly as we grow older.

5

The greatest desire of men is for eternal youth. From Merlin down to Cagliostro, Brown-Séquard, and Voronoff, charlatans and scientists have pursued the same dream and suffered the same defeat. No one has discovered the supreme secret. Meanwhile, our need of it is becoming more and more urgent. Scientific civilization has destroyed the world of the soul. But the realm of matter is widely opened to man. He must, then, keep intact the vigor of his body and of his intelligence. Only the strength of youth gives him the power to satisfy his physiological appetites and to conquer the outer world. In some measure, however, we have realized the ancestral dream. We enjoy youth, or its appearance, for a much longer time than our fathers did. But we have not succeeded in increasing the duration of our existence. A man of forty-five has no more chance of dying at the age of eighty years now than in the last century.

This failure of hygiene and medicine is a strange fact. In spite of the progress achieved in the heating, ventilation, and lighting of houses, of dietary hygiene, bathrooms, and sports, of periodical medical examinations, and increasing numbers of medical specialists, not even one day has been added to the span of human life. Are we to believe that hygienists, chemists, and physicians are mistaken in their ruling of the existence of the individual, like politicians, economists, and financiers in the organization of the life of the nation? After all, it may be that modern comfort and habits imposed upon the dwellers of the new city do not agree with natural laws. However, a marked change has taken place in the appearance of men and women. Owing to hygiene, athletics, alimentary restrictions, beauty parlors, and to the superficial activity engendered by telephone and automobile, all are more alert than in former times. At fifty, women are still young. Modern progress, however, has brought in its train counterfeit money as well as gold. When their visages, lifted and smoothed by the beauty surgeon, again become flabby, when massage no longer prevails against invading fat, those women whose appearance has been girlish for so many years look older than their grandmothers did at the same age. The pseudo-young men, who play tennis and dance as at twenty years, who discard their old wife and marry a young woman, are liable to softening of the brain, and to diseases of the heart and the kidneys. Sometimes they die suddenly in their bed, in their office, on the golf-links, at an age when their ancestors were still tilling their land or managing their business with a firm hand. The causes of this failure of modern life are not exactly known. Indeed, hygienists and physicians cannot be held responsible for it. The premature wearing out of modern men is probably due to worries, lack of economic security, overwork, absence of moral discipline, and excesses of all sorts.

A better knowledge of the mechanisms of physiological duration could bring a solution of the problem of longevity. But the science of man is still too rudimentary to be useful. We must, then, ascertain, in a purely empirical manner, whether life can be made longer. The presence of a few centenarians in every country demonstrates the extent of our temporal potentialities. No practical conclusions, however, have resulted so far from the observation of these centenarians. Obviously, longevity is hereditary. But it depends also on the conditions of development. When descendants of families where longevity is usual come to dwell in large cities, they generally lose, in one or two generations, the capacity of living to be old. A study of animals of pure stock and of well-known ancestral constitution would probably show in what measure environment may augment the span of existence. In certain races of mice, mated between brothers and sisters over many generations, the duration of life remains quite constant. However, if one places the animals in large pens, in a state of semi-liberty, instead of keeping them in cages, and allows them to burrow and return to more primitive conditions of existence, they die much earlier. When certain substances are removed from the diet, longevity is also found to decrease. On the contrary, life lengthens if the animals are given certain food or subjected to fasting during certain fixed periods for several generations. It is evident that simple changes in the mode of existence are capable of influencing the duration of life. Man's longevity could probably be augmented by analogous, or other, procedures.

We must not yield to the temptation to use blindly for this purpose the means placed at our disposal by medicine. Longevity is only desirable if it increases the duration of youth, and not that of old age. The lengthening of the senescent period would be a calamity. The aging individual, when not capable of providing for himself, is an encumbrance to his family and to the community. If all men lived to be one hundred years old, the younger members of the population could not support such a heavy burden. Before attempting to prolong life, we must discover methods for conserving organic and mental activities to the eve of death. It is imperative that the number of the diseased, the paralyzed, the weak, and the insane should not be augmented. Besides, it would not be wise to give everybody a long existence. The danger of increasing the quantity of human beings without regard to their quality is well known. Why should more years be added to the life of persons who are unhappy, selfish, stupid, and useless? The number of centenarians must not be augmented until we can prevent intellectual and moral decay, and also the lingering diseases of old age.

6

It would be more useful to discover a method for rejuvenating individuals whose physiological and mental qualities justify such a measure. Rejuvenation can be conceived as a complete reversal of inward time. The subject would be carried back to a previous stage of his life by some operation. One would amputate a part of his fourth dimension. However, for practical purposes, rejuvenation should be given a more restricted meaning and be considered as an incomplete reversal of duration. The direction of psychological time would not be changed. Memory would persist. Tissues and humors would be rejuvenated. With the help of organs in possession of their youthful vigor, the subject could utilize the experience acquired in the course of a long life. The word rejuvenation, when used in connection with the experiments and operations carried out by Steinach, Voronoff, and others, refers to an improvement in the general condition of the patients, to a feeling of strength and of sprightliness, to a revival of the sexual functions. But such changes occurring in an old man after the treatment do not mean that rejuvenation has taken place. Studies of the chemical composition of the blood serum, and of its physiological reactions, are the only means of detecting a reversal of physiological age. A permanent increase in the growth index of serum would demonstrate the reality of results claimed by the surgeons. For rejuvenation is equivalent to certain physiological and chemical modifications measurable in blood plasma. Nevertheless, the absence of such findings does not necessarily mean that the age of the subject has not decreased. Our techniques are still far from perfect. They cannot reveal, in an old individual, a reversal of physiological time of less than several years. If a fourteen-year-old dog were brought back to the age of ten, the change in the growth index of his serum would be hardly discernible.

Among the ancient medical superstitions, there was a persistent belief in the virtue of young blood, in its power to impart youth to an old and worn-out body. Pope Innocent VIII had the blood of three young men transfused into his veins. But after this operation, he died. As it is quite likely that death was due to a technical accident, perhaps the idea deserves reconsideration. The introduction of young blood into an old organism might bring about favorable changes. It is strange that such an operation has not been tried again. This omission is due, possibly, to the fact that endocrine glands have gained the favor of the physicians. Brown-Séquard, after having injected into himself a fresh extract of testicle, believed that he was rejuvenated. This discovery brought him very great fame. However, he died shortly afterwards. But faith in the testicle as an agent of rejuvenation survived. Steinach attempted to demonstrate that the ligature of its duct stimulates the gland. He performed this operation on many old men. But the results were doubtful. Brown-Séquard's idea was taken up again and extended by Voronoff. The latter, instead of simply injecting testicular extracts, grafted in old men, or men prematurely aged, testicles from chimpanzees. It is incontestable that the operation was followed by an improvement in the general condition and the sexual functions of the patients. But the testicle of a chimpanzee does not live long in a man. During the process of degeneration, it may set free certain secretory products, and these substances, passing into the circulating blood, probably activate the sexual and other endocrine glands of the subject. Such operations do not give lasting results. Old age, as we know, is due to profound modifications of all the tissues and humors, and not to the deficiency of a single gland. The loss of activity of the sexual glands is not the cause of senescence, but one of its consequences. It is probable that neither Steinach nor Voronoff has ever observed true rejuvenation. But their failure does not by any means signify that rejuvenation is forever impossible to obtain.

We can believe that a partial reversal of physiological time will become realizable. Duration, as already mentioned, consists of certain structural and functional processes. True age depends on progressive changes of the tissues and humors. Tissues and humors are one and the same system. If an old man were given the glands of a still-born infant and the blood of a young man, he would possibly be rejuvenated. Many technical difficulties remain to be overcome before such an operation can be undertaken. We have no way of selecting organs suitable to a given individual. There is no procedure for rendering tissues capable of adapting themselves to the body of their host in a definitive manner. But the progress of science is swift. With the aid of the methods already existing, and of those which will be discovered, we must pursue the search for the great secret.

Man will never tire of seeking immortality. He will not attain it, because he is bound by certain laws of his organic constitution. He may succeed in retarding, perhaps even in reversing in some measure, the inexorable advance of physiological time. Never will he vanquish death. Death is the price he has to pay for his brain and his personality. But some day, medicine will teach him that old age, free from diseases of the body and the soul, is not to be feared. To illness, and not to senescence, are due most of our woes.

7

The human significance of physical time is bound necessarily to the nature of inner time. We have already mentioned that physiological time is a flux of irreversible changes of the tissues and humors. It may be approximately measured in special units, each unit being equivalent to a certain functional modification of blood serum. Its characteristics depend on the structure of the organism and on the physiological processes connected with such structure. They are specific of each species, of each individual, and of the age of each individual.

Physiological time is generally referred to physical time, to the time of a clock, inasmuch as we are part of the material world. The natural periods of our life are measured in days or years. Infancy, childhood, and adolescence last about eighteen years. Maturity and old age, fifty or sixty years. Thus, man consists of a brief period of development and of a long period of completion and decay. On the contrary, physical time may be referred to physiological time, and the time of a clock expressed in terms of human duration. Then, a strange phenomenon occurs. Physical time loses the uniformity of its value. The content of a year in units of physiological time becomes variable. It is different for each individual, and for each period of an individual's life.

One perceives, more or less clearly, the changes in the

value of physical time, which occur in the course of one's life. The days of our childhood seemed very slow, and those of our maturity are disconcertingly rapid. Possibly we experience this feeling because we unconsciously place physical time in the frame of our duration. And, naturally, physical time seems to vary inversely to it. The rhythm of our duration slows down progressively. Physical time glides along at a uniform rate. It is like a large river flowing through a plain. At the dawn of his life, man briskly runs along the bank. And he goes faster than the stream. Toward midday, his pace slackens. The waters now glide as speedily as he walks. When night falls, man is tired. The stream accelerates the swiftness of its flow. Man drops far behind. Then he stops, and lies down forever. And the river inexorably continues on its course. In fact, the river never accelerates its flow. Only the progressive slackening of our pace is responsible for this illusion. The seeming length of the first part of our existence and the brevity of the last may also be due to the well-known fact that, for the child and for the old man, a year represents quite different proportions of the past. It is more probable, however, that our consciousness vaguely perceives the slowing down of our time, that is, of our physiological processes. And that each one of us runs along the bank and looks at the streaming waters of physical time.

The value of the days of early childhood is very great. Every moment should be utilized for education. The waste of this period of life can never be compensated. Instead of being allowed to grow like plants or little animals, children should be the object of the most enlightened training. But this training calls for a profound knowledge of physiology and psychology, which modern educators have not yet been given the opportunity of acquiring. The declining years of maturity and senescence have little physiological value. They are almost empty of organic and mental changes. They have to be filled with artificial activities. The aging man should neither stop working nor retire. Inaction further impoverishes the content of time. Leisure is even more dangerous for the old than for the young. To those whose forces are declining, appropriate work should be given. But not rest. Neither should physiological processes be stimulated at this moment. It is preferable to hide their slowness under a number of psychological events. If our days are filled with mental and spiritual adventures, they glide much less rapidly. They may even recover the plenitude of those of youth.

8

Duration is wedded to man, like the shape to the marble of the statue. Man refers all the events of his world to himself. He uses his span of life as a time unit in his estimation of the age of the earth, of the human race, of civilization, of the length of his own undertakings. Nevertheless, an individual and a nation cannot be placed in the same temporal scale. Social problems should not be considered in the same light as individual ones. They evolve very slowly. Our observations and our experiences are always too short. For this reason, they have little significance. The results of a modification in the material and mental conditions of the existence of a population rarely manifest themselves in less than a century. However, the investigation of the great biological questions is confined to isolated individuals. There is no provision for the continuation of their work when they die. In a like manner, scientific and political institutions are conceived in terms of individual duration. The Roman Catholic Church is the only organization to have realized that the progress of humanity is very slow, that the passing of a generation is an insignificant event in the history of the world. In the evolution of mankind, the duration of the individual is inadequate as a unit of temporal measure. The advent of scientific civilization necessitates a fresh discussion of all fundamental subjects. We are witnessing our own moral, intellectual, and social failure. We have been living under the delusion that democracies would survive through the weak and short-sighted efforts of the ignorant. We begin to understand that they are decaying. Problems involving the future of the great races demand a solution. It is now imperative to prepare for distant events, to mold young generations with a different ideal. The government of nations by men who estimate time in function of their own duration leads, as we well know, to confusion and to failure. We have to stretch our temporal outlook beyond ourselves.

On the contrary, in the organization of transitory social groups, such as a class of children, or a gang of workmen, individual time alone must be taken into account. The members of a group are obliged to work at the same rhythm. The intellectual activity of school children composing a class must be of practically the same standard. In factories, banks, stores, universities, etc., the workers are supposed to accomplish a certain task in a certain time. Those whose strength declines on account of age or illness impede the progress of the whole. So far, human beings are classified according to their chronological age. Children of the same age are placed in the same class. The date of retirement is also determined by the age of the worker. It is known, however, that the true condition of an individual does not depend on his chronological age. In certain types of occupation, individuals should be grouped according to physiological age. Puberty has been used as a way of classifying children in some New York schools. But there are still no means of ascertaining at what time a man should be pensioned. Neither is there any general method of measuring the rate of the organic and mental decline of a given individual. However, physiological tests have been developed by which the condition of a flyer can be accurately estimated. Pilots are retired according to their physiological, and not their chronological, age.

Young and old people, although in the same region of space, live in different temporal worlds. We are inexorably separated by age from one another. A mother never succeeds in being a sister to her daughter. It is impossible for children to understand their parents, and still less their grandparents. Obviously, the individuals belonging to four successive generations are profoundly heterochronic. An old man and his great-grandson are complete strangers. The shorter the temporal distance separating two generations, the stronger may be the moral influence of the older over the younger. Women should be mothers when they are still very young. Thus, they would not be isolated from their children by a temporal gap too great to be bridged, even by love.

9

From the concept of physiological time derive certain rules of our action on human beings. Organic and mental developments are not inexorable. They can be modified, in some measure, according to our will, because we are a movement, a succession of superposed patterns in the frame of our identity. Although man is a closed world, his outside and inside frontiers are open to many physical, chemical, and psychological agents. And those agents are capable of modifying our tissues and our mind. The moment, the mode, and the rhythm of our interventions depend on the structure of physiological time. Our temporal dimension extends chiefly during childhood, when functional processes are most active. Then, organs and mind are plastic. Their formation can effectively be aided. As organic events happen each day in great numbers, their growing mass can receive such shape as it seems proper to impress permanently upon the individual. The molding of the organism according to a selected pattern must take into account the nature of duration, the constitution of our temporal dimension. Our interventions have to be made in the cadence of inner time. Man is like a viscous liquid flowing into the physical continuum. He cannot instantaneously change his direction. We should not endeavor to modify his mental and structural form by rough procedures, as one shapes a statue of marble by blows of the hammer. Surgical operations alone produce in tissues sudden alterations which are beneficial. And still, recovery from the quick work of the knife is slow. No profound changes of the body as a whole can be obtained rapidly. Our action must blend with the physiological processes, substratum of inner time, by following their own rhythm. For instance, it is useless to administer to a child a large quantity of cod-liver oil in a single dose. But a small amount of this remedy, given each day for several months, modifies the dimensions and the form of the skeleton. Likewise, the mental factors act only in a progressive manner. Our interventions in the building up of body and consciousness have their full effects only when they conform to the laws of our duration.

A child may be compared to a brook, which follows any change in its bed. The brook persists in its identity, in spite of the diversity of its forms. It may become a lake or a torrent. Under the influence of environment, personality may spread and become very thin, or concentrate and acquire great strength. The growth of personality involves a constant trimming of our self. At the beginning of life, man is endowed with vast potentialities. He is limited in his development only by the extensible frontiers of his ancestral predispositions. But at each instant he has to make a choice. And each choice throws into nothingness one of his potentialities. He has of necessity to select one of the several roads open to the wanderings of his existence, to the exclusion of all others. Thus, he deprives himself of seeing the countries wherein he could have traveled along the other roads. In our infancy we carry within ourselves numerous virtual beings, who die one by one. In our old age, we are surrounded by an escort of those we could have been, of all our aborted potentialities. Every man is a fluid that becomes solid, a treasure that grows poorer, a history in the making, a personality that is being created. And our progress, or our disintegration, depends on physical, chemical, and physiological factors, on viruses and bacteria, on psychological influences, and, finally, on our own will. We are constantly being made by our environment and by our self. And duration is the very material of organic and mental life, as it means "invention, creation of forms, continual elaboration of the absolutely new."[1]

[1] Bergson, Henri, *loc. cit.*, 11.

Chapter VI

ADAPTIVE FUNCTIONS

---

1. *Adaptive functions are responsible for duration.* 2. *Intraorganic adaptation. Automatic regulation of the volume and composition of blood and humors. Its physicochemical and physiological nature.* 3. *Organic correlations. Teleological aspect of the phenomenon. Adaptation to future events. Adaptation to hemorrhage. Correlation of the structures of the eye.* 4. *Repair of tissues.* 5. *Adaptive phenomena and modern surgery.* 6. *Significance of diseases. Natural and acquired immunities.* 7. *Infectious and degenerative diseases. Artificial and natural health.* 8. *Extraorganic adaptation. Adaptation to physical environment.* 9. *Permanent changes imposed upon body and consciousness by adaptation.* 10. *Adaptation to social environment. Effort, conquest, flight. Lack of adaptation.* 11. *Characteristics of adaptive functions. Principle of Le Chatelier. Steady states. The law of effort.* 12. *Disuse of adaptive functions in modern civilization.* 13. *Activity of adaptive mechanisms necessary for the optimum development of man.* 14. *Practical significance of adaptive functions.*

I

THERE is a striking contrast between the durability of our body and the transitory character of its elements. Man is composed of a soft, alterable matter, susceptible of disintegrating in a few hours. However, he lasts longer than if made of steel. Not only does he last, but he ceaselessly overcomes the difficulties and dangers of the outside world. He accommodates himself, much better than the other animals do, to the changing conditions of his environment. He persists in living, despite physical, economic, and social upheavals. Such endurance is due to a very particular mode of activity of his tissues and humors. The body seems to mold itself on events. Instead of wearing out, it changes. Our organs always improvise means of meeting every new situation. And these means are such that they tend to give us a maximum duration. The physiological processes, which are the substratum of inner time, always incline in the direction leading to the longest survival of the individual. This strange function, this watchful automatism, makes possible human existence with its specific characters. It is called adaptation.

All physiological activities are endowed with the property of being adaptive. Adaptation, therefore, assumes innumerable forms. However, its aspects may be grouped into two categories, intraorganic and extraorganic. Intraorganic adaptation is responsible for the constancy of the organic medium and of the relations of tissues and humors. It determines the correlation of the organs. It brings about the automatic repair of tissues and the cure of diseases. Extraorganic adaptation adjusts the individual to the physical, psychological, and economic world. It allows him to survive in spite of the unfavorable conditions of his environment. Under these two aspects, the adaptive functions are at work during each instant of our whole life. They are the indispensable basis of our duration.

2

Whatever our sufferings, our joys, and the agitation of the world may be, our organs do not modify their inward rhythm to any great extent. The chemical exchanges of the cells and the humors continue imperturbably. The blood pulsates in the arteries and flows at an almost constant speed in the innumerable capillaries of the tissues. There is an impressive difference between the regularity of the phenomena taking place within our body and the extreme variability of our environment. Our organic states are very steady. But this stability is not equivalent to a condition of rest, or equilibrium. It is due, on the contrary, to the unceasing activity of the entire organism. To maintain the constancy of the blood's composition and the regularity of its circulation, an immense number of physiological processes are required. The tranquillity of the tissues is assured by the converging efforts of all the functional systems. And the more irregular and violent our life, the greater are these efforts. For the brutality of our relations with the cosmic world must never trouble the peace of the cells and humors of our inner world.

The blood is not subjected to large variations of pressure and volume. However, it receives and loses a great deal of water in an irregular manner. After each meal, it takes in the fluids absorbed by the intestinal mucosa from the food and the digestive juices. At other moments its volume tends to decrease. In the course of digestion, it loses several liters of water, which are used by the stomach, intestines, liver, and pancreas for manufacturing their secretions. An analogous phenomenon occurs during violent muscular exercise, a boxing-match for example, if the perspiration glands work actively. Blood also diminishes in volume in the course of certain diseases, such as dysentery or cholera, when a great deal of liquid passes from the capillary vessels into the lumen of the intestine. The administration of a purgative is followed by a similar waste of water. The gains and losses are exactly counterbalanced by mechanisms regulating the blood volume.

These mechanisms extend over the whole body. They maintain constant both the pressure and the volume of the blood. The pressure does not depend on the absolute amount of the blood, but on the relation of this amount to the capacity of the circulatory apparatus. This apparatus, however, is not comparable to a system of pipes fed by a pump. It has no analogy with the machines constructed by man. Arteries and veins automatically modify their caliber. They contract or dilate under the influence of the nerves of their muscular envelope. In addition, the walls of the capillaries are permeable. The water of the blood is thus free to enter or to leave the circulatory apparatus. It also escapes from the body through the kidneys, the pores of the skin, the intestinal mucosa, and evaporates in the lungs. The heart realizes the miracle of maintaining constant the pressure of the blood in a system of vessels whose capacity and permeability ceaselessly vary. When blood tends to accumulate in too large a quantity in the right heart, a reflex, starting from the right auricle, increases the rate of cardiac pulsations, and blood escapes more rapidly from the heart into the vessels. Moreover, serum traverses the wall of the capillaries and inundates connective tissue and muscles. In this manner, the circulatory system automatically ejects all excess of fluid. If, on the contrary, the volume and the pressure of the blood diminish, the change is recorded by nerve endings hidden in the wall of the sinus of the carotid artery. This reflex determines a contraction of the vessels and a reduction in the capacity of the circulatory apparatus. At the same time, the fluids of the tissues and those contained in the stomach pass into the vascular system by filtering through the wall of the capillaries. Such are the mechanisms responsible for the nearly perfect constancy of the amount and the tension of the blood.

The composition of the blood is also very stable. Under normal conditions, the quantity of red cells, plasma, salts, proteins, fats, and sugars varies only in a small measure. It always remains higher than is really necessary for the usual requirements of the tissues. Consequently, unforeseen events, such as privation of food, hemorrhages, or intense and prolonged muscular efforts do not modify in a dangerous manner the state of the organic fluids. The tissues contain abundant reserves of water, salts, fats, proteins, and sugar. Oxygen, however, is not stored anywhere. It must be unceasingly supplied to the blood by the lungs. The organism needs variable quantities of this gas, according to the activity of its chemical exchanges. At the same time it produces more or less carbon dioxide. However, the tension of these gases in the blood remains constant. This phenomenon is due to a mechanism both physicochemical and physiological. A physicochemical equilibrium determines the amount of oxygen taken up by the red corpuscles during their passage through the lungs, and carried by those corpuscles to the tissues. During its journey through the peripheral capillary vessels, the blood absorbs the carbon dioxide set free by the tissues. This acid decreases the affinity of hemoglobin for oxygen. It promotes the passing of the gas from the red corpuscles to the cells of the organs. The exchange of oxygen and carbon dioxide between tissues and blood is due exclusively to the chemical properties of the hemoglobin, the proteins, and the salts of blood plasma.

A physiological process is responsible for the quantity of oxygen carried by the blood to the tissues. The activity of the respiratory muscles, which give a more or less rapid motion to the thorax and control the penetration of air into the lungs, depends on nervous cells situated in the upper part of the spinal cord. The activity of this center is regulated by the tension of carbon dioxide in the blood. And also by the temperature of the body and by the excess or insufficiency of oxygen in the circulation. A similar mechanism, both physicochemical and physiological, regulates the ionic alkalinity of blood plasma. The intraorganic medium never becomes acid. This fact is all the more surprising as tissues unceasingly produce large quantities of carbonic, lactic, sulphuric acids, etc., which are set free into the lymph. These acids do not modify the reaction of blood plasma, because they are neutralized, or rather buffered, by the presence of bicarbonates and phosphates. Although blood plasma can accept a large quantity of acids without increasing its actual acidity, it must, nevertheless, get rid of them. Carbon dioxide escapes from the body by the lungs. Non-volatile acids are eliminated through the kidneys. The discharge of carbon dioxide by the pulmonary mucosa is a mere physicochemical phenomenon, while the secretion of urine and the motion of the thorax and the lungs require the intervention of physiological processes. The physicochemical equilibria, which assure the constancy of the organic medium, ultimately depend on the automatic intervention of the nervous system.

3

The organs are correlated by the organic fluids and the nervous system. Each element of the body adjusts itself to the others, and the others to it. This mode of adaptation is essentially teleological. If we attribute to tissues an intelligence of the same kind as ours, as mechanists and vitalists do, the physiological processes appear to associate together in view of the end to be attained. The existence of finality within the organism is undeniable. Each part seems to know the present and future needs of the whole, and acts accordingly. The significance of time and space is not the same for our tissues as for our mind. The body perceives the remote as well as the near, the future as well as the present. When pregnancy is nearly completed, the tissues of the vulva and vagina are invaded by fluids. They become soft and extensible. Such a change in their consistency renders the passage of the fetus possible a few days later. At the same time, the mammary glands multiply their cells. Before confinement, they begin to function. They are ready and waiting to feed the child. All these processes are obviously a preparation for a future event.

When one half of the thyroid gland is removed, the remaining half increases in volume. Generally, it even increases more than is necessary. The organism, as Meltzer has shown, is abundantly provided with factors of safety. In the same way, the extirpation of a kidney is followed by the enlargement of the other one, although the secretion of urine is amply assured by a single normal kidney. If at any time the organism calls upon the thyroid or the kidney for an exceptional effort, these organs will be capable of satisfying the unforeseen demand. During the entire history of the embryo the tissues seem to prepare for the future. Organic correlations take place as easily between different periods of time as between different regions of space. These facts are a primary datum of observation. But they cannot be interpreted with the help of our naïve mechanistic and vitalistic concepts. The teleological correlation of organic processes is evident in the regeneration of blood after a hemorrhage. First, all the vessels contract. The relative volume of the remaining blood automatically increases. Thus, arterial pressure is sufficiently restored for blood circulation to continue. The fluids of the tissues and the muscles pass through the wall of the capillary vessels and invade the circulatory system. The patient feels intense thirst. The blood immediately absorbs the fluids that enter the stomach and reëstablishes its normal volume. The reserves of red cells escape from the organs where they were stored. Finally, the bone marrow begins manufacturing red corpuscles, which will complete the regeneration of the blood. In sum, all parts of the body contribute a concatenation of physiological, physicochemical, and structural phenomena. These phenomena constitute the adaptation of the whole to hemorrhage.

The component parts of an organ, of the eye, for example, appear to associate for a definite, although future, purpose. The skin covering the young retina becomes transparent, as already mentioned, and metamorphoses into cornea and lens. This transformation is considered as due to substances set free by the cerebral part of the eye, the optic vesicle. But the solution of the problem is not given by this explanation. How does it happen that the optic vesicle secretes a substance endowed with the property of rendering the skin translucid? By what means does the future retina induce the skin to manufacture a lens capable of projecting upon its nerve endings the image of the outer world? In front of the lens, the iris shapes itself into a diaphragm. This diaphragm dilates or contracts according to the intensity of the light. At the same time, the sensitivity of the retina increases or decreases. In addition, the form of the lens automatically adjusts itself to near or distant vision. These correlations are obvious facts. But, as yet, they cannot be explained. Possibly they are not what they seem to be. The phenomena may be fundamentally simple. We may miss their oneness. In fact, we divide a whole into parts. And we are astonished that the parts, thus separated, exactly fit each other when they are put together again by our mind. We probably give to things an artificial individuality. Perhaps the frontiers of the organs and of the body are not where we believe them to be located. Neither do we understand the correlations between different individuals, for example, the corresponding existence of the penis and the vagina. Nor the coöperation of two individuals in the same physiological process, such as the fecundation of the egg by the spermatozoon. Those phenomena are not intelligible by the light of our present concepts of individuality, organization, space, and time.

4

When skin, muscles, blood vessels, or bones are injured by a blow, a flame, or a projectile, the organism immediately adapts itself to such a new situation. Everything happens as if a series of measures, some immediate, some delayed, were taken by the body in order to repair the lesions of the tissues. As in blood regeneration, heterogeneous and converging mechanisms come into play. They all turn toward the end to be attained, the reconstruction of the destroyed structures. An artery is cut. Blood gushes in abundance. Arterial pressure is lowered. The patient has a syncope. The hemorrhage decreases. A clot forms in the wound. Fibrin occludes the opening of the vessel. Then the hemorrhage definitely stops. During the following days, leucocytes and tissue cells invade the clot of fibrin and progressively regenerate the wall of the artery. Likewise, the organism may heal a small wound of the intestines by its own means. The wounded loop first becomes immobile. It is temporarily paralyzed, and fecal matter is thus prevented from running into the abdomen. At the same time, some other intestinal loop, or the surface of the omentum, approaches the wound and, owing to a known property of peritoneum, adheres to it. Within four or five hours the opening is occluded. Even if the surgeon's needle has drawn the edges of the wound together, healing is due to spontaneous adhesion of the peritoneal surfaces.

When a limb is broken by a blow, the sharp ends of the fractured bones tear muscles and blood vessels. They are soon surrounded by a bloody clot of fibrin, and by osseous and muscular debris. Then, circulation becomes more active. The limb swells. The nutritive substances necessary for the regeneration of the tissues are brought into the wounded area by the blood. At the seat of the fracture and around it, all structural and functional processes are directed toward repair. Tissues become what they have to be in order to accomplish the common task. For example, a shred of muscle close to the focus of fracture metamorphoses into cartilage.

Cartilage, as is well known, is the forerunner of bone in the soft mass temporarily uniting the broken ends. Later, cartilage transforms into osseous tissue. The skeleton is thus regenerated by a substance of exactly the same nature as its own. During the few weeks necessary for the completion of repair, an immense number of chemical, nervous, circulatory, and structural phenomena take place. They are all concatenated. The blood flowing from the vessels at the time of the accident, and the juices from the bone marrow and lacerated muscles, set in motion the physiological processes of regeneration. Each phenomenon results from the preceding one. To the physicochemical conditions and to the chemical composition of the fluids set free in the tissues must be attributed the actualization within the cells of certain potential properties. And these potential properties give to anatomical structures the power to regenerate. Each tissue is capable of responding, at any moment of the unpredictable future, to all physicochemical or chemical changes of the intraorganic medium in a manner consistent with the interests of the whole body.

The adaptive aspect of cicatrization is evident in superficial wounds. These wounds are exactly measurable. Their rate of healing can be calculated by Lecomte du Noüy's formulas. And the process of cicatrization thus analyzed. First, we observe that a wound only cicatrizes if cicatrization is advantageous to the body. When the tissues uncovered by the extirpation of the skin are completely protected against microbes, air, and other causes of irritation, regeneration does not take place. In fact, under such conditions it is useless. The wound, therefore, does not heal and remains in its initial state. Such a state is maintained as long as the tissues are guarded against the attacks of the outer world as perfectly as they would be by the regenerated skin. As soon as some blood, a few microbes, or an ordinary dressing is allowed to come in contact with the damaged surface and to irritate it, the process of healing starts and continues irresistibly until cicatrization is complete.

Skin, as we know, consists of superposed sheets of flat cells, the epithelial cells. These cells lie on the dermis—that is, on a soft and elastic layer of connective tissue containing many small blood vessels. When a piece of skin is removed, the bottom of the wound is seen to consist of fatty tissue and muscles. After three or four days its surface becomes smooth, glistening, and red. Then it abruptly begins to decrease with great rapidity. This phenomenon is due to a sort of contraction of the new tissue covering the wound. At the same time, the skin cells commence to glide over the red surface as a white edge. Finally, they cover its entire area. A definitive scar is formed. This scar is due to the collaboration of two types of tissue, the connective tissue filling the wound, and the epithelial cells, which advance over its surface from the borders. Connective tissue is responsible for the contraction of the wound. Epithelial tissue, for the membrane that ultimately covers it. The progressive decrease of the wounded area in the course of repair is expressed by an exponential curve. However, if one prevents either the epithelial tissue or the connective tissue from accomplishing its respective tasks, the curve does not change. It does not change because the deficiency of one of the factors of repair is compensated by the acceleration of the other. Obviously, the progress of the phenomenon depends on the end to be attained. If one of the regenerating mechanisms fails, it is replaced by the other. The result alone is invariable. And not the procedure. In a like manner, after a hemorrhage, arterial pressure and blood volume are reëstablished by two converging mechanisms. On one side, by contraction of the blood vessels and by diminution of their capacity. On the other side, by the bringing of a quantity of liquid from the tissues and the digestive apparatus. But each of these mechanisms is capable of compensating the failure of the other.

5

The knowledge of the processes of healing has brought modern surgery into being. Surgeons would not be able to treat wounds if adaptation did not exist. They have no influence on the healing mechanisms. They content themselves with guiding the spontaneous activity of those mechanisms. For example, they manage to bring the edges of a wound, or the ends of a broken bone, into such a position that regeneration takes place without defective scar and deformity. In order to open a deep abscess, treat an infected fracture, perform a Cesarean operation, extirpate a uterus, a portion of the stomach or of the intestines, or raise the roof of the skull and remove a tumor from the brain, they have to make long incisions and extensive wounds. The most accurate sutures would not suffice definitely to close such openings if the organism were not capable of making its own repairs. Surgery is based on the existence of this phenomenon. It has learned to turn adaptation to account. Owing to the extreme ingeniousness and audacity of its methods, it has surpassed the most ambitious hopes of medicine of former times. Its attainments are the purest triumph of biology. He who has completely mastered its techniques, who understands its spirit, who has acquired the knowledge of human beings and the science of their diseases, truly becomes like God. He possesses the power to open the body, explore the organs, and repair their lesions, almost without risk to the patient. To many people he restores strength, health, and the joy of living. Even to those tortured by incurable diseases, he is always capable of bringing some relief. Men of such type are rare. But their number could easily be increased by a better technical, moral, and scientific education.

The reason behind such success is simple. Surgery has merely learned that the normal processes of healing must not be hindered. It has succeeded in preventing microbes from getting into wounds. Operations, before the discoveries of Pasteur and Lister, were always followed by invasion of bacteria. Such attacks caused suppuration, gaseous gangrene, and infection of the whole body. They often ended in death. Modern techniques have practically eliminated microbes from operative wounds. In this manner they save the life of the patient and lead him to a rapid recovery. For microbes have the power to obstruct or delay adaptive processes and repair. As soon as wounds were protected against bacteria surgery began to grow. Its methods rapidly developed in the hands of Ollier, Billroth, Kocher, and their contemporaries. In a quarter of a century of stupendous progress they blossomed into the mighty art of Halsted, Tuffier, Harvey Cushing, the Mayos, and of all the great modern surgeons.

This success came from the clear understanding of certain adaptive phenomena. It is indispensable, not only to preserve the wounds from infection, but also to respect, in the course of operative handling, their structural and functional conditions. Tissues are endangered by most antiseptic substances. They must not be crushed by forceps, compressed by apparatuses, or pulled about by the fingers of a brutal operator. Halsted and the surgeons of his school have shown how delicately wounds must be treated if they are to keep intact their regenerative power. The result of an operation depends both on the state of the tissues and on that of the patient. Modern techniques take into consideration every factor capable of modifying physiological and mental activities. The patient is protected against the dangers of fear, cold, and anesthesia, as well as against infection, nervous shock, and hemorrhages. And if, through some mistake, infection sets in, it can be effectively dealt with. Some day, perhaps, when the nature of healing processes is better known, it will become possible to increase their rapidity. The rate of repair, as we know, varies according to definite qualities of the humors, and especially to their youthfulness. If such qualities could temporarily be given to the blood and the tissues of the patient, recovery from surgical operations would be made much easier. Certain chemical substances are known to accelerate cell multiplication. Possibly, they will be utilized for this purpose. Each step forward in the knowledge of the mechanisms of regeneration will bring about a corresponding progress in surgery. But in the best hospital, as in the desert or the primitive forest, the healing of wounds depends, above all, on the efficiency of the adaptive functions.

6

All organic functions are modified, as soon as microbes or viruses cross the frontiers of the body and invade the tissues.

Illness sets in. Its characteristics depend on the mode of adjustment of the tissues to the pathological changes of their medium. For instance, fever is the reply of the body to the presence of bacteria and viruses. Other adaptive reactions are determined by the production of poisons by the organism itself, the lack of certain substances indispensable to nutrition, and the disturbances in the activities of various glands. The symptoms of Bright's disease, of scurvy, of exophthalmic goiter, express the accommodation of the organism to substances which diseased kidneys are no longer able to eliminate, to the absence of a vitamine, to the secretion of toxic products by the thyroid gland. The accommodation to pathogenic agents assumes two different aspects. On one side, it opposes their invasion of the body and tends to bring about their destruction. On the other, it repairs the lesions the organism has suffered, and causes the poisons generated by the bacteria or by the tissues themselves to disappear. Disease is nothing but the development of these processes. It is equivalent to the struggle of the body against a disturbing agent and to its effort to persist in time. But it may be, as in cancer or insanity, the expression of the passive decay of an organ, or of consciousness.

Microbes and viruses are to be found everywhere, in the air, in water, in our food. They are always present at the surface of the skin, and of the digestive and respiratory mucosas. Nevertheless, in many people they remain inoffensive. Among human beings, some are subject to diseases, and others are immune. Such a state of resistance is due to the individual constitution of the tissues and the humors, which oppose the penetration of pathogenic agents or destroy them when they have invaded our body. This is natural immunity. This form of immunity may preserve certain individuals from almost any disease. It is one of the most precious qualities for which man could wish. We are still ignorant of its nature. It appears to depend on some properties of ancestral origin, as well as on others acquired in the course of development. Certain families are observed to be susceptible to tuberculosis, appendicitis, cancer, or mental disorders. Others resist all diseases except the degenerative ones occurring during old age. But natural immunity does not exclusively derive from our ancestral constitution. It may come also from the mode of life and alimentation, as Reid Hunt showed long ago. Some diets were found to increase the susceptibility of mice to experimental typhoid fever. The frequency of pneumonia may also be modified by food. The mice belonging to one of the strains kept in the mousery of the Rockefeller Institute died of pneumonia in the proportion of fifty-two per cent while subjected to the standard diet. Several groups of these animals were given different diets. The mortality from pneumonia fell to thirty-two per cent, fourteen per cent, and even zero, according to the food. We should ascertain whether natural resistance to infections could be conferred on man by definite conditions of life. Injections of specific vaccine or serum for each disease, repeated medical examinations of the whole population, construction of gigantic hospitals, are expensive and not very effective means of preventing diseases and of developing a nation's health. Good health should be natural. Such innate resistance gives the individual a strength, a boldness, which he does not possess when his survival depends on physicians.

In addition to an inherent resistance to maladies, there is also an acquired resistance. The latter may be spontaneous or artificial. The organism is known to adapt itself to bacteria and viruses by the production of substances capable of directly or indirectly destroying the invaders. Thus, diphtheria, typhoid fever, smallpox, measles, etc., render their victims immune to a second attack of the disease, at least for some time. This spontaneous immunity expresses the adaptation of the organism to a new situation. If a fowl is injected with the serum of a rabbit, the serum of the fowl acquires, after a few days, the property of bringing about an abundant precipitate in the serum of the rabbit. In this way the fowl has been rendered immune to the albumins of the rabbit. Likewise, when bacterial toxins are injected into an animal, this animal produces antitoxins. The phenomenon becomes more complex if the bacteria themselves are injected. These bacteria compel the animal to manufacture substances by which they are agglutinated and destroyed. At the same time, the leucocytes of blood and tissues acquire the power of devouring them, as was discovered by Metchnikoff. Independent phenomena, whose effects are converging, take place under the influence of the pathogenic agent and bring about the destruction of the invading microbes. These processes are endowed with the same characteristics of simplicity, complexity, and finality as other physiological processes.

The adaptive responses of the organism are due to definite chemical substances. Certain polysaccharids, present in the bodies of bacteria, determine specific reactions of the cells and the humors when they are united with a protein. Instead of the polysaccharids of the bacteria, the tissues of our body manufacture some carbohydrates and lipoids, which possess similar properties. These substances give to the organism the power to attack foreign proteins or foreign cells. In the same way as the microbes, the cells of an animal determine in the organism of another animal the appearance of antibodies. And those cells are finally destroyed by their antibodies. For this reason, the transplantation into a man of a chimpanzee's testicles is not successful. The existence of these adaptive reactions has led to vaccination and to the use of therapeutic serums. Ultimately, to artificial immunity. A great quantity of antibodies develops in the blood of an animal injected with dead or attenuated microbes, viruses, or bacterial poisons. The serum of the animal rendered immune to a disease may sometimes cure patients suffering from the disease in question. It supplies their blood with the antitoxic antibacterial substances which are lacking. Thus, it gives them the power, which most individuals do not possess, to overcome the infection.

7

Either alone or with the aid of specific serums and of nonspecific chemical and physical medications, the patient fights against the invading microbes. Meanwhile, lymph and blood are modified by poisons set free by the bacteria and by the waste products of the diseased organism. Profound alterations take place in the whole body. Fever, delirium, and acceleration of the chemical exchanges occur. In dangerous infections, in typhoid fever, pneumonia, and septicemias, for instance, lesions develop in various organs, such as heart, lungs, and liver. The cells then actualize certain properties which, in ordinary life, remain potential. They tend to render the humors deleterious to bacteria, and to stimulate all organic activities. The leucocytes multiply, secrete new substances, undergo precisely such metamorphoses as are needed by the tissues, adapt themselves to the unforeseen conditions created by the pathogenic factors, the defection of organs, the virulence of bacteria, and their local accumulation. They form abscesses in the infected regions, and the ferments contained in the pus of the abscesses digest the microbes. These ferments also possess the power of dissolving living tissues. They thus open a way for the abscess, either toward the skin or some hollow organ. In this manner, pus is eliminated from the body. The symptoms of bacterial diseases express the effort made by tissues and humors to adapt themselves to the new conditions, to resist them, and to return to a normal state.

In degenerative diseases, such as arteriosclerosis, myocarditis, nephritis, diabetes, and cancer, and those due to alimentary deficiencies, the adaptive functions likewise enter into play. The physiological processes become modified in the manner best suited to the survival of the organism. If the secretion of a gland is insufficient, some other glands augment their activity and volume in order to supplement its work. When the valve protecting the orifice of communication of the left auricle and ventricle allows the blood to flow back, the heart increases in size and strength. Thus, it succeeds in pumping into the aorta an almost normal quantity of blood. This adaptive phenomenon enables the patient to continue to lead a normal existence for several years. When the kidneys are impaired, the arterial pressure rises in order that a larger volume of blood may pass through the defective filter. During the first stage of diabetes, the organism endeavors to compensate the decrease in the quantity of insulin secreted by the pancreas. These diseases generally represent an attempt made by the body to adapt itself to a defective function.

There are pathogenic agents against which the tissues do not react, which do not elicit any response from the adaptive mechanisms. Such is, for instance, *Treponema pallidum,* the agent of syphilis. Once *Treponema* has penetrated the body, it never spontaneously leaves its victim. It takes up its abode in the skin, the blood vessels, the brain, or the bones. Neither the cells nor the humors are able to destroy it. Syphilis yields only to prolonged treatment. Likewise, cancer meets with no opposition from the organism. Tumors, whether benign or malignant, are so much like normal tissues that the body is not aware of their presence. They often develop in individuals who for a long time show no evidence of being affected. The symptoms, when they appear, are not the expression of a reaction of the organism. They are the direct result of the misdoings of the tumor, of its toxic products, of the destruction of an essential organ, or of the compression of a nerve. The progress of cancer is inexorable, because tissues and humors do not react against the invasion of the diseased cells.

In the course of an illness, the body meets with situations never previously encountered. It tends, nevertheless, to adapt itself to these new conditions by eliminating the pathogenic agents and repairing the lesions they have caused. In the absence of such adaptive power, living beings could not endure, because they are ceaselessly exposed to the attacks of viruses or bacteria, and to the structural failure of innumerable elements of the organic systems. An individual's survival was formerly wholly due to his adaptive capacity. Modern civilization, with the help of hygiene, comfort, good food, soft living, hospitals, physicians, and nurses, has kept alive many human beings of poor quality. These weaklings and their descendants contribute, in a large measure, to the enfeeblement of the white races. We should perhaps renounce this artificial form of health and exclusively pursue natural health, which results from the excellence of the adaptive functions and from the inherent resistance to disease.

8

Extraorganic adaptation consists in the adjustment of the inner state of the body to the variations of the environment. This adjustment is brought about by the mechanisms responsible for stabilizing physiological and mental activities, and for giving the body its unity. To each change of the surroundings the adaptive functions furnish an appropriate reply. Man can, therefore, stand the modifications of the outside world. The atmosphere is always either warmer or colder than the skin. Nevertheless, the temperature of the humors bathing the tissues, and of the blood circulating in the vessels, remains unchanged. Such a phenomenon depends on the continuous work of the entire organism. Our temperature has a tendency to rise with that of the atmosphere, or when our chemical exchanges become more active, as, for instance, in fever. Pulmonary circulation and respiratory movements then accelerate. A larger quantity of water is evaporated from the pulmonary alveoli. Consequently, the temperature of the blood in the lungs is lowered. At the same time, the subcutaneous vessels dilate and the skin becomes red. The blood rushes to the surface of the body and cools by contact with atmospheric air. If the air is too warm, the skin becomes covered by thin streams of perspiration produced by the sweat glands. This perspiration, in evaporating, brings about a fall in the temperature. The central nervous system and the sympathetic nerves come into play. They increase the rapidity of cardiac pulsations, dilate blood-vessels, bring on the sensation of thirst, etc. On the contrary, when the outer temperature falls, the vessels of the skin contract, and the skin itself becomes white. The blood circulates sluggishly in the capillaries. It takes refuge in the inner organs, whose circulation and chemical exchanges are accelerated. Thus, we fight external cold, as we fight heat, by nervous, circulatory, and nutritive changes of our whole body. All the organs, as well as the skin, are maintained in constant activity by exposure to heat, cold, wind, sun, and rain. When we spend our life sheltered from the inclemencies of the weather, the processes regulating the temperature of the blood, its volume, its alkalinity, etc., are rendered useless.

We become adapted to excitations emanating from the outer world, even when their violence or their weakness modifies, in an exaggerated or insufficient manner, the nerve endings of the sense organs. Excessive light is dangerous. In primitive surroundings men instinctively hide from it. There is a large number of mechanisms capable of protecting the organism from sun rays. The eye is defended by the eyelids and the diaphragm of the iris against any increase in light intensity. Simultaneously, the retina becomes less sensible. The skin opposes the penetration of solar radiations by manufacturing pigment. When these natural defenses are insufficient, lesions of the retina or of the skin occur, and also certain disorders of the viscera and the nervous system.

It is possible that lessened reactivity of the nervous system and of the intelligence may eventually result from too strong a light. We must not forget that the most highly civilized races—the Scandinavians, for example—are white, and have lived for many generations in a country where the atmospheric luminosity is weak during a great part of the year. In France, the populations of the north are far superior to those of the Mediterranean shores. The lower races generally inhabit countries where light is violent and temperature equal and warm. It seems that the adaptation of white men to light and to heat takes place at the expense of their nervous and mental development.

In addition to light rays, the nervous system receives from the cosmic world various excitations. These stimuli are sometimes strong, sometimes weak. Man may be compared to a photographic plate, which must record different intensities of light in the same way. The effect of light on the plate is regulated by a diaphragm and a proper duration of exposure. The organism uses another method. Its adaptation to the unequal intensity of the excitations is obtained by an increase or a decrease of its receptivity. It is well known that the retina becomes much less sensitive when exposed to intense light. Likewise, the mucosa of the nose, after a short time, no longer perceives a bad odor. An intense noise, if produced continuously or at a uniform rhythm, causes little inconvenience. The roaring of the ocean as it pounds the rocks, or the rumbling of a train, does not disturb our sleep. We chiefly notice variations in the intensity of the excitations. Weber thought that, when stimulus increases in geometrical progression, sensation increases only in arithmetical progression. The intensity of sensation augments, therefore, much more slowly than that of excitation. Since we are affected, not by the absolute intensity of a stimulus, but by the difference in intensity of two successive excitations, such mechanism effectively protects our nervous system. Weber's law, although not exact, approximately expresses what takes place. However, the adaptive mechanisms of our nervous systems are not as developed as those of the other organic apparatuses. Civilization has created new stimuli against which we have no defense. Our organism tries in vain to adapt itself to the noises of the large cities and factories, to the agitation of modern life, the worries and the crowding of our days. We do not get used to lack of sleep. We are incapable of resisting hypnotic poisons, such as opium or cocaine. Strange to say, we adjust ourselves without suffering to most of these conditions. But such adjustment is far from being a victorious adaptation. It brings about organic and mental changes, which are equivalent to a degradation of civilized man.

9

Permanent modifications of body and consciousness may be produced by adaptation. In this manner, environment stamps human beings with its mark. When young people are subjected to its influence over lengthy periods, they may be indelibly modified by it. Thus, new structural and mental aspects appear in the individual and also in the race. It seems that environment gradually affects the cells of the sexual glands. Such modifications are naturally hereditary. Indeed, the individual does not transmit his acquired characteristics to his descendants. But when in the course of life his humors are modified by the environment, his sexual tissues may adapt themselves, by corresponding structural changes, to the state of their humoral medium. For instance, the plants, trees, animals, and men of Normandy differ greatly from those of Brittany. They bear the specific mark of the soil. In former times, when the food of the inhabitants of a village consisted exclusively of local products, the aspect of the population showed still greater differences from one province to another.

Adaptation of animals to thirst and to hunger is easily noticeable. The cattle of the Arizona deserts can go three or four days without water. A dog may remain fat and in perfect health, although eating only twice a week. Animals unable to quench their thirst except at rare intervals learn to drink abundantly. They adapt their tissues to store large quantities of water over lengthy periods. Likewise, those subjected to fasting become accustomed to absorbing in one or two days enough food for the rest of the week. It is the same with sleep. We can train ourselves to do without sleep, or to sleep very little during some periods, and a great deal during others. We indulge quite easily in an excess of nourishment and of drink. If a child is given as much food as he can absorb, he rapidly gets used to eating exaggerated quantities. Later on, he finds it very difficult to break himself of the habit. All the organic and mental consequences of alimentary excesses are not yet exactly understood. They seem to be manifested by an increase in the volume and the height of the body, and by a decrease in its general activity. A similar phenomenon occurs in wild rabbits when they become transformed into domestic rabbits. It is not certain that the standardized habits of modern life lead to the optimum development of human beings. The present ways of living have been adopted because they are easy and pleasant. Indeed, they differ profoundly from those of our ancestors and of the human groups which have so far resisted industrial civilization. We do not know, as yet, whether they are better or worse.

Man becomes acclimatized to high altitudes through certain modifications of his blood and of his circulatory, respiratory, skeletal, and muscular systems. The red corpuscles respond to the lowering of the barometric pressure by multiplying. Adaptation rapidly takes place. In a few weeks, soldiers transported to the summits of the Alps walk, climb, and run as actively as at lower altitudes. At the same time, the skin produces a great deal of pigment as a protection against the glare of the snow. The thorax and the muscles of the chest develop markedly. After some months in the high mountains, the muscular system is inured to the greater efforts required for active life. The shape and the posture of the body become modified. The circulatory apparatus and the heart accustom themselves to the ceaseless work they are called upon to do. The processes that regulate the temperature of the blood improve. The organism learns to resist cold and to support easily all inclemencies of the weather. When mountaineers descend to the plains, the number of their blood corpuscles becomes normal. But the adaptation of the thorax, lungs, heart, and vessels to a rarefied atmosphere, to the effects of cold, to the exertions made in the daily ascension of mountains, leaves its mark forever on the body. Intense muscular activity also brings about permanent changes. For example, on the Western ranches, the cowpunchers acquire strength, resistance, and litheness such as no athlete ever attains in the comfort of a modern university. It is the same with intellectual work. Man is indelibly marked by prolonged and intense mental struggle. This type of activity is almost impossible in the state of mechanization reached by education. It can only take place in small groups, such as that of the first disciples of Pasteur, inspired by an ardent ideal, by the will to know. The young men who gathered around Welch, at the beginning of his career at the Johns Hopkins University, have been strengthened during their whole lives and made greater by the intellectual discipline into which they were initiated under his guidance.

There is also a more subtle, less known aspect of the adaptation of organic and mental activities to environment. It consists of the response of the body to the chemical substances contained in the food. We know that in countries where water is rich in calcium, the skeleton becomes heavier than it does in regions where the water is quite pure. We also know that individuals fed on milk, eggs, vegetables, and cereals differ from those fed mostly on meat, that many substances may influence the shape of the body and consciousness. But we ignore the mechanism of this adaptation. Endocrine glands and nervous system probably become modified according to the forms of alimentation. Mental activities seem to vary with the constitution of the tissues. It is not wise to follow blindly the doctrines of physicians and hygienists, whose horizon is limited to their specialty—that is, to one aspect of the individual. The progress of man certainly will not come from an increase in weight, or in longevity.

It seems that the work of the adaptive mechanisms stimulates all organic functions. A temporary change of climate is of benefit to debilitated individuals and to convalescents. Some variations in the mode of life, in food, sleep, and habitat, are useful. The accommodation to new conditions of existence momentarily increases the activity of physiological and mental processes. The rate of adaptation to any factor depends on the rhythm of physiological time. Children respond immediately to a change of climate. Adults, much more slowly. In order to produce lasting results, the action of the environment must be prolonged. During youth, a new country and new habits are able to determine permanent adaptive changes. For this reason, conscription greatly helps the development of the body by imposing on each individual a new type of life, certain exercises, and a certain discipline. Rougher conditions of existence and more responsibility would restore moral energy and audacity to the majority of those who have lost them. More virile habits should be substituted for the uniformity and softness of life in schools and universities. The adaptation of the individual to a physiological, intellectual, and moral discipline determines definite changes in the nervous system, the endocrine glands, and the mind. The organism acquires, in this way, a better integration, greater vigor, and more ability to overcome the difficulties and dangers of existence.

10

Man adapts himself to social environment as to physical environment. Mental activities, like physiological activities, tend to become modified in the way best suited to the survival of the body. They determine our adjustment to our surroundings. The individual does not generally get without effort the position he covets in the group of which he is a member. He wants wealth, knowledge, power, pleasures. He is driven by his greed, his ambition, his curiosity, his sexual appetite. But he finds himself in an environment always indifferent, sometimes hostile. He quickly realizes that he must fight for what he wants. His mode of reaction to his social surroundings depends on his specific constitution. Some people become accommodated to the world by conquering it. Others by escaping from it. Still others refuse to accept its rules. The natural attitude of the individual toward his fellow men is one of strife. Consciousness responds to the enmity of the environment by an effort directed against it. Intelligence and cunning then develop, as well as the desire to learn, the will to work, to possess, and to dominate. The passion for conquest assumes diverse aspects according to individuals and circumstances. It inspires all great adventures. Such passion led Pasteur to the renovation of medicine, Mussolini to the building up of a great nation, Einstein to the creation of a universe. The same spirit drives the modern human being to robbery, to murder, and to the great financial and economic enterprises characterizing our civilization. But its impulse also builds hospitals, laboratories, universities, and churches. It impels men to fortune and to death, to heroism and to crime. But never to happiness.

The second mode of adaptation is flight. Some abandon the struggle and descend to a social level where competition is no longer necessary. They become factory workers, proletarians. Others take refuge within their own self. At the same time they can adapt themselves, in some measure, to the social group, and even conquer it through the superiority of their intelligence. But they do not fight. They are members of the community only in appearance. In fact, they live in an inner world of their own. Still others forget their surroundings in ceaseless toil. Those who are obliged to work uninterruptedly accommodate themselves to all events. A woman whose child dies, and who has to look after several other children, has no time to brood over her grief. Work is more effective than alcohol and morphine in helping people to bear adverse conditions. Certain individuals spend their lives in dreaming, in hoping for fortune, health, and happiness. Illusions and hope are also a powerful means of adaptation. Hope generates action. It is rightly looked upon by Christian morals as a great virtue. It contributes in a powerful manner to the adjustment of the individual to unfavorable circumstances. Habit is another aspect of adaptation. Sorrows are more quickly forgotten than joys. But inaction augments all sufferings.

Many people never adjust themselves to the social group. Among those unadapted are the feeble-minded. Except in special institutions, they have no place in modern society. A number of normal children are born in the families of degenerates and criminals. In such a mold they shape their body and their consciousness. They become unadaptable to normal life. They supply the prisons with most of their inmates. They also constitute the far larger population that remains free to live by burglary and murder. These human beings are the fatal result of physiological and moral degradation brought about by industrial civilization. They are irresponsible. Irresponsible, also, is the youth brought up in modern schools by teachers ignorant of the necessity for effort, for intellectual concentration, for moral discipline.

Later on in life, when these young men and women encounter the indifference of the world, the material and mental difficulties of existence, they are incapable of adaptation, save by asking for relief, for protection, for doles, and, if relief cannot thus be obtained, by crime. Although having strong muscles, they are deprived of nervous and moral resistance. They shrink from effort and privation. In periods of stress they demand food and shelter from their parents or from the community. Like the offspring of the wretched and the criminals, they are unfit to have a place in the new city.

Certain forms of modern life lead directly to degeneration. There are social conditions as fatal to white men as are warm and humid climates. We react to poverty, anxieties, and sorrows by working and struggling. We can stand tyranny, revolution, and war. But we are not able to fight successfully against misery or prosperity. The individual and the race are weakened by extreme poverty. Wealth is just as dangerous. Nevertheless, there are still families which, in spite of having had money and power for centuries, have kept their strength. But, in former times, power and money derived from the ownership of land. To hold the land required struggle, administrative ability, and leadership. This indispensable effort prevented degeneration. Today, wealth does not bring in its train any responsibility toward the community. Irresponsibility, even in the absence of wealth, is harmful. In the poor, as well as in the rich, leisure engenders degeneration. Cinemas, concerts, radios, automobiles, and athletics are no substitutes for intelligent work. We are far from having solved this momentous problem of idleness created by prosperity, modern machinery, or unemployment. By imposing leisure upon man, scientific civilization has brought him great misfortune. We are as incapable of fighting the consequences of indolence and irresponsibility as cancer and mental diseases.

II

Adaptive functions assume as many different aspects as tissues and humors encounter new situations. They are not the particular expression of any organic system. They are definable only by their end. Their means vary. But their end always remains the same. Such an end is the survival of the individual. Adaptation, considered in its various manifestations and its oneness, appears as an agent of stabilization and organic repair, as the cause of the molding of organs by function, as the link that integrates tissues and humors in a whole enduring in spite of the attacks of the outer world. Thus, it appears as an entity. This abstraction is convenient for describing its characteristics. In fact, adaptation is an aspect of all physiological processes and of their physicochemical components.

When a system is in equilibrium, and a factor tends to modify the equilibrium, there occurs a reaction that opposes this factor. If sugar is dissolved in water, the temperature falls, and the lowering of the temperature diminishes the solubility of sugar. Such is the principle of Le Chatelier. When violent muscular exercise greatly increases the quantity of venous blood flowing into the heart, the central nervous system is informed of this event by the nerves of the right auricle. At once it determines an acceleration of the cardiac pulsations. The excess of venous blood is thus carried away. There is only a superficial analogy between the principle of Le Chatelier and such physiological adaptation. In the first case, an equilibrium is maintained by physical means. In the second case, a steady state, and not an equilibrium, persists with the help of physiological processes. If, instead of blood, a tissue modifies its state, a similar phenomenon occurs. The extirpation of a fragment of skin sets in motion a complex reaction which, through converging mechanisms, brings about the repair of the lesion. In both instances, the excess of venous blood and the wound are the factors tending to modify the state of the organism. These factors are opposed by a concatenation of physiological processes leading, in the first case, to acceleration of the heart and, in the second case, to cicatrization.

The more a muscle works, the more it develops. Activity strengthens it, instead of wearing it out. An organ atrophies when not used. It is a primary datum of observation that physiological and mental functions are improved by work. Also, that effort is indispensable to the optimum development of the individual. Like muscles and organs, intelligence and moral sense become atrophied for want of exercise. The law of effort is still more important than the law of the constancy of the organic states. Steadiness of the inner medium is, without any doubt, indispensable to the survival of the organism. But the physiological and mental progress of the individual depends on his functional activity and on his efforts. We become adapted to the lack of use of our organic and mental systems by degenerating.

Adaptation employs multiple processes to attain its end. It never localizes in one region or one organ. It mobilizes the entire body. For example, anger profoundly modifies all the organic apparatuses. The muscles contract. The sympathetic nerves and the suprarenal glands come into action. Their intervention brings about an increase of the blood pressure, an acceleration of the heart pulsations, the setting free by the liver of glucose, which will be used by the muscles as fuel. In a like manner, when the body strives against outside cold, its circulatory, respiratory, digestive, muscular, and nervous apparatuses are forced to act. In sum, the organism responds to changes in the outer world by setting in motion all its activities. The exercise of adaptive functions is as necessary to the development of body and consciousness as physical effort to that of the muscles. Accommodation to inclemency of the weather, to lack of sleep, to fatigue, and to hunger stimulates every physiological process. In order to reach his optimum state, the human being must actualize all his potentialities.

Adaptive phenomena always tend toward a certain end. But they do not always attain their goal. They do not work accurately. They operate within certain limits. Each individual withstands only a given number of bacteria and a given virulence of these bacteria. Beyond such number and virulence, the adaptive functions become insufficient to protect the body. Disease breaks out. It is the same with resistance to fatigue, to heat, or to cold. There is no doubt that adaptive power, as well as other physiological activities, increases with exercise. Like these activities, it is perfectible. Instead of preventing diseases only by protecting the individual against their agents, we must, by artificially increasing the efficiency of his adaptive functions, render each man capable of protecting himself.

To summarize. We have considered adaptation as an expression of fundamental properties of the tissues, as an aspect of nutrition. Physiological processes are modified in as many different ways as new and unforeseen situations occur. Strange to say, they shape themselves for the goal to be attained. They do not seem to estimate time and space in the same manner as our intelligence does. The tissues organize with equal ease relative to spatial configurations already existing and to those which do not as yet exist. During embryonic growth, the retina and the lens associate for the benefit of the still potential eye. Adaptability is a property of the components of tissues, as well as of the tissues themselves and of the entire organism. Individual cells appear to act in the interest of the whole, just as bees work for the good of the hive. They seem to know the future. And they prepare for this future by anticipated changes of their structure and functions.

12

We utilize our adaptive functions much less than our ancestors did. For a quarter of a century, especially, we have accommodated ourselves to our environment through mechanisms created by our intelligence, and no longer through physiological mechanisms. Science has supplied us with means for keeping our intraorganic equilibrium, which are more agreeable and less laborious than the natural processes. We have mentioned how the physical conditions of our daily life are prevented from varying. How muscular exercise, food, and sleep are standardized. How modern civilization has done away with effort and moral responsibility, and transformed the modes of activity of our muscular, nervous, circulatory, and glandular systems.

We have also drawn attention to the fact that the inhabitants of the modern city no longer suffer from changes of atmospheric temperature. That they are protected by modern houses, clothes, and automobiles. That during the winter they are not subjected, as their ancestors were, to alternatives of prolonged cold and of brutal heat from stoves and open fireplaces. The organism does not have to fight cold by setting in motion the chain of the associated physiological processes, which increase the chemical exchanges and modify the circulation of all the tissues. When an individual, insufficiently clothed, has to maintain his inner temperature by violent exercise, all his organic systems work with great intensity. On the contrary, these systems remain in a condition of repose if cold weather is fought by furs and warm clothing, by the heating apparatus of a closed car, or by the walls of a steam-heated room. The skin of modern man is never whipped by the wind. It never has to defend itself for long and tiring hours against snow, rain, or sun. In former times the mechanisms responsible for regulating the temperature of blood and humors were maintained in constant activity by the struggle against the rigors of the weather. Today they are in a state of perpetual rest. However, their work is probably indispensable to the optimum development of the body and the mind. We must realize that the adaptive functions do not correspond to a particular structure which, when not needed, could be dispensed with. They are, on the contrary, the expression of the whole body.

Muscular effort has not been completely eliminated from modern life, but it is not frequent. It has been replaced in our daily existence by that of machines. Muscles are now used only in athletic games. Their mode of acting is standardized and subjected to arbitrary rules. It is doubtful whether these artificial exercises completely replace the hardships of a more primitive condition of life. For women, dancing and playing tennis for a few hours every week are not the equivalent of the effort required to climb up and down stairs, to carry out their domestic duties without the help of machines, to walk along the streets. Nowadays, they live in houses provided with an elevator, walk with difficulty on high heels, and almost constantly use an automobile or a trolley car. It is the same with men. Golf on Saturdays and Sundays does not compensate for the complete inaction of the rest of the week. By doing away with muscular effort in daily life, we have suppressed, without being aware of it, the ceaseless exercise required from our organic systems in order that the constancy of the inner medium be maintained. As is well known, muscles, when they work, consume sugar and oxygen, produce heat, and pour lactic acid into the circulating blood. To adapt itself to these changes, the organisms must set in action the heart, the respiratory apparatus, the liver, the pancreas, the kidneys, the sweat glands, and the cerebrospinal and sympathetic systems. In sum, the intermittent exercises of modern man, such as golf and tennis, are not equivalent to the continuous muscular activity required by the existence of our ancestors. Today, physical effort only takes place at certain moments and on certain days. The customary state of the organic systems, of blood vessels, of sweat and endocrine glands, is that of repose.

The usage of the digestive functions has also been modified. Hard foods, such as stale bread or tough meat, are no longer permitted in our diet. Likewise, physicians have forgotten that jaws are made to grind resistant matter, and that the stomach is constructed to digest natural products. As previously mentioned, children are fed chiefly on soft, mashed, pulped food, and milk. Their jaws, their teeth, and the muscles of their face are not subjected to sufficiently hard work. It is the same with the muscles and glands of their digestive apparatus. The frequency, the regularity, and the abundance of meals render useless an adaptive function that has played an important part in the survival of human races, the adaptation to lack of food. In primitive life men were subjected to long periods of fasting. When want did not compel them to starve, they voluntarily deprived themselves of food. All religions have insisted upon the necessity of fasting. Privation of food at first brings about a sensation of hunger, occasionally some nervous stimulation, and later a feeling of weakness. But it also determines certain hidden phenomena which are far more important. The sugar of the liver, the fat of the subcutaneous deposits, are mobilized, and also the proteins of the muscles and the glands. All the organs sacrifice their own substances in order to maintain blood, heart, and brain in a normal condition. Fasting purifies and profoundly modifies our tissues.

Modern man sleeps too much or not enough. He does not easily adapt himself to too much sleep. He fares still worse if he sleeps too little during prolonged periods. It is, however, useful to accustom oneself to remain awake when one wants to sleep. The struggle against sleep sets in motion organic apparatuses whose strength develops by exercise. It also calls for an effort of the will. This effort, together with many others, has been suppressed by modern habits. In spite of the restlessness of existence, the false activity of sports and rapid transportation, the great organic systems responsible for our adaptive functions remain idle. In short, the mode of life created by scientific civilization has rendered useless a number of mechanisms whose activities had never ceased during the millenniums of the existence of the human race.

13

The exercise of the adaptive functions appears to be indispensable to the optimum development of man. Our body is placed in a physical medium whose conditions are variable. The constancy of our inner states is maintained through ceaseless organic activity. Such activity is not localized in a single system. It extends to the entire body. All our anatomical apparatuses react against the outside world in the sense most favorable to our survival. Is it possible that such a fundamental property may remain virtual without inconvenience to our body? Are we not organized to live under changing and irregular conditions? Man attains his highest development when he is exposed to the rigors of the seasons, when he sometimes goes without sleep and sometimes sleeps for long hours, when his meals are sometimes abundant and sometimes scanty, when he conquers food and shelter at the price of strenuous efforts. He has also to train his muscles, to tire himself and rest, to fight, suffer, and be happy, to love and to hate. His will needs alternately to strain and to relax. He must strive against his fellow men or against himself. He is made for such an existence, just as the stomach is made for digesting food. When his adaptive processes work most intensely, he develops his virility to the fullest extent. It is a primary datum of observation that hardships make for nervous resistance and health. We know how strong physically and morally are those who, since childhood, have been submitted to intelligent discipline, who have endured some privations and adapted themselves to adverse conditions.

However, we observe human beings who develop fully even though they are not obliged by poverty to fight against their environment. But these individuals are also molded by adaptation, although in a different way. Generally, they have imposed upon themselves, or have accepted from others, a discipline, a sort of asceticism, which has protected them against the deleterious effects of wealth and leisure. The sons of feudal lords were subjected to a hard physical and moral training. One of Brittany's heroes, Bertrand du Guesclin, compelled himself every day to face the inclemencies of the weather and to fight with children of his own age. Although small and ill-formed, he acquired such endurance and strength as are still legendary. During the early period of the development of the United States, the men who built the railroads, laid the foundations of the large industries, and opened the West to civilization, triumphed over all obstacles by their will and their audacity. Today most of the sons of these great men possess wealth, without having had to earn it. They have never struggled against their environment. Generally, they lack the ancestral strength. A similar phenomenon occurred in Europe among the descendants of the feudal aristocracy and of the great financiers and manufacturers of the nineteenth century.

The effect of the deficiencies of adaptation upon the development of man is not as yet completely known. In the large cities, there are many individuals whose adaptive activities are permanently at rest. Sometimes the consequences of this phenomenon become obvious. They manifest themselves especially in the children of rich families. And, likewise, in those who are brought up in the same way as the rich. From their birth, these children live under conditions that bring about the atrophy of their adaptive systems. They are kept in warm rooms and, when they go out, dressed like little Eskimos. They are crammed with food, they sleep as much as they like, have no responsibility, never make an intellectual or moral effort, learn only what amuses them, and struggle against nothing. The result is well known. They generally become pleasant and handsome, often strong, easily tired, extremely selfish, without intellectual acuteness, moral sense, and nervous resistance. These defects are not of ancestral origin. They are observed in the descendants of the men who built up American industries, as well as in those of the newcomers. Obviously, a function as important as adaptation cannot be left in disuse with impunity. The law of the struggle for life must, above all, be obeyed. Degeneration of body and soul is the price paid by the individuals and the races who have forgotten the existence of this law.

As optimum development requires the activity of all organic systems, a decrease in the value of man necessarily follows the decay of the adaptive functions. In the process of education, these functions must be kept constantly at work. Each one of them is equally useful. Muscles are no more important than brains. They only contribute strength and harmony to the body. Instead of training athletes, we have to construct modern men. And modern men need more nervous resistance, intelligence, and moral energy than muscular power. The acquisition of these qualities calls for effort, struggle, and discipline. It also demands that human beings should not be exposed to conditions of existence to which they are unadaptable. Apparently, there is no adaptation possible to ceaseless agitation, intellectual dispersion, alcoholism, precocious sexual excesses, noise, polluted air, and adulterated foods. If such is the case, we must modify our mode of life and our environment, even at the cost of a destructive revolution. After all, the purpose of civilization is not the progress of science and machines, but the progress of man.

14

In conclusion. Adaptation is a mode of being of all organic and mental processes. It is not an entity. It is equivalent to the automatic grouping of our activities in such a manner as to assure the survival of the individual. It is essentially teleological. Owing to the adaptive activities, the organic medium remains constant, the body conserves its unity and recovers from diseases. It is for the same reason that we endure, in spite of the fragility and the transitory character of our tissues. Adaptation is as indispensable as nutrition. In fact, it is only an aspect of nutrition. However, in the organization of modern life no account has ever been taken of such an important function. Its use has been almost completely given up. And this neglect has brought about a deterioration of the body and of the mind.

This mode of activity is necessary to the complete development of the human being. Its deficiency determines the atrophy of the nutritive and mental functions from which it is not distinct. Adaptation causes the organic processes to move simultaneously according to the rhythms of physiological time and of the unforeseeable variations of the environment. Any change in the environment elicits a response of all physiological and mental processes. Those movements of the functional systems express the apprehension by man of the outer reality. They act as a buffer for the material and psychological shocks which he unceasingly receives. They not only permit him to endure, but they also are the agents of his formation and of his progress. They are endowed with a property of capital importance. The property of being easily modified by certain chemical, physical, and psychological factors, which we know well how to handle. We can use these factors as tools, and thus successfully intervene in the development of human activities. In fact, the knowledge of the mechanisms of adaptation gives man the power of renovating and of constructing himself.

Chapter VII

THE INDIVIDUAL

---

1. *The human being and the individual. The quarrel between realists and nominalists. Confusion of symbols and concrete facts.* 2. *Individuality of tissues and humors.* 3. *Psychological individuality. Characteristics of personality.* 4. *Individuality of disease. Medicine and the reality of Universals.* 5. *Origin of individuality. The quarrel between behaviorists and geneticists. Relative importance of heredity and environment. Influence of hereditary factors on the individual.* 6. *Influence of developmental factors on the individual. Variations in the effect of these factors according to immanent characteristics of tissues.* 7. *Spatial frontiers of the individual. Anatomical and psychological limits. Extension of the individual beyond his anatomical structure.* 8. *Temporal frontiers of the individual. Links of organism and mind with the past and the future.* 9. *The individual.* 10. *Man consists of the human being and of the individual. Realism and nominalism are both indispensable.* 11. *Practical significance of such knowledge.*

I

HUMAN beings are not found anywhere in nature. There are only individuals. The individual differs from the human being because he is a concrete event. He is the one who acts, loves, suffers, fights, and dies. On the contrary, the human being is a Platonic Idea living in our minds and in our books. He consists of the abstractions studied by physiologists, psychologists, and sociologists. His characteristics are expressed by Universals. Today we are again facing a problem which engrossed the philosophical minds of the Middle Ages, the problem of the reality of general ideas. In defense of the Universals, Anselm sustained against Abélard an historical fight, whose echoes are still heard after eight hundred years. Abélard was defeated. However, Anselm and Abélard, the realists who believed in the existence of the Universals and the nominalists who did not believe in it, were equally right.

Indeed, we need both the general and the particular, the human being and the individual. The reality of the general—that is, of the Universals—is indispensable to the construction of science, because our mind readily moves only among abstractions. For modern scientists, as for Plato, Ideas are the sole reality. This abstract reality leads our mind to the knowledge of the concrete. The general helps us to grasp the particular. Owing to the abstractions created by the sciences of the human being, each individual can be clothed in convenient schemata. Although not made to his measure, these schemata approximately fit him. At the same time, the empirical consideration of the concrete facts determines the evolution and the progress of the schemas, of the Ideas, of the Universals. It continually enriches these abstractions. The study of a multitude of individuals develops a more and more complete science of the human being. The Ideas, instead of being immutable in their beauty, as Plato thought, move and expand as soon as our mind becomes immersed in the ever-flowing waters of empirical reality.

We live in two different worlds—the world of facts and that of their symbols. In order to acquire knowledge of ourselves, we utilize both observation and scientific abstractions. But the abstract may be mistaken for the concrete. In such an instance, facts are treated as symbols and the individual is likened to the human being. Most of the errors made by educators, physicians, and sociologists come from such confusion. Scientists accustomed to the techniques of mechanics, chemistry, physics, and physiology, and unfamiliar with philosophy and intellectual culture, are liable to mingle the concepts of the different disciplines and not to distinguish clearly the general from the particular. However, in the concept of man, it is important to define exactly the part of the human being and that of the individual. Education, medicine, and sociology are concerned with the individual. They are guilty of a disastrous error when they look upon him only as a symbol, as a human being. Indeed, individuality is fundamental in man. It is not merely a certain aspect of the organism. But it permeates our entire being. It makes the self a unique event in the history of the world. It stamps its mark on the whole of body and consciousness, and, although remaining indivisible, on each component of this whole. For the sake of convenience we will consider separately the organic, humoral, and mental aspects of the individual, instead of apprehending him in his oneness.

2

Individuals are easily distinguished from one another by the lineaments of their visages, their gestures, their way of walking, their intellectual and moral characters. Time causes many changes in their appearance. Despite these changes, each individual can always be identified, as Bertillon has shown long since, by the dimensions of certain parts of his skeleton. The lines of the finger tips are also indelible characteristics. Fingerprints are the genuine signature of man. However, the configuration of the skin is only one of the aspects of the individuality of tissues. In general, the latter is not evidenced by any morphological peculiarity. The cells of the thyroid gland, the liver, the skin, etc., of one individual appear to be identical with those of another individual. In every one the pulsations of the heart are nearly, although not quite, the same. The structure and functions of organs do not seem to be marked by individual properties. However, their specificity would doubtless be evidenced by more subtle methods of examination. Certain dogs are endowed with such a sharp olfactory sense that they recognize the specific smell of their master among a crowd of other men. Likewise, the tissues of one individual are capable of perceiving the specificity of his humors and the foreign character of the humors of another.

The individuality of tissues may manifest itself in the following way. Fragments of skin, some supplied by the patient himself and others by a friend or a relative, are grafted on the surface of a wound. After a few days the grafts coming from the patient are adherent to the wound and grow larger, whereas those taken from the other people loosen and grow smaller. The former survive, and the latter die. One very rarely finds two individuals so closely alike that they are able to exchange their tissues. Many years ago, Cristiani transplanted into a little girl, whose thyroid function was deficient, a few fragments of the thyroid gland of her mother. The child was cured. Some ten years later she married and became pregnant. Not only were the grafts still alive, but they increased in size, as normal thyroid glands do in like circumstances. Such a result is quite exceptional. However, between identical twins, glandular transplantation would doubtless succeed. As a rule, the tissues of one individual refuse to accept those of another individual. When, by the suture of the vessels, blood circulates again in a transplanted kidney, the organ immediately secretes urine. At first, it behaves normally. After a few weeks, however, albumin, then blood, appear in the urine. And a disease similar to nephritis rapidly brings on atrophy of the kidney. However, if the grafted organ comes from the animal itself, its functions are permanently reëstablished. Obviously, the humors recognize, in foreign tissues, certain differences of constitution, which are not revealed by any other test. Cells are specific of the individual to whom they belong. This peculiarity of our body has so far prevented the wide use of the transplantation of organs for therapeutic purposes.

The humors possess a similar specificity. This specificity is detected by a definite effect of the blood serum of one individual upon the red corpuscles of another individual. Under the influence of serum the corpuscles often agglutinate. The accidents noticed after blood transfusion are due to such a phenomenon. It is, therefore, indispensable that the corpuscles of the donor should not be agglutinated by the serum of the patient. According to a remarkable discovery made by Landsteiner, human beings are divided into four groups, the knowledge of which is essential to the success of transfusion. The serum of the members of certain groups agglutinates the corpuscles of the members of certain other groups. One of the groups is composed of universal donors, whose cells are not agglutinated by the serum of any other group. No inconvenience results from the mingling of their blood with that of any other person. These characteristics persist during the entire life. They are transmitted from generation to generation, according to the laws of Mendel. In addition, Landsteiner discovered about thirty sub-groups, by using special serological methods. In transfusion, their influence is negligible. But it is indicative of the existence of resemblances and differences between smaller groups of individuals. The test of agglutination of blood corpuscles by serum, although most useful, is still imperfect. It only brings to light certain relations between categories of individuals. It does not disclose the more subtle characteristics that single out each individual from all others in his category.

The properties specific to each animal are evidenced by the results of the transplantation of organs. There is no means by which they can easily be detected. Repeated injections of one individual's serum into the veins of another, belonging to the same blood group, bring about no reaction, no formation of antibodies in measurable amount. A patient, therefore, can be subjected without danger to several consecutive transfusions. His humors react against neither the corpuscles nor the serum of the donor. However, the differences specific of the individual, which preclude successful exchanges of organs, would probably be revealed by sufficiently delicate tests. The specificity of tissues and humors depends on proteins and chemical groups called haptens by Landsteiner. Haptens are carbohydrates and fatty substances. The compounds resulting from the union of a hapten with a protein, when injected into an animal, determine the appearance in its serum of antibodies specifically opposed to the hapten. The specificity of the individual depends on the inner structure of the large molecules resulting from haptens and proteins. Individuals of the same race are more similar to each other than to individuals belonging to other races. The protein and carbohydrate molecules are made up of a large number of groups of atoms. The possible permutations of these groups are practically infinite. It is probable that, among the gigantic crowds of human beings who have inhabited the earth, no two individuals have ever been of identical chemical constitution. The personality of the tissues is linked in a manner still unknown with the molecules entering into the construction of the cells and the humors. Our individuality takes its roots in the very depths of ourself.

Individuality stamps all the component parts of the body. It is present in the physiological processes, as well as in the chemical structure of the humors and cells. Everyone reacts in his own way to the events of the outside world—to noise, to danger, to food, to cold, to heat, to the attacks of microbes and viruses. When animals of pure stock are injected with equal quantities of a foreign protein, or of a suspension of bacteria, they never respond to those injections in an identical manner. A few do not respond at all. During great epidemics human beings behave according to their individual characteristics. Some fall ill and die. Some fall ill, but recover. Others are entirely immune. Still others are slightly affected by the disease, but without presenting any specific symptoms. Each one manifests a different adaptivity to the infective agent. As Richet said, there is a humoral personality just as there is a mental personality.

Physiological duration bears also the mark of our individuality. Its value, as we know, is not the same for every human being. Besides, it does not remain constant during the course of our life. As each event is recorded within the body, our organic and humoral personality becomes more and more specific during the process of aging. It is enriched by all the happenings of our inner world. For cells and humors, like mind, are endowed with memory. The body is permanently modified by each disease, each injection of serum or of vaccine, each invasion of the tissues by bacteria, viruses, or foreign chemical substances. These events determine within ourselves allergic states—that is, states in which our reactivity is modified. In this manner, tissues and humors acquire a progressively growing individuality. Old people differ from one another far more than children do. Every man is a history unlike all others.

3

Mental, structural, and humoral individualities blend in an unknown manner. They bear to one another the same relations as do psychological activities, cerebral processes, and organic functions. They give us our uniqueness. They cause every man to be himself and nobody else. Identical twins coming from the same ovum, having the same genetical constitution, are, however, two quite different persons. Mental characteristics are a more delicate reagent of individuality than organic and humoral characteristics. Everyone is defined simultaneously by the number, quality, and intensity of his psychological activities. There are no individuals of identical mentality. Indeed, those whose consciousness is rudimentary closely resemble each other. The richer the personality, the greater the individual differences. All the activities of consciousness rarely develop at the same time in one individual. In most men, some of them are weak or lacking. There is a marked difference not only in the intensity of those functions, but also in their quality. Moreover, the number of their possible combinations is infinite. No task is more difficult than to analyze the constitution of a given individual. The complexity of mental personality being extreme, and the psychological tests insufficient, it is impossible to classify individuals accurately. They can, however, be divided into categories according to their intellectual, affective, moral, esthetic, and religious characteristics, to the combinations of these characteristics, and to their relations with the various types of physiological activities. There are also some obvious relations between psychological and morphological types. The physical aspect of an individual is an indication of the constitution of his tissues, humors, and mind. Between the more definite types there are many intermediate ones. The possible classifications are almost innumerable. They are, consequently, of little value.

Individuals have been separated into intellectual, sensitive, and voluntary types. In each category, there are the hesitating, the annoying, the impulsive, the incoherent, the weak, the dispersed, the restless, and also the reflective, the self-controlled, the honest, the well balanced. Among the intellectual, several distinct groups are observed. The broad-minded, whose ideas are numerous, who assimilate, coördinate, and unite a most varied knowledge. The narrow-minded, incapable of grasping vast ensembles, but who master perfectly the details of one subject. Intelligence is more frequently precise and analytical than capable of great syntheses. There are also the group of the logicians and that of the intuitives. Most of the great men belong to this latter group. There are many combinations of the intellectual and affective types. The intellectual may be emotional, passionate, enterprising, and also cowardly, irresolute, and weak. Among them, the mystical type is exceptional. The same multiplicity of combinations exists in the groups characterized by moral, esthetic, and religious tendencies. Such a classification evidences the prodigious variety of the human types.[1] The study of psychological individuality is as deceptive as would be that of chemistry, if the number of the elements should become infinite.

Each individual is conscious of being unique. Such uniqueness is real. But there are great differences in the degree of individualization. Certain personalities are very rich, very strong. Others are weak, easily modified by environment and circumstances. Between simple weakening of the personality and psychoses, there are many intermediate states. People suffering from certain neuroses have the feeling that their personality is being dissolved. Other diseases really destroy personality. Encephalitis lethargica brings about cerebral lesions which may profoundly modify the individual. The same may be said of dementia præcox and general paralysis. In other diseases the psychological changes are only temporary. Hysteria engenders double personality. The patient seems to become two different individuals. Each of these artificial persons ignores the thoughts and acts of the other. Likewise, one can, during hypnotic sleep, modify the identity of the subject. If another personality is imposed upon him by suggestion, he takes the attitudes and feels the emotions of his second self. In addition to those who thus become two persons, there are others whose personalities are

[1] Dumas, Georges. *Traité de Psychologie,* 1924, t. II, livre II. chapitre III, p. 575.

incompletely disassociated. In this category are many types of neurotics, those who practice automatic writing, a number of mediums, and also the queer, weak, unsteady beings who are so numerous in modern society.

It is not yet possible to make a complete survey of psychological individuality, and to measure its component parts. Neither can we exactly determine its nature, and how one individual differs from another. We are not even capable of discovering the essential characteristics of a given man. And still less his potentialities. Each youth, however, should insert himself in his social group according to his aptitudes and to his specific mental and physiological activities. But he cannot do it, because he is ignorant of himself. Parents and educators share with him such ignorance. They do not know how to detect the nature of the individuality of children. And they endeavor to standardize them. Modern business methods take no account of the personality of the workers. They ignore the fact that all men are different. Most of us are unaware of our own aptitudes. However, everybody cannot do everything. According to his characteristics, each individual adjusts himself more easily to a certain type of work or a certain mode of living. His success and happiness depend on the affinity between himself and his environment. He should fit into his social group as a key fits into its lock. Parents and school-teachers should set themselves first and foremost to acquire a knowledge of the inherent qualities and the potentialities of each child. Unfortunately, scientific psychology cannot give them very effective help. The tests applied to school children and students by inexperienced psychologists have no great significance. They give an illusive confidence to those unacquainted with psychology. In fact, they should be accorded less importance. Psychology is not yet a science. Today, individuality and its potentialities are not measurable. But a wise observer, trained in the study of human beings, is sometimes capable of discovering the future in the present characteristics of a given individual.

4

A disease is not an entity. We observe individuals suffering from pneumonia, syphilis, diabetes, typhoid fever, etc. Then, we construct in our mind certain Universals, certain abstractions, which we call diseases. Illness expresses the adaptation of the organism to a pathogenic agent, or its passive destruction by this agent. Adaptation and destruction assume the form of the sick individual and the rhythm of his inner time. The body is more rapidly destroyed by degenerative diseases during youth than during old age. It replies to all enemies in a specific manner. The form of its reply depends on the inherent properties of the tissues. Angina pectoris, for example, announces its presence by acute suffering. The heart seems to be gripped in steel claws. But the intensity of the pain varies according to the sensitiveness of the individual. When the patient is not sensitive, the disease takes another aspect. Without warning, without pain, it kills its victim. Typhoid fever, as we know, is accompanied by high temperature, headache, diarrhea, general depression. It is a serious illness necessitating a long sojourn in the hospital. However, certain individuals, although suffering from this malady, continue to attend to their usual occupations. In the course of epidemics of influenza, diphtheria, yellow fever, etc., some patients feel only a slight fever, a little discomfort. In spite of the lack of symptoms, they are affected by the disease. Their mode of response to the infection is due to the inherent resistance of their tissues. As we know, the adaptive mechanisms which protect the body from microbes and viruses differ in each individual. When the organism is incapable of resistance, as in cancer, it is being destroyed at a rhythm and in a manner determined by its own properties. In a young woman, a cancer of the breast rapidly brings on death. On the contrary, in extreme old age, it evolves very slowly, as slowly as the body itself. Disease is a personal event. It consists of the individual himself. There are as many different diseases as patients.

However, it would have been impossible to build up a science of medicine merely by compiling a great number of individual observations. The facts had to be classified and simplified with the aid of abstractions. In this way disease was born. And medical treatises could be written. A kind of science was built up, roughly descriptive, rudimentary, imperfect, but convenient, indefinitely perfectible and easy to teach. Unfortunately, we have been content with this result. We did not understand that treatises describing pathological entities contain only a part of the knowledge indispensable to those who attend the sick. Medical knowledge should go beyond the science of diseases. The physician must clearly distinguish the sick human being described in his books from the concrete patient whom he has to treat, who must not only be studied, but, above all, relieved, encouraged, and cured. His rôle is to discover the characteristics of the sick man's individuality, his resistance to pathogenic factors, his sensibility to pain, the value of his organic activities, his past, and his future. The outcome of an illness in a given individual has to be predicted, not by a calculation of the probabilities, but by a precise analysis of the organic, humoral, and psychological personality of this individual. In fact, medicine, when confining itself to the study of diseases, amputates a part of its own body.

Many physicians still persist in pursuing abstractions exclusively. Some, however, believe that a knowledge of the patient is as important as that of the disease. The former desire to remain in the realm of symbols. The latter feel the necessity of apprehending the concrete. Today the old quarrel of the realists and the nominalists is being revived around the schools of medicine. Scientific medicine, installed in its palaces, defends, as did the church of the Middle Ages, the reality of the Universals. It anathematizes the nominalists who, following the example of Abélard, consider Universals and disease as creations of our mind, and the patient as the only reality. In fact, a physician has to be both realist and nominalist. He must study the individual as well as the disease. The distrust which the public feels toward medicine, the inefficiency, and sometimes the ridicule, of therapeutics, are, perhaps, due to the confusion of the symbols indispensable to the building up of medical sciences with the concrete patient who has to be treated and relieved. The physician's lack of success comes from his living in an imaginary world. Instead of his patients, he sees the diseases described in the treatises of medicine. He is a victim of the belief in the reality of Universals. Moreover, he mixes the concepts of principle and method, of science and technology. He does not realize sufficiently that the individual is a whole, that adaptive functions extend to all organic systems, and that anatomical divisions are artificial. The separation of the body into parts has so far been to his advantage. But it is dangerous and costly for the patient, and ultimately for the physician.

Medicine has to take into account the nature of man, of his unity, and of his uniqueness. Its sole purpose is to relieve the suffering of the individual, and to cure him. Indeed, physicians must use the spirit and the methods of science. They have to become capable of recognizing and treating diseases and, still better, of preventing them. Medicine is not a discipline of the mind. There is no valid motive for cultivating it for itself, or for the advantage of those who practice it. The goal of all our efforts should be exclusively the healing of the sick. But medicine is the most difficult of all human attainments. It should not be likened to any science. A professor of medicine is not an ordinary teacher. He differs profoundly from other professors. While the fields covered by his colleagues specialized in the study of anatomy, physiology, chemistry, pathology, pharmacology, etc., are limited and clearly defined, he must acquire an almost universal knowledge. In addition, he needs sound judgment, great physical endurance, and ceaseless activity. He should possess higher qualities than those of a laboratory worker. He is set a task very different from that of a man of science. The latter can confine himself entirely to the world of symbols. Physicians, on the contrary, have to face both concrete reality and scientific abstractions. Their mind must simultaneously grasp the phenomena and their symbols, search into organs and consciousness, and enter, with each individual, a different world. They are asked to realize the impossible feat of building up a science of the particular.

Of course, they might use the expedient of indiscriminately applying their scientific knowledge to each patient, as, for instance, a salesman trying to fit the same ready-made coat to people of different sizes. But they do not really fulfill their duty unless they discover the specific peculiarities of each patient. Their success depends not only on their knowledge, but also on their ability to grasp the characteristics which make each human being an individual.

5

The uniqueness of each man has a double origin. It comes simultaneously from the constitution of the ovum, from which he originates, and from his development and his history. We have already mentioned how, before fertilization, the ovum expels half of its nucleus, half of each chromosome —that is, half the hereditary factors, the genes, which are arranged in a linear series along the chromosomes. We know how the head of a spermatozoon penetrates the ovum, after having also lost half of its chromosomes, how the body, with all its characteristics and tendencies, derives from the union of the male and female chromosomes within the nucleus of the fertilized egg. At this moment the individual exists only in a potential state. He contains the dominant factors responsible for the visible characteristics of his parents. And also the recessive factors, which have remained hidden during their entire life. According to their relative position in the new individual's chromosomes, the recessive factors will manifest their activity or will be neutralized by dominant factors. These relations are described by the science of genetics as the laws of heredity. They merely express the origin of the inherent characteristics of each human being. But these characteristics are nothing but tendencies or potentialities. According to the circumstances encountered by the embryo, the fetus, the child, and the adolescent during their development, these tendencies become actual or remain virtual. And each man's history is as unique as were the nature and the arrangement of his constitutive genes when he was an ovum. Thus, the originality of the human being depends both on heredity and on development.

We know that individuality springs from these two sources. But not what part each of them plays in our formation. Is heredity more important than development, or vice versa? Watson and the behaviorists proclaim that education and environment are capable of giving human beings any desired form. Education would be everything, and heredity nothing. Geneticists believe, on the contrary, that heredity imposes itself on man like ancient fate, and that the salvation of the race lies, not in education, but in eugenics. Both schools forget that such a problem cannot be solved by arguments, but only by observations and experiments.

Observations and experiments teach us that the parts of heredity and of development vary in each individual, and that generally their respective values cannot be determined. However, in children conceived by the same parents, brought up together and in the same manner, there are striking differences in form, stature, nervous constitution, intellectual aptitudes, and moral qualities. It is obvious that these differences are of ancestral origin. Animals behave in a like way. Let us take as an example a litter of shepherd dogs, still being suckled by their mother. Each of the nine or ten puppies presents distinct characteristics. Some react to a sudden noise, to the report of a pistol, for example, by crouching on the ground, some by standing up on their little paws, others by advancing toward the noise. Some conquer the best teats, others let themselves be pushed out of their place. Some ramble away from their mother and explore the neighborhood of their kennel. Others stay with her. Some growl when touched. Others remain silent. When the animals brought up together under identical conditions have grown into adults, most of their characteristics are found unchanged by development. Shy and timorous dogs remain shy and timorous all their lives. Those that were fearless and alert sometimes lose these qualities as they grow older, but, in general, they become still more fearless and active. Among the characteristics of ancestral origin, some are not utilized, the others develop. Twins originating in the same ovum possess the same inherent characteristics. At first, they are quite identical. However, if they are parted right at the beginning of their lives and are brought up in different ways and in different countries, they lose such identity. After eighteen or twenty years, they show marked differences, and also great resemblances, especially from an intellectual point of view. From this it appears that, given dissimilar surroundings, identity of constitution does not determine the formation of identical individuals. It is also evident that disparity of environment does not efface identity of constitution. According to the conditions under which development takes place, some or others of the potentialities are actualized. And two beings, originally identical, become different.

What influence do the genes, those particles of nuclear substance originating from our ancestors, exert on the formation of the individual, on the building up of body and consciousness? In what measure does the constitution of the individual depend on that of the egg? Many observations and experiments have shown that certain aspects of the individual are already present in the ovum, that others are only potential. The genes, therefore, exercise their influence, either in an inexorable manner by imposing on the individual characteristics which develop fatally, or in the form of tendencies which become, or fail to become, effective, according to the circumstances of the development. Sex is inevitably determined from the time of the union of the paternal and maternal cells. The egg of the future male possesses one chromosome less than that of the female, or an atrophied chromosome. In this manner, all the cells of the body of the man differ from those of the body of the woman. Weakness of mind, insanity, hemophilia, deafmutism, as is known, are hereditary defects. Certain diseases, such as cancer, hypertension, tuberculosis, etc., are transmitted also from parents to children, but as a tendency. The conditions of development may impede or favor their actualization. It is the same with strength, alertness, will power, intelligence, and judgment. The value of each individual is determined in a large measure by his hereditary predispositions. But as human beings are not of pure breed, the characteristics of the products of a given marriage cannot be predicted. However, it is known that children born in families of superior people are more likely to be of a superior type than those born in an inferior family. Owing to the hazards of the nuclear unions, a great man's descendants may include mediocre children, or an obscure family may give birth to a great man. The tendency to superiority is by no means irresistible, like that to insanity, for example. Eugenics succeeds in producing superior types only under certain conditions of development and education. It has no magic power, and is not capable, when unaided, of greatly improving the individuals.

6

The ancestral tendencies, transmitted according to the laws of Mendel and other laws, give a special aspect to the development of each man. In order to manifest themselves, they naturally require the coöperation of the environment. The potentialities of tissues and consciousness actualize only through the chemical, physical, physiological, and mental factors of such environment. One cannot distinguish, in general, the inherited from the acquired. Indeed, certain peculiarities, such as the color of eyes and of hair, short-sightedness, and feeble-mindedness, are evidently of hereditary origin. But many other characteristics depend on the influence environment has upon body and mind. The development of the organism bends in different directions, in compliance with its surroundings. And its inherent properties become actual or remain virtual. It is certain that hereditary tendencies are profoundly modified by the circumstances of our formation. But we must also realize that each individual develops according to his own rules, to the specific qualities of his tissues. Moreover, the original intensity of our tendencies, their capacity for actualization, varies. The destiny of certain individuals is inexorably determined. That of others more or less depends on the conditions of their development.

It is impossible to predict in what measure a child's hereditary tendencies will be affected by his education, mode of life, and social surroundings. The genetical constitution of the tissues of a human being is always a mystery. We do not know how the genes of his parents, grandparents, and great-grandparents are grouped in the egg from which he originated. Neither do we know whether certain nuclear particles of some distant and forgotten ancestor are not present in him. Nor whether spontaneous changes in the genes themselves may not cause the appearance of some unforeseen characteristics. It sometimes happens that a child, whose ancestral tendencies have been known for several generations, manifests completely new and unexpected aspects. However, the probable results of a given environment upon a given individual can be anticipated in a certain measure. A seasoned observer is able to grasp the significance of the growing characteristics of a child, as well as of a puppy, very early in its life. Developmental conditions cannot transform a weak, apathetic, dispersed, timid, inactive child into an energetic man, a powerful and audacious leader. Vitality, imagination, boldness are never entirely due to environment. Neither can they be repressed by it. Indeed, the circumstances of development are efficient only within the limits of the hereditary predispositions, of the immanent qualities of tissues and consciousness. But we never know the exact nature of these predispositions. We must, however, presume them to be favorable, and act accordingly. It is imperative that each individual should receive an education conducive to the growth of his virtual qualities, until the qualities in question are proven not to exist.

The chemical, physiological, and psychological factors of the environment favor or hinder the development of the inherent tendencies. In fact, these tendencies can express themselves only by certain organic forms. If the body is deprived of the calcium and phosphorus indispensable to the building up of the skeleton, or of the vitamines and glandular secretions which permit the utilization of this material by cartilage in the formation of bones, the limbs become deformed and the pelvis narrow. Such a commonplace accident may prevent the actualization of potentialities which destined this or that woman to be a prolific mother, perhaps to beget a new Lincoln or a new Pasteur. The lack of a vitamine or an infectious disease may cause the testicles, or any other gland, to atrophy and, in this manner, stop the development of an individual who, owing to his ancestral qualities, could have become the leader of a nation. All the physical and chemical conditions of the environment are capable of affecting the actualization of our potentialities. To their molding influence is due, in a large measure, the organic and mental aspect of each human being.

Psychological factors act still more effectively on the individual. They give to our life its intellectual and moral form. They induce discipline or dispersion. They lead us to the neglect or the mastery of ourselves. Through circulatory and glandular changes, they also transform the activities and the constitution of the body. The discipline of the mind and of the physiological appetites has a definite effect, not only on the psychological attitude of the individual, but also on his organic and humoral structure. We do not know in what measure the mental influences emanating from the environment are capable of promoting or stifling ancestral tendencies. Without any doubt, they play a leading part in the destiny of the individual. They sometimes annihilate the highest mental qualities. They develop certain individuals beyond all expectations. They help the weak, and render the strong yet stronger. Young Bonaparte read Plutarch and endeavored to think and to live as the great men of antiquity did. It is not immaterial that a child idolize Babe Ruth or George Washington, Charlie Chaplin or Lindbergh. To play at being a gangster is not the same thing as to play at being a soldier. Whatever his ancestral tendencies may be, each individual is started by his developmental conditions upon a road which may lead him either to the solitude of the mountains, to the beauty of the hills, or to the mud of the marshes where most civilized men delight in living.

The influence of environment upon individualization varies according to the state of tissues and consciousness. In other words, the same factor, acting on several individuals, or upon the same individual at different periods of his existence, does not have identical effects. It is well known that the response of a given organism to environment depends on its hereditary tendencies. For example, the obstacle that stops one man stimulates another to a greater effort, and determines in him the actualization of potentialities which so far had remained hidden. Likewise, at successive periods of life, before or after certain diseases, the organism responds to a pathogenic influence in different ways. The effect of an excess of food or sleep is not the same on a young man as on an old one. Measles are an insignificant disease in children and a serious one in adults. In addition, the reactivity of a subject varies according to his physiological age, and also to all his previous history. It depends on the nature of his individualization. In sum, the part of environment in the actualization of the hereditary tendencies of a given subject is not exactly definable. The immanent properties of the tissues and the conditions of their development are inextricably mingled in the formation of the body and the soul of each individual.

7

The individual is obviously a center of specific activities. He appears as distinct from the inanimate world and also from other living beings. At the same time, he is linked to his environment and to his fellow men. He could not exist without them. He is characterized by being independent of, and dependent on, the cosmic universe. But we do not know how he is bound to other beings, where his spatial and temporal frontiers are. Personality is rightly believed to extend outside the physical continuum. Its limits seem to be situated beyond the surface of the skin. The definiteness of the anatomical contours is partly an illusion. Each one of us is certainly far larger and more diffuse than his body.

We know that our visible frontiers are, on one side, the skin and, on the other side, the digestive and respiratory mucosas. Our anatomical and functional integrity, as also our survival, depends on their inviolability. Their destruction and the invasion of the tissues by bacteria bring on death and disintegration of the individual. We also know that they can be crossed by cosmic rays, oxygen from the atmosphere, light, heat, and sound waves, and substances resulting from the intestinal digestion of food. Through these surfaces the inner world of our body is in continuity with the cosmic world. But this anatomical frontier is only that of one aspect of the individual. It does not enclose our mental personality. Love and hatred are realities. Through these feelings, men are bound to one another in a positive manner, whatever may be the distance between them. To a woman, the loss of her child causes greater suffering than the loss of a limb. The breaking of an affective bond may even bring about death. If we could visualize those immaterial links, human beings would assume new and strange aspects. Some would hardly extend beyond their anatomical limits. Others would stretch out as far as a safe in a bank, the sexual organs of another individual, certain foods or beverages, perhaps to a dog, a jewel, some object of art. Others would appear immense. They would expand in long tentacles attached to their family, to a group of friends, to an old homestead, to the sky and the mountains of their native country. Leaders of nations, great philanthropists, saints, would look like fairy-tale giants, spreading their multiple arms over a country, a continent, the entire world. There is a close relation between us and our social environment. Each human being occupies a certain place in his group. He is shackled to it by mental chains. His position may appear to him as more important than life itself. If he is deprived of it by financial losses, illness, persecution, scandal, or crime, he may prefer suicide to such a change. Obviously, the individual projects on all sides beyond his anatomical frontiers.

But man diffuses through space in a still more positive way.[1] In telepathic phenomena, he instantaneously sends

[1] The psychological frontiers of the individual in space and time are obviously suppositions. But suppositions, even when very strange, are convenient and help to group together facts that are temporarily unexplainable. Their purpose is merely to inspire new experiments. The author realizes clearly that his conjectures will be considered naïve or heretical by the layman, as well as by the scientist. That they will equally displease materialists and spiritualists, vitalists and mechanicists. That the equilibrium of his intellect will be doubted. However, one cannot neglect facts because they are strange. On the contrary, one must investigate them. Metapsychics

out a part of himself, a sort of emanation, which joins a faraway relative or friend. He thus expands to great distances. He may cross oceans and continents in a time too short to be estimated. He is capable of finding in the midst of a crowd the person whom he must meet. Then he communicates to this person certain knowledge. He can also discover in the immensity and confusion of a modern city the house, the room of the individual whom he seeks, although acquainted neither with him nor with his surroundings. Those endowed with this form of activity behave like extensible beings, amebas of a strange kind, capable of sending pseudopods to prodigious distances. The hypnotist and his subject are sometimes observed to be linked together by an invisible bond. This bond seems to emanate from the subject. When communication is established between the hypnotist and his subject, the former can, by suggestion from a distance, command the latter to perform certain acts. At this moment, a telepathic relation is established between them. In such an instance, two distant individuals are in contact with each

---

may bring to us more important information on the nature of man than normal psychology does. The societies of psychical research, and especially the English Society, have attracted to clairvoyance and telepathy the attention of the public. The time has come to study these phenomena as one studies physiological phenomena. But metapsychical researches must not be undertaken by amateurs, even when those amateurs are great physicists, great philosophers, or great mathematicians. To go beyond one's own field and to dabble in theology or spiritism is dangerous, even for men as illustrious as Isaac Newton, William Crookes, or Oliver Lodge. Experimenters trained in clinical medicine, having a profound knowledge of the human being, of his physiology and psychology, of his neuroses, of his aptitude to lie, of his susceptibility to suggestion, of his skill at prestidigitation, are alone qualified to investigate this subject. The author hopes that his suppositions about the spatial and temporal limits of the individual will possibly inspire, instead of smiles or futile discussions, experiments made with the techniques of physiology and physics.

other, although both appear to be confined within their respective anatomical limits.

Thought seems to be transmitted, like electromagnetic waves, from one region of space to another. We do not know its velocity. So far, it has not been possible to measure the speed of telepathic communications. Neither biologists, physicists, nor astronomers have taken into account the existence of metapsychical phenomena. Telepathy, however, is a primary datum of observation. If, some day, thought should be found to travel through space as light does, our theories about the constitution of the universe would have to be modified. But it is not sure that telepathic phenomena are due to the transmission of a physical agent. Possibly there is no spatial contact between individuals who are in communication. In fact, we know that mind is not entirely described within the four dimensions of the physical continuum. It is situated simultaneously within the material universe and elsewhere. It may insert itself into the cerebral cells and stretch outside space and time, like an alga, which fastens to a rock and lets its tendrils drift out into the mystery of the ocean. We are totally ignorant of the realities that lie outside space and time. We may suppose that a telepathic communication is an encounter, beyond the four dimensions of our universe, between the immaterial parts of two minds. But it is more convenient to consider these phenomena as being brought about by the expansion of the individual into space.

The spatial extensibility of personality is an exceptional fact. Nevertheless, normal individuals may sometimes read the thoughts of others, as clairvoyants do. In a perhaps analogous manner some men have the power of carrying away and convincing great multitudes with seemingly commonplace words, of leading people to happiness, to battle, to sacrifice, to death. Caesar, Napoleon, Mussolini, all great leaders of nations, grow beyond human stature. They encircle innumerable throngs of men in the net of their will and their ideas. Between certain individuals and nature there are subtle and obscure relations. Such men are able to spread across space and time and to grasp concrete reality. They seem to escape from themselves, and also from the physical continuum. Sometimes they project their tentacles in vain beyond the frontiers of the material world, and they bring back nothing of importance. But, like the great prophets of science, art, and religion, they often succeed in apprehending in the abysses of the unknown, elusive and sublime beings called mathematical abstractions, Platonic Ideas, absolute beauty, God.

8

In time, as in space, the individual stretches out beyond the frontiers of his body. His temporal frontiers are neither more precise nor more fixed than his spatial ones. He is linked to the past and to the future, although his self does not extend outside the present. Our individuality, as we know, comes into being when the spermatozoon enters the egg. But before this moment, the elements of the self are already in existence, scattered in the tissues of our parents, of our parents' parents, and of our most remote ancestors. We are made of the cellular substances of our father and our mother. We depend on the past in an organic and indissoluble manner. We bear within ourselves countless fragments of our ancestors' bodies. Our qualities and defects proceed from theirs. In men, as in race-horses, strength and courage are hereditary qualities. History cannot be set aside. We must, on the contrary, make use of the past to foresee the future and to prepare our destiny.

It is well known that characteristics acquired by the individual in the course of his life are not transmitted to his descendants. However, germ-plasm is not immutable. It may change under the influence of the organic medium. It can be altered by disease, poison, food, and secretions of endocrine glands. Syphilis in parents may cause profound disorders in the body and consciousness of their children. For this reason, the descent of men of genius sometimes consists of inferior beings, weak and unbalanced. *Treponema pallidum* has exterminated more great families than have all the wars of the world. Likewise, alcoholics, morphinomaniacs, and cocaine addicts may beget defectives, who pay during their entire life for the vices of their fathers. Indeed, the consequences of one's faults are easily passed on to one's descendants. But it is far more difficult to give them the benefit of one's virtues. Each individual puts his mark on his environment, his house, his family, his friends. He lives as if surrounded by himself. Through his deeds, he may transfer his qualities to his descendants. The child depends on his parents for a long period. He has time to learn all that they can teach him. He uses his innate capacity for imitation and tends to become like them. He takes on their true visage, and not the mask that they wear in social life. In general, his feeling toward his father and mother is one of indifference and of some contempt. But he willingly imitates their ignorance, vulgarity, selfishness, and cowardice.

Of course, there are many types of parents. Some of them leave their offspring a heritage of intelligence, goodness, esthetic sense, and courage. After their death their personality goes on living through their scientific discoveries, their artistic production, the political, economic, or social institutions they have founded, or more simply through the house which they have built, and the fields which they have cultivated with their own hands. It is by such people that our civilization has been created.

The influence of the individual upon the future is not equivalent to an extension of the self in time. It takes place by means of the fragments of cell substance directly transmitted by him to his children, or of his creations in the domains of art, religion, science, philosophy, etc. Sometimes, however, personality seems really to extend beyond physiological duration. There is in certain individuals a psychical element capable of traveling in time.[1] As already mentioned, clairvoyants perceive not only events spatially remote, but also past and future events. They seem to wander as easily in time as in space. Or to escape from the physical continuum and contemplate the past and the future as a fly could contemplate a picture if, instead of walking on its surface, it flew at some distance above it. The facts of prediction of the future lead us to the threshold of an unknown world. They seem to point to the existence of a psychic principle capable of evolving outside the limits of our bodies. The specialists of spiritism interpret certain of these phenomena as proof of the survival of consciousness after death. The medium believes himself to be inhabited by the spirit of the deceased. He may reveal to the experimenters some details

[1] See note, page 259.

known only to the dead man, and the exactness of which is verified later. According to Broad, these facts could be interpreted as indicating the persistence after death, not of the mind, but of a psychic factor capable of grafting itself temporarily upon the organism of the medium. This psychic factor, in uniting with a human being, would constitute a sort of consciousness belonging both to the medium and to the defunct. Its existence would be transitory. It would progressively break up and finally disappear. The results obtained by the spiritists' experiments are of great importance. But their significance is not precise. For the clairvoyant there are no secrets. At the present time, therefore, it does not seem possible to make a distinction between the survival of a psychic principle and a phenomenon of mediumistic clairvoyance.

9

To summarize. Individuality is not merely an aspect of the organism. It also constitutes an essential characteristic of each component part of this organism. It remains virtual in the fertilized ovum, and progressively unfolds its characteristics as the new being extends into time. The ancestral tendencies of this being are forced to actualize by his conflict with the environment. They incline his adaptive activities in a certain direction. In fact, the mode of utilization of its surroundings by the body is determined by its innate properties. Each individual responds to these surroundings in his own way. He chooses among the things of the outer world those which increase his individualization. He is a focus of specific activities. These activities are distinct but indivisible. The soul cannot be separated from the body, the structure from the function, the cell from its medium, the multiplicity from the unity, or the determining from the determined. We are beginning to realize that our surface is not our real frontier, that it merely sets up between us and the cosmic universe a plane of cleavage indispensable to our action. We are constructed like the castles of the Middle Ages, whose dungeons were surrounded by several lines of fortifications. Our inner defenses are numerous and entangled one with another. The skin is the barrier that our microscopic enemies must not traverse. But we extend much farther beyond it. Beyond space and time. We know the individual's center, yet ignore where his outer limits are located. These limits, in fact, are hypothetical. Perhaps they do not exist. Each man is bound to those who precede and follow him. He fuses in some manner into them. Humanity does not appear to be composed of separate particles, as a gas is of molecules. It resembles an intricate network of long threads extending in space-time and consisting of series of individuals. Individuality is doubtless real. But it is much less definite than we believe. And the independence of each individual from the others and from the cosmos is an illusion.

Our body is made up of the chemical substances of the environment. These substances enter it and become modified according to its individuality. They are built up into temporary edifices, tissues, humors, and organs, which ceaselessly disintegrate and are reconstructed during our whole life. After our death, they return to the world of inert matter. Certain chemical compounds assume our racial and individual peculiarities. They become truly ourselves.

Others only pass through the body. They participate in the existence of our tissues without taking any of their characteristics, just as wax does not modify its chemical composition when made into statues of different shapes. They flow through the organism like a large river, from which cells draw the substances required for their growth, their maintenance, and their expenditure of energy. According to Christian mystics, we receive from the outer world certain spiritual elements. The grace of God permeates soul and body, just as atmospheric oxygen, or nitrogen from the food, diffuses in our tissues.

Individual specificity persists during the entire life, although tissues and humors continually change. The organs and their medium move at the rhythm of physiological time, that is, at the rhythm of irreversible processes, towards definitive transformations and death. But they always keep their inherent qualities. They are not modified by the stream of matter in which they are immersed, any more than the spruce trees on the mountains by the clouds passing through their branches. However, individuality grows stronger or weaker according to environmental conditions. When these conditions are particularly unfavorable, it dissolves. Sometimes, mental personality is less marked than organic personality. One may rightly ask whether it still exists in modern men. Some observers doubt its reality. Theodore Dreiser considers it a myth. It is certain that the inhabitants of the new city show great uniformity in their mental and moral weakness. Most of the individuals belong to the same type. A mixture of nervousness and apathy, of vanity and lack of confidence in themselves, of muscular strength and tendency to fatigue. Of genesic impulses, both irresistible and not strong, sometimes homosexual. Such a state is due to profound disorders in the formation of personality. It does not consist only in an attitude of mind, a fashion which could easily change. It expresses either a degeneration of the race, or a defective development of the individual, or both these phenomena.

This debasement is, in a certain measure, of hereditary origin. The suppression of natural selection, as already mentioned, has caused the survival of children whose tissues and consciousness are defective. The race has been weakened by the preservation of such reproducers. The relative importance of this factor of degeneration is not yet known. As we have already mentioned, the influence of heredity cannot be distinguished clearly from that of environment. Feeblemindedness and insanity surely have an ancestral cause. The intellectual weakness observed in schools and universities, and in the population in general, comes from developmental disorders, and not from hereditary defects. When these flabby, silly young people are removed from their customary environment and placed in more primitive conditions of life, they sometimes change for the better and recover their virility. The atrophic character of the products of our civilization, therefore, is not incurable. It is far from being always the expression of a racial degeneration.

Among the multitude of weak and defective there are, however, some completely developed men. These men, when closely observed, appear to be superior to the classical schemata. In fact, the individual whose potentialities are all actualized does not resemble the human being pictured by the specialists. He is not the fragments of consciousness which psychologists attempt to measure. He is not to be found in the chemical reactions, the functional processes, and the organs which physicians have divided between themselves. Neither is he the abstraction whose concrete manifestations the educators try to guide. He is almost completely wanting in the rudimentary being manufactured by social workers, prison wardens, economists, sociologists, and politicians. In fact, he never appears to a specialist unless this specialist is willing to look at him as a whole. He is much more than the sum of all the facts accumulated by the particular sciences. We never apprehend him in his entirety. He contains vast, unknown regions. His potentialities are almost inexhaustible. Like the great natural phenomena, he is still unintelligible. When one contemplates him in the harmony of all his organic and spiritual activities, one experiences a profound esthetic emotion. Such an individual is truly the creator and the center of the universe.

10

Modern society ignores the individual. It only takes account of human beings. It believes in the reality of the Universals and treats men as abstractions. The confusion of the concepts of individual and of human being has led industrial civilization to a fundamental error, the standardization of men. If we were all identical, we could be reared and made to live and work in great herds, like cattle. But each one has his own personality. He cannot be treated like a symbol. Children should not be placed, at a very early age, in schools where they are educated wholesale. As is well known, most great men have been brought up in comparative solitude, or have refused to enter the mold of the school.

Of course, schools are indispensable for technical studies. They also fill, in a certain measure, the child's need of contact with other children. But education should be the object of unfailing guidance. Such guidance belongs to the parents. They alone, and more especially the mother, have observed, since their origin, the physiological and mental peculiarities whose orientation is the aim of education. Modern society has committed a serious mistake by entirely substituting the school for the familial training. The mothers abandon their children to the kindergarten in order to attend to their careers, their social ambitions, their sexual pleasures, their literary or artistic fancies, or simply to play bridge, go to the cinema, and waste their time in busy idleness. They are, thus, responsible for the disappearance of the familial group where the child was kept in contact with adults and learned a great deal from them. Young dogs brought up in kennels with others of the same age do not develop as well as puppies free to run about with their parents. It is the same with children living in a crowd of other children, and with those living in the company of intelligent adults. The child easily molds his physiological, affective, and mental activities upon those of his surroundings. He learns little from children of his own age. When he is only a unit in a school he remains incomplete. In order to reach his full strength, the individual requires the relative isolation and the attention of the restricted social group consisting of the family.

The neglect of individuality by our social institutions is, likewise, responsible for the atrophy of the adults. Man does not stand, without damage, the mode of existence and the uniform and stupid work imposed on factory and office workers, on all those who take part in mass production. In the immensity of modern cities he is isolated and as if lost. He is an economic abstraction, a unit of the herd. He gives up his individuality. He has neither responsibility nor dignity. Above the multitude stand out the rich men, the powerful politicians, the bandits. The others are only nameless grains of dust. On the contrary, the individual remains a man when he belongs to a small group, when he inhabits a village or a small town where his relative importance is greater, when he can hope to become, in his turn, an influential citizen. The contempt for individuality has brought about its factual disappearance.

Another error, due to the confusion of the concepts of human being and individual, is democratic equality. This dogma is now breaking down under the blows of the experience of the nations. It is, therefore, unnecessary to insist upon its falseness. But its success has been astonishingly long. How could humanity accept such faith for so many years? The democratic creed does not take account of the constitution of our body and of our consciousness. It does not apply to the concrete fact which the individual is. Indeed, human beings are equal. But individuals are not. The equality of their rights is an illusion. The feeble-minded and the man of genius should not be equal before the law. The stupid, the unintelligent, those who are dispersed, incapable of attention, of effort, have no right to a higher education. It is absurd to give them the same electoral power as the fully developed individuals. Sexes are not equal. To disregard all these inequalities is very dangerous. The democratic principle has contributed to the collapse of civilization in opposing the development of an élite. It is obvious that, on the contrary, individual inequalities must be respected. In modern society the great, the small, the average, and the mediocre are needed. But we should not attempt to develop the higher types by the same procedures as the lower. The standardization of men by the democratic ideal has already determined the predominance of the weak. Everywhere, the weak are preferred to the strong. They are aided and protected, often admired. Like the invalid, the criminal, and the insane, they attract the sympathy of the public. The myth of equality, the love of the symbol, the contempt for the concrete fact, are, in a large measure, guilty of the collapse of individuality. As it was impossible to raise the inferior types, the only means of producing democratic equality among men was to bring all to the lowest level. Thus vanished personality.

Not only has the concept of the individual been confused with that of the human being, but the latter has been adulterated by the introduction of foreign elements, and deprived of certain of its own elements. We have applied to man concepts belonging to the mechanical world. We have neglected thought, moral suffering, sacrifice, beauty, and peace. We have treated the individual as a chemical substance, a machine, or a part of a machine. We have amputated his moral, esthetic, and religious functions. We have also ignored certain aspects of his physiological activities. We have not asked how tissues and consciousness would accommodate themselves to the changes in the mode of life imposed upon us. We have totally forgotten the important rôle of the adaptive functions, and the momentous consequences of their enforced rest. Our present weakness comes both from our unappreciation of individuality and from our ignorance of the constitution of the human being.

II

Man is the result of heredity and environment, of the habits of life and thought imposed upon him by modern society. We have described how these habits affect his body and his consciousness. We know that he cannot adapt himself to the environment created by technology, that such environment brings about his degradation. Science and machines are not responsible for his present state. We alone are guilty. We have not been capable of distinguishing the prohibited from the lawful. We have infringed natural laws. We have thus committed the supreme sin, the sin that is always punished. The dogmas of scientific religion and industrial morals have fallen under the onslaught of biological reality. Life always gives an identical answer when asked to trespass on forbidden ground. It weakens. And civilizations collapse. The sciences of inert matter have led us into a country that is not ours. We have blindly accepted all their gifts. The individual has become narrow, specialized, immoral, unintelligent, incapable of managing himself and his own institutions. But at the same time the biological sciences have revealed to us the most precious of all secrets—the laws of the development of our body and of our consciousness. This knowledge has brought to humanity the means of renovating itself. As long as the hereditary qualities of the race remain present, the strength and the audacity of his forefathers can be resurrected in modern man by his own will. But is he still capable of such an effort?

Chapter VIII

THE REMAKING OF MAN

1. Can the science of man lead to his renovation? 2. Necessity of a change in our intellectual outlook. The error of the Renaissance. The supremacy of the quantitative over the qualitative, of matter over spirit, to be rejected. 3. How to render utilizable our knowledge of man. How to construct a synthesis. Can any one scientist master this mass of knowledge? 4. The institutions required for the development of the science of man. 5. The task of constructing man according to the rules of his nature. Necessity of acting on the individual through his environment. 6. The selection of individuals. Social and biological classes. 7. The construction of an élite. Voluntary eugenics. Hereditary aristocracy. 8. Physical and chemical factors in the formation of the individual. 9. Physiological factors. 10. Mental factors. 11. Health. 12. Development of personality. 13. The human universe. 14. The remaking of man.

I

SCIENCE, which has transformed the material world, gives man the power of transforming himself. It has unveiled some of the secret mechanisms of his life. It has shown him how to alter their motion, how to mold his body and his soul on patterns born of his wishes. For the first time in history, humanity, helped by science, has become master of its destiny. But will we be capable of using this knowledge of ourselves to our real advantage? To progress again, man must remake himself. And he cannot remake himself without suffering. For he is both the marble and the sculptor.

In order to uncover his true visage he must shatter his own substance with heavy blows of his hammer. He will not submit to such treatment unless driven by necessity. While surrounded by the comfort, the beauty, and the mechanical marvels engendered by technology, he does not understand how urgent is this operation. He fails to realize that he is degenerating. Why should he strive to modify his ways of being, living, and thinking?

Fortunately, an event unforeseen by engineers, economists, and politicians took place. The superb edifice of American finance and economics suddenly collapsed. At first, the public did not believe in the reality of such a catastrophe. Its faith was not disturbed. The explanations given by the economists were heard with docility. Prosperity would return. But prosperity has not returned. Today, the more intelligent heads of the flock are beginning to doubt. Are the causes of the crisis uniquely economic and financial? Should we not also incriminate the corruption and the stupidity of the politicians and the financiers, the ignorance and the illusions of the economists? Has not modern life decreased the intelligence and the morality of the whole nation? Why must we pay several billions of dollars each year to fight criminals? Why do the gangsters continue victoriously to attack banks, kill policemen, kidnap, ransom, or assassinate children, in spite of the immense amount of money spent in opposing them? Why are there so many feeble-minded and insane among civilized people? Does not the world crisis depend on individual and social factors that are more important than the economic ones? It is to be hoped that the spectacle of civilization at this beginning of its decline will compel us to ascertain whether the causes of the catastrophe do not lie within ourselves, as well as in our institutions. And that we will fully realize the imperativeness of our renovation.

Then, we will be faced by a single obstacle, our inertia. And not by the incapacity of our race to rise again. In fact, the economic crisis came before the complete destruction of our ancestral qualities by the idleness, corruption, and softness of life. We know that intellectual apathy, immorality, and criminality are not, in general, hereditary. Most children, at their birth, are endowed with the same potentialities as their parents. We can develop their innate qualities if we wish earnestly to do so. We have at our disposal all the might of science. There are still many men capable of using this power unselfishly. Modern society has not stifled all the focuses of intellectual culture, moral courage, virtue, and audacity. The flame is still burning. The evil is not irreparable. But the remaking of the individual demands the transformation of modern life. It cannot take place without a material and mental revolution. To understand the necessity of a change, and to possess the scientific means of realizing this change, are not sufficient. The spontaneous crash of technological civilization may help to release the impulses required for the destruction of our present habits and the creation of new modes of life.

Do we still have enough energy and perspicacity for such a gigantic effort? At first sight, it does not seem so. Man has sunk into indifference to almost everything except money. There are, however, some reasons for hope. After all, the races responsible for the construction of our world are not extinct. The ancestral potentialities still exist in the germplasm of their weak offspring. These potentialities can yet be actualized. Indeed, the descendants of the energetic strains are smothered in the multitude of proletarians whom industry has blindly created. They are in small number. But they will not succumb. For they possess a marvelous, although hidden, strength. We must not forget the stupendous task we have accomplished since the fall of the Roman Empire. In the small area of the states of western Europe, amid unceasing wars, famines, and epidemics, we have succeeded in keeping, throughout the Middle Ages, the relics of antique culture. During long, dark centuries we shed our blood on all sides in the defense of Christendom against our enemies of the north, the east, and the south. At the cost of immense efforts we succeeded in thrusting back the sleep of Islamism. Then a miracle happened. From the mind of men sharpened by scholastic discipline, sprang science. And, strange to say, science was cultivated by those men of the Occident for itself, for its truth and its beauty, with complete disinterestedness. Instead of stagnating in individual egoism, as it did in the Orient and especially in China, this science, in four hundred years, has transformed the world. Our fathers have made a prodigious effort. Most of their European and American descendants have forgotten the past. History is also ignored by those who now profit from our material civilization. By the white who, in the Middle Ages, did not fight beside us on the European battlefields, by the yellow, the brown, and the black, whose mounting tide exaggeratedly alarms Spengler. What we accomplished once we are capable of accomplishing again. Should our civilization collapse, we would build up another one. But is it indispensable to suffer the agony of chaos before reaching order and peace? Can we not rise again, without undergoing the bloody regeneration of total overthrow? Are we capable of renovating ourselves, of avoiding the cataclysms which are imminent, and of continuing our ascension?

2

We cannot undertake the restoration of ourselves and of our environment before having transformed our habits of thought. Modern society has suffered, ever since its origin, from an intellectual fault—a fault which has been constantly repeated since the Renaissance. Technology has constructed man, not according to the spirit of science, but according to erroneous metaphysical conceptions. The time has come to abandon these doctrines. We should break down the fences which have been erected between the properties of concrete objects, and between the different aspects of ourselves. The error responsible for our sufferings comes from a wrong interpretation of a great idea of Galileo. Galileo, as is well known, distinguished the primary qualities of things, dimensions and weight, which are easily measurable, from their secondary qualities, form, color, odor, which cannot be measured. The quantitative was separated from the qualitative. The quantitative, expressed in mathematical language, brought science to humanity. The qualitative was neglected. The abstraction of the primary qualities of objects was legitimate. But the overlooking of the secondary qualities was not. This mistake had momentous consequences. In man, the things which are not measurable are more important than those which are measurable. The existence of thought is as fundamental as, for instance, the physicochemical equilibria of blood serum. The separation of the qualitative from the quantitative grew still wider when Descartes created the dualism of the body and the soul. Then, the manifestations of the mind became inexplicable. The material was definitely isolated from the spiritual. Organic structures and physiological mechanisms assumed a far greater reality than thought, pleasure, sorrow, and beauty. This error switched civilization to the road which led science to triumph and man to degradation.

In order to find again the right direction we must return in thought to the men of the Renaissance, imbue ourselves with their spirit, their passion for empiric observation, and their contempt for philosophical systems. As they did, we have to distinguish the primary and secondary qualities of things. But we must radically differ from them and attribute to secondary qualities the same importance as to primary qualities. We should also reject the dualism of Descartes. Mind will be replaced in matter. The soul will no longer be distinct from the body. Mental manifestations, as well as physiological processes, will be within our reach. Indeed, the qualitative is more difficult to study than the quantitative. Concrete facts do not satisfy our mind, which prefers the definitive aspect of abstractions. But science must not be cultivated only for itself, for the elegance of its methods, for its light and its beauty. Its goal is the material and spiritual benefit of man. As much importance should be given to feelings as to thermodynamics. It is indispensable that our thought embraces all aspects of reality. Instead of discarding the residues of scientific abstractions we will utilize those residues as fully as the abstractions. We will not accept the tyranny of the quantitative, the superiority of mechanics, physics, or chemistry. We will renounce the intellectual attitude generated by the Renaissance, and its arbitrary definition of the real. But we must retain all the conquests made since Galileo's day. The spirit and the techniques of science are our most precious possessions.

It will be difficult to get rid of a doctrine which, during more than three hundred years, has dominated the intelligence of the civilized. The majority of men of science believe in the reality of the Universals, the exclusive right to existence of the quantitative, the supremacy of matter, the separation of the mind from the body, and the subordinated position of the mind. They will not easily give up this faith. For such a change would shake pedagogy, medicine, hygiene, psychology, and sociology to their foundations. The little garden which each scientist easily cultivates would be turned into a forest, which would have to be cleared. If scientific civilization should leave the road that it has followed since the Renaissance and return to the naïve observation of the concrete, strange events would immediately take place. Matter would lose its supremacy. Mental activities would become as important as physiological ones. The study of moral, esthetic, and religious functions would appear as indispensable as that of mathematics, physics, and chemistry. The present methods of education would seem absurd. Schools and universities would be obliged to modify their programs. Hygienists would be asked why they concern themselves exclusively with the prevention of organic diseases, and not with that of mental and nervous disturbances. Why they pay no attention to spiritual health. Why they segregate people ill with infections, and not those who propagate intellectual and moral maladies. Why the habits responsible for organic diseases are considered dangerous, and not those which bring on corruption, criminality, and insanity. The public would refuse to be attended by physicians knowing nothing but a small part of the body. Specialists would have to learn general medicine, or work as units of a group under the direction of a general practitioner. Pathologists would be induced to study the lesions of the humors as well as those of the organs. To take into account the influence of the mental upon the tissues, and vice versa. Economists would realize that human beings think, feel, and suffer, that they should be given other things than work, food, and leisure, that they have spiritual as well as physiological needs. And also that the causes of economic and financial crises may be moral and intellectual. We should no longer be obliged to accept the barbarous conditions of life in great cities, the tyranny of factory and office, the sacrifice of moral dignity to economic interest, of mind to money, as benefactions conferred upon us by modern civilization. We should reject mechanical inventions that hinder human development. Economics would no longer appear as the ultimate reason of everything. It is obvious that the liberation of man from the materialistic creed would transform most of the aspects of our existence. Therefore, modern society will oppose with all its might this progress in our conceptions.

However, we must take care that the failure of materialism does not bring about a spiritual reaction. Since technology and worship of matter have not been a success, the temptation may be great to choose the opposite cult, the cult of mind. The primacy of psychology would be no less dangerous than that of physiology, physics, and chemistry. Freud has done more harm than the most extreme mechanicists. It would be as disastrous to reduce man to his mental aspect as to his physiological and physicochemical mechanisms. The study of the physical properties of blood serum, of its ionic equilibria, of protoplasmic permeability, of the chemical constitution of antigens, etc., is as indispensable as that of dreams, libido, mediumistic states, psychological effects of prayer, memory of words, etc. Substitution of the spiritual for the material would not correct the error made by the Renaissance. The exclusion of matter would be still more detrimental to man than that of mind. Salvation will be found only in the relinquishing of all doctrines. In the full acceptation of the data of observation. In the realization of the fact that man is no less and no more than these data.

3

These data must be the basis of the construction of man. Our first task is to make them utilizable. Every year we hear of the progress made by eugenists, geneticists, statisticians, behaviorists, physiologists, anatomists, biological chemists, physical chemists, psychologists, physicians, hygienists, endocrinologists, psychiatrists, immunologists, educators, social workers, clergymen, sociologists, economists, etc. But the practical results of these accomplishments are surprisingly small. This immense amount of information is disseminated in technical reviews, in treatises, in the brains of men of science. No one has it in his possession. We have now to put together its disparate fragments, and to make this knowledge live within the mind of at least a few individuals. Then, it will become productive.

There are great difficulties in such an undertaking. How should we proceed to build up this synthesis? Around what aspect of man should the others be grouped? What is his most important activity? The economic, the political, the sociological, the mental, or the organic? What particular science should be caused to grow and absorb the others? Obviously, the remaking of man and of his economic and social world should be inspired by a precise knowledge of his body and of his soul—that is, of physiology, psychology, and pathology.

Medicine is the most comprehensive of all the sciences concerning man, from anatomy to political economy. However, it is far from apprehending its object in its full extent. Physicians have contented themselves with studying the structure and the activities of the individual in health and in disease, and attempting to cure the sick. Their effort has met, as we know, with modest success. Their influence on modern society has been sometimes beneficial, sometimes harmful, always secondary. Excepting, however, when hygiene aided industry in promoting the growth of civilized populations. Medicine has been paralyzed by the narrowness of its doctrines. But it could easily escape from its prison and help us in a more effective manner. Nearly three hundred years ago a philosopher, who dreamed of consecrating his life to the service of man, clearly conceived the high functions of which medicine is capable. "The mind," wrote Descartes in his *Discourse on Method,* "so strongly depends on temperament and the disposition of bodily organs, that if it is possible to find some means which will make men generally more wise and more clever than they have been till now, I believe that it is in medicine one should seek it. It is true that the medicine now practiced contains few things having so remarkable a usefulness. But, without having any intention of scorning it, I am confident that there is no one, even among those whose profession it is, who does not admit that everything already known about it is almost nothing in comparison with what remains to be learned, and that people could be spared an infinity of diseases, both bodily and mental, and perhaps even the weakening of old age, if the causes of those troubles and all the remedies with which nature has provided us were sufficiently well known."

Medicine has received from anatomy, physiology, psychology, and pathology the more essential elements of the knowledge of ourselves. It could easily enlarge its field, embrace, in addition to body and consciousness, their relations with the material and mental world, take in sociology and economics, and become the very science of the human being. Its aim, then, would be not only to cure or prevent diseases, but also to guide the development of all our organic, mental, and sociological activities. It would become capable of building the individual according to natural laws. And of inspiring those who will have the task of leading humanity to a true civilization. At the present time, education, hygiene, religion, town planning, and social and economic organizations are entrusted to individuals who know but a single aspect of the human being. No one would ever dream of substituting politicians, well-meaning women, lawyers, literary men, or philosophers for the engineers of the steel-works or of the chemical factories. However, such people are given the incomparably heavier responsibility of the physiological, mental, and sociological guidance of civilized men, and even of the government of great nations. Medicine aggrandized according to the conception of Descartes, and extended in such a manner as to embrace the other sciences of man, could supply modern society with engineers understanding the mechanisms of the body and the soul of the individual, and of his relations with the cosmic and social world.

This superscience will be utilizable only if, instead of being buried in libraries, it animates our intelligence. But is it possible for a single brain to assimilate such a gigantic amount of knowledge? Can any individual master anatomy, physiology, biological chemistry, psychology, metapsychics, pathology, medicine, and also have a thorough acquaintance with genetics, nutrition, development, pedagogy, esthetics, morals, religion, sociology, and economics? It seems that such an accomplishment is not impossible. In about twenty-five years of uninterrupted study, one could learn these sciences. At the age of fifty, those who have submitted themselves to this discipline could effectively direct the construction of the human being and of a civilization based on his true nature. Indeed, the few gifted individuals who dedicate themselves to this work will have to renounce the common modes of existence. They will not be able to play golf and bridge, to go to cinemas, to listen to radios, to make speeches at banquets, to serve on committees, to attend meetings of scientific societies, political conventions, and academies, or to cross the ocean and take part in international congresses. They must live like the monks of the great contemplative orders, and not like university professors, and still less like business men. In the course of the history of all great nations, many have sacrificed themselves for the salvation of the community. Sacrifice seems to be a necessary condition of progress. There are now, as in former times, men ready for the supreme renunciation. If the multitudes inhabiting the defenseless cities of the seacoast were menaced by shells and gases, no army aviator would hesitate to thrust himself, his plane, and his bombs against the invaders. Why should not some individuals sacrifice their lives to acquire the science indispensable to the making of man and of his environment? In fact, the task is extremely difficult. But minds capable of undertaking it can be discovered. The weakness of many of the scientists whom we meet in universities and laboratories is due to the mediocrity of their goal and to the narrowness of their life. Men grow when inspired by a high purpose, when contemplating vast horizons. The sacrifice of oneself is not very difficult for one burning with the passion for a great adventure. And there is no more beautiful and dangerous adventure than the renovation of modern man.

4

The making of man requires the development of institutions wherein body and mind can be formed according to natural laws, and not to the prejudices of the various schools of educators. It is essential that the individual, from infancy, be liberated from the dogmas of industrial civilization and the principles which are the very basis of modern society. The science of the human being does not need costly and numerous organizations in order to start its constructive work. It can utilize those already existing, provided they are rejuvenated. The success of such an enterprise will depend, in certain countries, on the attitude of the government and, in others, on that of the public. In Italy, Germany, or Russia, if the dictator judged it useful to condition children according to a definite type, to modify adults and their ways of life in a definite manner, appropriate institutions would spring up at once. In democratic countries progress has to come from private initiative. When the failure of most of our educational, medical, economic, and social beliefs becomes more apparent, the public will probably feel the necessity of a remedy for this situation.

In the past, the efforts of isolated individuals have caused the ascent of religion, science, and education. The development of hygiene in the United States is entirely due to the inspiration of a few men. For instance, Hermann Biggs made New York one of the most healthful cities of the world. A group of unknown young men, under the guidance of Welch, founded the Johns Hopkins Medical School, and initiated the astonishing progress of pathology, surgery, and hygiene in the United States. When bacteriology sprang from Pasteur's brain, the Pasteur Institute was created in Paris by national subscription. The Rockefeller Institute for Medical Research was founded in New York by John D. Rockefeller, because the necessity for new discoveries in the domain of medicine had become evident to Welch, Theobald Smith, T. Mitchell Prudden, Simon Flexner, Christian Herter, and a few other scientists. In many American universities, research laboratories, destined to further the progress of physiology, immunology, chemistry, etc., were established and endowed by enlightened benefactors. The great Carnegie and Rockefeller Foundations were inspired by more general ideas. To develop education, raise the scientific level of universities, promote peace among nations, prevent infectious diseases, improve the health and the welfare of everybody with the help of scientific methods. Those movements have always been started by the realization of a need, and the establishment of an institution responding to that need. The state did not help in their beginnings. But private institutions forced the progress of public institutions. In France, for example, bacteriology was at first taught exclusively at the Pasteur Institute. Later, chairs and laboratories of bacteriology were established in all state universities.

The institutions necessary for the rebuilding of man will probably develop in a similar manner. Some day, a school, a college, a university may understand the importance of the subject. Slight efforts in the right direction have already been made. For instance, Yale University has created an Institute for the study of human relations. The Macy Foundation was established for the development of integrative ideas concerning man, his health, and his education. Greater advance has been realized in Genoa by Nicola Pende in his Institute for the study of the human individual. Many American physicians begin to feel the necessity for a broader comprehension of man. However, this feeling has by no means been formulated as clearly here as in Italy. The already existing organizations have to undergo important changes in order to become fitted for the work of human renovation. They must, for instance, eliminate the remnants of the narrow mechanisticism of the last century, and understand the imperativeness of a clarification of the concepts used in biology, of a reintegration of the parts into the whole, and of the formation of true scholars, as well as of scientific workers. The direction of the institutions of learning, and of those which apply to man the results of the special sciences, from biological chemistry to political economy, should not be given to specialists, because specialists are exaggeratedly interested in the progress of their own particular studies, but to individuals capable of embracing all sciences. The specialists must be only the tools of a synthetic mind. They will be utilized by him in the same way as the professor of medicine of a great university utilizes the services of pathologists, bacteriologists, physiologists, chemists, and physicists in the laboratories of his clinic. None of these scientists is ever given the direction of the treatment of the patients. An economist, an endocrinologist, a social worker, a psychoanalyst, a biological chemist, are equally ignorant of man. They cannot be trusted beyond the limits of their own field.

We should not forget that our knowledge of man is still rudimentary, that most of the great problems mentioned at the beginning of this book remain unsolved. However, an answer must be given to the questions which concern the fate of hundreds of millions of individuals and the future of civilization. Such an answer can be elaborated only in research institutes dedicated to the promotion of the science of man. Our biological and medical laboratories have so far devoted their activities to the pursuit of health, to the discovery of the chemical and physicochemical mechanisms underlying physiological phenomena. The Pasteur Institute has followed with great success the road opened by its founder. Under the direction of Duclaux and of Roux, it has specialized in the investigation of bacteria and viruses, in the means of protecting human beings from their attacks, in the discovery of vaccines, sera, and chemicals for the prevention or the cure of diseases. The Rockefeller Institute undertook the survey of a broader field. The study of the agents responsible for diseases, and of their effects on animals and men, was pursued simultaneously with that of the physical, chemical, physicochemical, and physiological activities manifested by the body. Such investigations should now progress further. The entire man has to be brought into the domain of biological research. Each specialist must freely continue the exploration of his own field. But no important aspect of the human being should remain ignored. The method used by Simon Flexner in the direction of the Rockefeller Institute could be profitably extended to the organization of the biological or medical institutes of tomorrow. At the Rockefeller Institute, living matter is being studied in an exhaustive manner, from the structure of the molecules to that of the human body. However, in the organization of this vast ensemble of researches, Flexner did not impose any program on the staff of his Institute. He was content with selecting scientists who had a natural propensity for the exploration of these different fields. A similar policy could lead to the development of laboratories for the investigation of the psychological and sociological activities, as well as the chemical and physiological.

The biological institutes of the future, in order to be productive, will have to guard against the confusion of concepts, which we have mentioned as one of the causes of the sterility of medical research. The supreme science, psychology, needs the methods and the concepts of physiology, anatomy, mechanics, chemistry, physical chemistry, physics, and mathematics—that is, of all sciences occupying a lower rank in the hierarchy of knowledge. We know that the concepts of a science of higher rank cannot be reduced to those of a science of lower rank, that large-scale phenomena are no less fundamental than small-scale phenomena, that psychological events are as real as physicochemical ones. Mathematics, physics, and chemistry are indispensable but not basic sciences in the researches concerning living organisms. They are as indispensable as, but not more basic than, speaking and writing are, for instance, to a historian. They are not capable of constructing the concepts specific to the human being. Like the universities, the research institutions entrusted with the study of man in health and disease should be led by scientists possessing a broad knowledge of physiology, chemistry, medicine, and psychology. The biological workers of tomorrow must realize that their goal is the living organism and not merely artificially isolated systems or models. That general physiology, as considered by Bayliss, is a very small part of physiology. That organismal and mental phenomena cannot be dismissed. The studies to be undertaken in the laboratories for medical research should include all the subjects pertaining to the physical, chemical, structural, functional, and psychological activities of man, and to the relations of those activities with the cosmic and social environment.

We know that the evolution of humanity is very slow, that the study of its problems demands the lifetime of several generations of scientists. We need, therefore, an institution capable of providing for the uninterrupted pursuit for at least a century of the investigations concerning man. Modern society should be given an intellectual focus, an immortal brain, capable of conceiving and planning its future, and of promoting and pushing forward fundamental researches, in spite of the death of the individual researchers, or the bankruptcy of the research institutes. Such an organization would be the salvation of the white races in their staggering advance toward civilization. This thinking center would consist, as does the Supreme Court of the United States, of a few individuals; the latter being trained in the knowledge of man by many years of study. It should perpetuate itself automatically, in such a manner as to radiate ever young ideas. Democratic rulers, as well as dictators, could receive from this source of scientific truth the information that they need in order to develop a civilization really suitable to man.

The members of this high council would be free from research and teaching. They would deliver no addresses. They would dedicate their lives to the contemplation of the economic, sociological, psychological, physiological, and pathological phenomena manifested by the civilized nations and their constitutive individuals. And to that of the development of science and of the influence of its applications to our habits of life and of thought. They would endeavor to discover how modern civilization could mold itself to man without crushing any of his essential qualities. Their silent meditation would protect the inhabitants of the new city from the mechanical inventions which are dangerous for their body or their mind, from the adulteration of thought as well as food, from the whims of the specialists in education, nutrition, morals, sociology, etc., from all progress inspired, not by the needs of the public, but by the greed or the illusions of their inventors. An institution of this sort would acquire enough knowledge to prevent the organic and mental deterioration of civilized nations. Its members should be given a position as highly considered, as free from political intrigues and from cheap publicity, as that of the justices of the Supreme Court. Their importance would, in truth, be much greater than that of the jurists who watch over the Constitution. For they would be the defenders of the body and the soul of a great race in its tragic struggle against the blind sciences of matter.

5

We must rescue the individual from the state of intellectual, moral, and physiological atrophy brought about by modern conditions of life. Develop all his potential activities. Give him health. Reëstablish him in his unity, in the harmony of his personality. Induce him to utilize all the hereditary qualities of his tissues and his consciousness. Break the shell in which education and society have succeeded in enclosing him. And reject all systems. We have to intervene in the fundamental organic and mental processes. These processes are man himself. But man has no independent existence. He is bound to his environment. In order to remake him, we have to transform his world.

Our social frame, our material and mental background, should be rebuilt. But society is not plastic. Its form cannot be changed in an instant. Nevertheless, the enterprise of our restoration must start immediately, in the present conditions of our existence. Each individual has the power to modify his way of life, to create around him an environment slightly different from that of the unthinking crowd. He is capable of isolating himself in some measure, of imposing upon himself certain physiological and mental disciplines, certain work, certain habits, of acquiring the mastery of his body and mind. But if he stands alone, he cannot indefinitely resist his material, mental, and economic environment. In order to combat this environment victoriously, he must associate with others having the same purpose. Revolutions often start with small groups in which the new tendencies ferment and grow. During the eighteenth century such groups prepared the overthrow of absolute monarchy in France. The French Revolution was due to the encyclopedists far more than to the Jacobins. Today, the principles of industrial civilization should be fought with the same relentless vigor as was the *ancien régime* by the encyclopedists. But the struggle will be harder because the mode of existence brought to us by technology is as pleasant as the habit of taking alcohol, opium, or cocaine. The few individuals who are animated by the spirit of revolt might organize in secret groups. At present, the protection of children is almost impossible. The influence of the school, private as well as public, cannot be counterbalanced. The young who have been freed by intelligent parents from the usual medical, pedagogical, and social superstitions, relapse through the example of their comrades. All are obliged to conform to the habits of the herd. The renovation of the individual demands his affiliation with a group sufficiently numerous to separate from others and to possess its own schools. Under the impulse of the centers of new thought, some universities may perhaps be led to abandon the classical forms of education and prepare youth for the life of tomorrow with the help of disciplines based on the true nature of man.

A group, although very small, is capable of eluding the harmful influence of the society of its epoch by imposing upon its members rules of conduct modeled on military or monastic discipline. Such a method is far from being new. Humanity has already lived through periods when communities of men or women separated from others and adopted strict regulations, in order to attain their ideals. Such groups were responsible for the development of our civilization during the Middle Ages. There were the monastic orders, the orders of chivalry, and the corporations of artisans. Among the religious organizations, some took refuge in monasteries, while others remained in the world. But all submitted to strict physiological and mental discipline. The knights complied with rules varying according to the aims of the different orders. In certain circumstances, they were obliged to sacrifice their lives. As for the artisans, their relations between themselves and with the public were determined by exacting legislation. Each corporation had its customs, its ceremonies, and its religious celebrations. In short, the members of these communities renounced the ordinary forms of existence. Are we not capable of repeating, in a different form, the accomplishments of the monks, the knights, and the artisans of the Middle Ages? Two essential conditions for the progress of the individual are relative isolation and discipline. Each individual, even in the new city, can submit himself to these conditions. One has the power of refusing to go to certain plays or cinemas, to send one's children to certain schools, to listen to radio programs, to read certain newspapers, certain books, etc. But it is chiefly through intellectual and moral discipline, and the rejection of the habits of the herd, that we can reconstruct ourselves. Sufficiently large groups could lead a still more personal life. The Doukhobors of Canada have demonstrated that those whose will is strong can secure complete independence, even in the midst of modern civilization.

The dissenting groups would not need to be very numerous to bring about profound changes in modern society. It is a well-established fact that discipline gives great strength to men. An ascetic and mystic minority would rapidly acquire an irresistible power over the dissolute and degraded majority. Such a minority would be in a position to impose, by persuasion or perhaps by force, other ways of life upon the majority. None of the dogmas of modern society are immutable. Gigantic factories, office buildings rising to the sky, inhuman cities, industrial morals, faith in mass production, are not indispensable to civilization. Other modes of existence and of thought are possible. Culture without comfort, beauty without luxury, machines without enslaving factories, science without the worship of matter, would restore to man his intelligence, his moral sense, his virility, and lead him to the summit of his development.

6

A choice must be made among the multitude of civilized human beings. We have mentioned that natural selection has not played its part for a long while. That many inferior individuals have been conserved through the efforts of hygiene and medicine. But we cannot prevent the reproduction of the weak when they are neither insane nor criminal. Or destroy sickly or defective children as we do the weaklings in a litter of puppies. The only way to obviate the disastrous predominance of the weak is to develop the strong. Our efforts to render normal the unfit are evidently useless. We should, then, turn our attention toward promoting the optimum growth of the fit. By making the strong still stronger, we could effectively help the weak. For the herd always profits by the ideas and inventions of the élite. Instead of leveling organic and mental inequalities, we should amplify them and construct greater men.

We must single out the children who are endowed with high potentialities, and develop them as completely as possible. And in this manner give to the nation a non-hereditary aristocracy. Such children may be found in all classes of society, although distinguished men appear more frequently in distinguished families than in others. The descendants of the founders of American civilization may still possess the ancestral qualities. These qualities are generally hidden under the cloak of degeneration. But this degeneration is often superficial. It comes chiefly from education, idleness, lack of responsibility and moral discipline. The sons of very rich men, like those of criminals, should be removed while still infants from their natural surroundings. Thus separated from their family, they could manifest their hereditary strength. In the aristocratic families of Europe there are also individuals of great vitality. The issue of the Crusaders is by no means extinct. The laws of genetics indicate the probability that the legendary audacity and love of adventure can appear again in the lineage of the feudal lords. It is possible also that the offspring of the great criminals who had imagination, courage, and judgment, of the heroes of the French or Russian Revolutions, of the high-handed business men who live among us, might be excellent building stones for an enterprising minority. As we know, criminality is not hereditary if not united with feeble-mindedness or other mental or cerebral defects. High potentialities are rarely encountered in the sons of honest, intelligent, hard-working men who have had ill luck in their careers, who have failed in business or have muddled along all their lives in inferior positions. Or among peasants living on the same spot for centuries. However, from such people sometimes spring artists, poets, adventurers, saints. A brilliantly gifted and well-known New York family came from peasants who cultivated their farm in the south of France from the time of Charlemagne to that of Napoleon.

Boldness and strength suddenly appear in families where they have never before been observed. Mutations may occur in man, just as they do in other animals and in plants. Nevertheless, one should not expect to find among peasants and proletarians many subjects endowed with great developmental possibilities. In fact, the separation of the population of a free country into different classes is not due to chance or to social conventions. It rests on a solid biological basis, the physiological and mental peculiarities of the individuals. In democratic countries, such as the United States and France, for example, any man had the possibility during the last century of rising to the position his capacities enabled him to hold. Today, most of the members of the proletarian class owe their situation to the hereditary weakness of their organs and their mind. Likewise, the peasants have remained attached to the soil since the Middle Ages, because they possess the courage, judgment, physical resistance, and lack of imagination and daring which render them apt for this type of life. These unknown farmers, anonymous soldiers, passionate lovers of the soil, the backbone of the European nations, were, despite their great qualities, of a weaker organic and psychological constitution than the medieval barons who conquered the land and defended it victoriously against all invaders. Originally, the serfs and the chiefs were really born serfs and chiefs. Today, the weak should not be artificially maintained in wealth and power. It is imperative that social classes should be synonymous with biological classes. Each individual must rise or sink to the level for which he is fitted by the quality of his tissues and of his soul. The social ascension of those who possess the best organs and the best minds should be aided. Each one must have his natural place. Modern nations will save themselves by developing the strong. Not by protecting the weak.

7

Eugenics is indispensable for the perpetuation of the strong. A great race must propagate its best elements. However, in the most highly civilized nations reproduction is decreasing and yields inferior products. Women voluntarily deteriorate through alcohol and tobacco. They subject themselves to dangerous dietary regimens in order to obtain a conventional slenderness of their figure. Besides, they refuse to bear children. Such a defection is due to their education, to the progress of feminism, to the growth of short-sighted selfishness. It also comes from economic conditions, nervous unbalance, instability of marriage, and fear of the burden imposed upon parents by the weakness or precocious corruption of children. The women belonging to the oldest stock, whose children would, in all probability, be of good quality, and who are in a position to bring them up intelligently, are almost sterile. It is the newcomers, peasants and proletarians from primitive European countries, who beget large families. But their offspring are far from having the value of those who came from the first settlers of North America. There is no hope for an increase in the birth rate before a revolution takes place in the habits of thinking and living, and a new ideal rises above the horizon.

Eugenics may exercise a great influence upon the destiny of the civilized races. Of course, the reproduction of human beings cannot be regulated as in animals. The propagation of the insane and the feeble-minded, nevertheless, must be prevented. A medical examination should perhaps be imposed on people about to marry, as for admission into the army or the navy, or for employees in hotels, hospitals, and department stores. However, the security given by medical examination is not at all positive. The contradictory statements made by experts before the courts of justice demonstrate that these examinations often lack any value. It seems that eugenics, to be useful, should be voluntary. By an appropriate education, each one could be made to realize what wretchedness is in store for those who marry into families contaminated by syphilis, cancer, tuberculosis, insanity, or feeble-mindedness. Such families should be considered by young people at least as undesirable as those which are poor. In truth, they are more dangerous than gangsters and murderers. No criminal causes so much misery in a human group as the tendency to insanity. Voluntary eugenics is not impossible. Indeed, love is supposed to blow as freely as the wind. But the belief in this peculiarity of love is shaken by the fact that many young men fall in love only with rich girls, and vice versa. If love is capable of listening to money, it may also submit to a consideration as practical as that of health. None should marry a human being suffering from hidden hereditary defects. Most of man's misfortunes are due to his organic and mental constitution and, in a large measure, to his heredity. Obviously, those who are afflicted with a heavy ancestral burden of insanity, feeble-mindedness, or cancer should not marry. No human being has the right to bring misery to another human being. Still less, that of procreating children destined to misery. Thus, eugenics asks for the sacrifice of many individuals. This necessity, with which we meet for the second time, seems to be the expression of a natural law. Many living beings are sacrificed at every instant by nature to other living beings. We know the social and individual importance of renunciation. Nations have always paid the highest honors to those who gave up their lives to save their country. The concept of sacrifice, of its absolute social necessity, must be introduced into the mind of modern man.

Although eugenics may prevent the weakening of the strong, it is insufficient to determine their unlimited progress. In the purest races, individuals do not rise beyond a certain level. However, among men, as among thoroughbred horses, exceptional beings appear from time to time. The determining factors of genius are entirely unknown. We are incapable of inducing a progressive evolution of germ-plasm, of bringing about by appropriate mutations the appearance of superior men. We must be content with facilitating the union of the best elements of the race through education and certain economic advantages. The progress of the strong depends on the conditions of their development and the possibility left to parents of transmitting to their offspring the qualities which they have acquired in the course of their existence. Modern society must, therefore, allow to all a certain stability of life, a home, a garden, some friends. Children must be reared in contact with things which are the expression of the mind of their parents. It is imperative to stop the transformation of the farmer, the artisan, the artist, the professor, and the man of science into manual or intellectual proletarians, possessing nothing but their hands or their brains. The development of this proletariat will be the everlasting shame of industrial civilization. It has contributed to the disappearance of the family as a social unit, and to the weakening of intelligence and moral sense. It is destroying the remains of culture. All forms of the proletariat must be suppressed. Each individual should have the security and the stability required for the foundation of a family. Marriage must cease being only a temporary union. The union of man and woman, like that of the higher anthropoids, ought to last at least until the young have no further need of protection. The laws relating to education, and especially to that of girls, to marriage, and divorce should, above all, take into account the interest of children. Women should receive a higher education, not in order to become doctors, lawyers, or professors, but to rear their offspring to be valuable human beings.

The free practice of eugenics could lead not only to the development of stronger individuals, but also of strains endowed with more endurance, intelligence, and courage. These strains should constitute an aristocracy, from which great men would probably appear. Modern society must promote, by all possible means, the formation of better human stock. No financial or moral rewards should be too great for those who, through the wisdom of their marriage, would engender geniuses. The complexity of our civilization is immense. No one can master all its mechanisms. However, these mechanisms have to be mastered. There is need today of men of larger mental and moral size, capable of accomplishing such a task. The establishment of a hereditary biological aristocracy through voluntary eugenics would be an important step toward the solution of our present problems.

8

Although our knowledge of man is still very incomplete, nevertheless it gives us the power to intervene in his formation, and to help him unfold all his potentialities. To shape him according to our wishes, provided these wishes conform to natural laws. Three different procedures are at our disposal. The first comprises the physical and chemical factors, which cause definite changes in the constitution of the tissues, humors, and mind. The second sets in motion, through proper modifications in the environment, the adaptive mechanisms regulating all human activities. The third makes use of psychological factors, which influence organic development or induce the individual to build himself up by his own efforts. The handling of these agencies is difficult, empirical, and uncertain. We are not as yet well acquainted with them. They do not limit their effects to a single aspect of the individual. They act slowly, even during childhood and youth. But they always produce profound modifications of the body and of the mind.

The physical and chemical peculiarities of the climate, the soil, and the food can be used as instruments for modeling the individual. Endurance and strength generally develop in the mountains, in the countries where seasons are extreme, where mists are frequent and sunlight rare, where hurricanes blow furiously, where the land is poor and sown with rocks. The schools devoted to the formation of a hard and spirited youth should be established in such countries, and not in southern climates where the sun always shines and the temperature is even and warm. Florida and the French Riviera are suitable for weaklings, invalids, and old people, or normal individuals in need of a short rest. Moral energy, nervous equilibrium, and organic resistance are increased in children when they are trained to withstand heat and cold, dryness and humidity, burning sun and chilling rain, blizzards and fog—in short, the rigors of the seasons in northern countries. The resourcefulness and hardihood of the Yankee were probably due, in a certain measure, to the harshness of a climate where, under the sun of Spain, there are Scandinavian winters. But these climatic factors have lost their efficiency since civilized men are protected from inclemencies of the weather by the comfort and the sedentariness of their life.

The effect of the chemical compounds contained in food upon physiological and mental activities is far from being thoroughly known. Medical opinion on this point is of little value, for no experiments of sufficient duration have been made upon human beings to ascertain the influence of a given diet. There is no doubt that consciousness is affected by the quantity and the quality of the food. Those who have to dare, dominate, and create should not be fed like manual workers, or like contemplative monks who, in the solitude of monasteries, endeavor to repress in their inner self the turmoil of the secular passions. We have to discover what food is suitable for human beings vegetating in offices and factories. What chemical substances could give intelligence, courage, and alertness to the inhabitants of the new city. The race will certainly not be improved merely by supplying children and adolescents with a great abundance of milk, cream, and all known vitamines. It would be most useful to search for new compounds which, instead of uselessly increasing the size and weight of the skeleton and of the muscles, would bring about nervous strength and mental agility. Perhaps some day a scientist will discover how to manufacture great men from ordinary children, in the same manner that bees transform a common larva into a queen by the special food which they know how to prepare. But it is probable that no chemical agent alone is capable of greatly improving the individual. We must assume that the superiority of any organic and mental form is due to a combination of hereditary and developmental conditions. And that, during development, chemical factors are not to be separated from psychological and functional factors.

9

We know that adaptive processes stimulate organs and functions, that the more effective way of improving tissues and mind is to maintain them in ceaseless activity. The mechanisms, which determine in certain organs a series of reactions ordered toward an end, can easily be set in motion. As is well known, a muscular group develops by appropriate drill. If we wish to strengthen not only the muscles, but also the apparatuses responsible for their nutrition and the organs which enable the body to sustain a prolonged effort, exercises more varied than classical sports are indispensable. These exercises are the same as were practiced daily in a more primitive life. Specialized athletics, as taught in schools and universities, do not give real endurance. The efforts requiring the help of muscles, vessels, heart, lungs, brain, spinal cord, and mind—that is, of the entire organism—are necessary in the construction of the individual. Running over rough ground, climbing mountains, wrestling, swimming, working in the forests and in the fields, exposure to inclemencies, early moral responsibility, and a general harshness of life bring about the harmony of the muscles, bones, organs, and consciousness.

In this manner, the organic systems enabling the body to adapt itself to the outside world are trained and fully developed. The climbing of trees or rocks stimulates the activity of the apparatuses regulating the composition of plasma, the circulation of the blood, and the respiration. The organs responsible for the manufacture of red cells and hemoglobin are set in motion by life at high altitudes. Prolonged running and the necessity of eliminating acid produced by the muscles release processes extending over the entire organism. Unsatisfied thirst drains water from the tissues. Fasting mobilizes the proteins and fatty substances from the organs. Alternation from heat to cold and from cold to heat sets at work the multiple mechanisms regulating the temperature. The adaptive systems may be stimulated in many other ways. The whole body is improved when they are brought into action. Ceaseless work renders all integrating apparatuses stronger, more alert, and better fitted to carry out their many duties.

The harmony of our organic and psychological functions is one of the most important qualities that we may possess. It can be acquired by means varying according to the specific characteristics of each individual. But it always demands a voluntary effort. Equilibrium is obtained in a large measure by intelligence and self-control. Man naturally tends toward the satisfaction of his physiological appetites and artificial needs, such as a craving for alcohol, speed, and ceaseless change. But he degenerates when he satisfies these appetites completely. He must, then, accustom himself to dominate his hunger, his need of sleep, his sexual impulses, his laziness, his fondness for muscular exercise, for alcohol, etc. Too much sleep and food are as dangerous as too little. It is first by training and later by a progressive addition of intellectual motives to the habits gained by training, that individuals possessing strong and well-balanced activities may be developed.

A man's value depends on his capacity to face adverse situations rapidly and without effort. Such alertness is attained by building up many kinds of reflexes and instinctive reactions. The younger the individual, the easier is the establishment of reflexes. A child can accumulate vast treasures of unconscious knowledge. He is easily trained, incomparably more so than the most intelligent shepherd dog. He can be taught to run without tiring, to fall like a cat, to climb, to swim, to stand and walk harmoniously, to observe everything exactly, to wake quickly and completely, to speak several languages, to obey, to attack, to defend himself, to use his hands dexterously in various kinds of work, etc. Moral habits are created in an identical manner. Dogs themselves learn not to steal. Honesty, sincerity, and courage are developed by the same procedures as those used in the formation of reflexes—that is, without argument, without discussion, without explanation. In a word, children must be conditioned.

Conditioning, according to the terminology of Pavlov, is

nothing but the establishment of associated reflexes. It repeats in a scientific and modern form the procedures employed for a long time by animal trainers. In the construction of these reflexes, a relation is established between an unpleasant thing and a thing desired by the subject. The ringing of a bell, the report of a gun, even the crack of a whip, become for a dog the equivalent of the food he likes. A similar phenomenon takes place in man. One does not suffer from being deprived of food and sleep in the course of an expedition into an unknown country. Physical pain and hardship are easily supported if they accompany the success of a cherished enterprise. Death itself may smile when it is associated with some great adventure, with the beauty of sacrifice, or with the illumination of the soul that becomes immersed in God.

10

The psychological factors of development have a mighty influence on the individual, as is well known. They can be used at will for giving both to the body and to the mind their ultimate shape. We have mentioned how, by constructing proper reflexes in a child, one may prepare that child to face certain situations advantageously. The individual who possesses many acquired, or conditioned, reflexes reacts successfully to a number of foreseen stimuli. For instance, if attacked, he can instantaneously draw his pistol. But he is not prepared to respond properly to unforeseen stimuli, to unpredictable circumstances. The aptitude for improvising a fitting response to all situations depends on precise qualities of the nervous system, the organs, and the mind. These qualities can be developed by definite psychological agencies. We know that mental and moral disciplines, for instance, bring about a better equilibrium of the sympathetic system, a more complete integration of all organic and mental activities. These agencies can be divided into two classes: those acting from without, and those acting from within. To the first class belong all reflexes and states of consciousness imposed on the subject by other individuals or by his social environment. Insecurity or security, poverty or wealth, effort, struggle, idleness, responsibility, create certain mental states capable of molding human beings in an almost specific manner. The second class comprises the factors which modify the subject from within, such as meditation, concentration, will to power, asceticism, etc.

The use of mental factors in the making of man is delicate. We can, however, easily direct the intellectual shaping of a child. Proper teachers, suitable books, introduce into his inner world the ideas destined to influence the evolution of his tissues and his mind. We have already mentioned that the growth of other mental activities, such as moral, esthetic and religious senses, is independent of intelligence and formal teaching. The psychological factors instrumental in training these activities are parts of the social environment. The subjects, therefore, have to be placed in a proper setting. This includes the necessity of surrounding them with a certain mental atmosphere. It is extremely difficult today to give children the advantages resulting from privation, struggle, hardship, and real intellectual culture. And from the development of a potent psychological agency, the inner life. This private, hidden, not-to-be-shared, undemocratic thing appears to the conservatism of many educators to be a damnable sin. However, it remains the source of all originality. Of all great actions. It permits the individual to retain his personality, his poise, and the stability of his nervous system in the confusion of the new city.

Mental factors influence each individual in a different manner. They must be applied only by those who fully understand the psychological and organic peculiarities which distinguish human beings. The subjects who are weak or strong, sensitive or insensitive, selfish or unselfish, intelligent or unintelligent, alert or apathetic, etc., react in their own way to every psychological agency. There is no possibility of a wholesale application of these delicate procedures for the construction of the mind and the body. However, there are certain general conditions, both social and economic, which may act in a beneficial, or harmful, way on each individual in a given community. Sociologists and economists should never plan any change in the conditions of life without taking into consideration the mental effects of this change. It is a primary datum of observation that man does not progress in complete poverty, in prosperity, in peace, in too large a community, or in isolation. He would probably reach his optimum development in the psychological atmosphere created by a moderate amount of economic security, leisure, privation, and struggle. The effects of these conditions differ according to each race and to each individual. The events that crush certain people will drive others to revolt and victory. We have to mold on man his social and economic world. To provide him with the psychological surroundings capable of keeping his organic systems in full activity.

These factors are, of course, far more effective in children and adolescents than in adults. They should constantly be used during this plastic period. But their influence, although less marked, remains essential during the entire course of life. At the epoch of maturity, when the value of time decreases, their importance becomes greater. Their activity is most beneficial to aging people. Senescence seems to be delayed when body and mind are kept working. In middle and old age, man needs a stricter discipline than in childhood. The early deterioration of numerous individuals is due to self-indulgence. The same factors that determine the shaping of the young human being are able to prevent the deformation of the old. A wise use of these psychological influences would retard the decay of many men, and the loss of intellectual and moral treasures, which sink prematurely into the abyss of senile degeneration.

II

There are, as we know, two kinds of health, natural, and artificial. Scientific medicine has given to man artificial health, and protection against most infectious diseases. It is a marvelous gift. But man is not content with health that is only lack of malady and depends on special diets, chemicals, endocrine products, vitamines, periodical medical examinations, and the expensive attention of hospitals, doctors, and nurses. He wants natural health, which comes from resistance to infectious and degenerative diseases, from equilibrium of the nervous system. He must be constructed so as to live without thinking about his health. Medicine will achieve its greatest triumph when it discovers the means of rendering the body and the mind naturally immune to diseases, fatigue, and fear. In remaking modern human beings we must endeavor to give them the freedom and the happiness engendered by the perfect soundness of organic and mental activities.

This conception of natural health will meet with strong opposition because it disturbs our habits of thought. The present trend of medicine is toward artificial health, toward a kind of directed physiology. Its ideal is to intervene in the work of tissues and organs with the help of pure chemicals, to stimulate or replace deficient functions, to increase the resistance of the organism to infection, to accelerate the reaction of the humors and the organs to pathogenic agencies, etc. We still consider a human being to be a poorly constructed machine, whose parts must be constantly reënforced or repaired. In a recent address, Henry Dale has celebrated with great candor the triumphs of chemical therapeutics during the last forty years, the discovery of antitoxic sera and bacterial products, hormones, insulin, adrenalin, thyroxin, etc., of organic compounds of arsenic, vitamines, substances controlling sexual functions, of a number of new compounds synthetized in the laboratory for the relief of pain or the stimulation of some flagging natural activity. And the advent of the gigantic industrial laboratories where these substances are manufactured. There is no doubt that those achievements of chemistry and physiology are extremely important, that they throw much light on the hidden mechanisms of the body. But should they be hailed as great triumphs of humanity in its striving toward health? This is far from being certain. Physiology cannot be compared with economics. Organic, humoral, and mental processes are infinitely more complex than economic and sociological phenomena. While directed economics may ultimately be a success, directed physiology is a failure and will probably remain so.

Artificial health does not suffice for human happiness. Medical examinations, medical care, are troublesome and often ineffectual. Drugs and hospitals are expensive. Men and women are constantly in need of small repairs, although they appear to be in good health. They are not well and strong enough to play their part of human beings fully. The growing dissatisfaction of the public with the medical profession is, in some measure, due to the existence of this evil. Medicine cannot give to man the kind of health he needs without taking into consideration his true nature. We have learned that organs, humors, and mind are one, that they are the result of hereditary tendencies, of the conditions of development, of the chemical, physical, physiological, and mental factors of the environment. That health depends on a definite chemical and structural constitution of each part and on certain properties of the whole. We must help this whole to perform its functions efficiently rather than intervene ourselves in the work of each organ. Some individuals are immune to infections and degenerative diseases, and to the decay of senescence. We have to learn their secret. It is the knowledge of the inner mechanisms responsible for such endurance that we must acquire. The possession of natural health would enormously increase the happiness of man.

The marvelous success of hygiene in the fight against infectious diseases and great epidemics allows biological research to turn its attention partly from bacteria and viruses to physiological and mental processes. Medicine, instead of being content with masking organic lesions, must endeavor to prevent their occurrence, or to cure them. For instance, insulin brings about the disappearance of the symptoms of diabetes. But it does not cure the disease. Diabetes can be mastered only by the discovery of its causes and of the means of bringing about the repair or the replacement of the degenerated pancreatic cells. It is obvious that the mere administration to the sick of the chemicals which they need is not sufficient. The organs must be rendered capable of normally manufacturing these chemicals within the body. But the knowledge of the mechanisms responsible for the soundness of glands is far more profound than that of the products of these glands. We have so far followed the easiest road. We now have to switch to rough ground and enter uncharted countries. The hope of humanity lies in the prevention of degenerative and mental diseases, not in the mere care of their symptoms. The progress of medicine will not come from the construction of larger and better hospitals, of larger and better factories for pharmaceutical products. It depends entirely on imagination, on observation of the sick, on meditation and experimentation in the silence of the laboratory. And, finally, on the unveiling, beyond the proscenium of chemical structures, of the organismal and mental mysteries.

12

We now have to reëstablish, in the fullness of his personality, the human being weakened and standardized by modern life. Sexes have again to be clearly defined. Each individual should be either male or female, and never manifest the sexual tendencies, mental characteristics, and ambitions of the opposite sex. Instead of resembling a machine produced in series, man should, on the contrary, emphasize his uniqueness. In order to reconstruct personality, we must break the frame of the school, factory, and office, and reject the very principles of technological civilization.

Such a change is by no means impracticable. The renovation of education requires chiefly a reversal of the respective values attributed to parents and to school-teachers in the formation of the child. We know that it is impossible to bring up individuals wholesale, that the school cannot be considered as a substitute for individual education. Teachers often fulfill their intellectual function well. But affective, esthetic, and religious activities also need to be developed. Parents have to realize clearly that their part is indispensable. They must be fitted for it. Is it not strange that the educational program for girls does not contain in general any detailed study of infants and children, of their physiological and mental characteristics? Her natural function, which consists not only of bearing, but also of rearing, her young, should be restored to woman.

Like the school, the factory and the office are not intangible institutions. There have been, in the past, industrial organizations which enabled the workmen to own a house and land, to work at home when and as they willed, to use their intelligence, to manufacture entire objects, to have the joy of creation. At the present time this form of industry could be resumed. Electrical power and modern machinery make it possible for the light industries to free themselves from the curse of the factory. Could not the heavy industries also be decentralized? Or would it not be possible to use all the young men of the country in those factories for a short period, just as for military service? In this or another way the proletariat could be progressively abolished. Men would live in small communities instead of in immense droves. Each would preserve his human value within his group. Instead of being merely a piece of machinery, he would become a person. Today, the position of the proletarian is as low as was that of the feudal serf. Like the serf, he has no hope of escaping from his bondage, of being independent, of holding authority over others. The artisan, on the contrary, has the legitimate hope that some day he may become the head of his shop. Likewise, the peasant owning his land, the fisherman owning his boat, although obliged to work hard, are, nevertheless, masters of themselves and of their time. Most industrial workers could enjoy similar independence and dignity. The white-collar people lose their personality just as factory hands do. In fact, they become proletarians. It seems that modern business organization and mass production are incompatible with the full development of the human self. If such is the case, then industrial civilization, and not civilized man, must go.

In recognizing personality, modern society has to accept its disparateness. Each individual must be utilized in accordance with his special characteristics. In attempting to establish equality among men, we have suppressed individual peculiarities which were most useful. For happiness depends on one being exactly fitted to the nature of one's work. And there are many varied tasks in a modern nation. Human types, instead of being standardized, should be diversified, and these constitutional differences maintained and exaggerated by the mode of education and the habits of life. Each type would find its place. Modern society has refused to recognize the dissimilarity of human beings and has crowded them into four classes—the rich, the proletarian, the farmer, and the middle class. The clerk, the policeman, the clergyman, the scientist, the school-teacher, the university professor, the shopkeeper, etc., who constitute the middle class, have practically the same standard of living. Such ill-assorted types are herded together according to their financial position and not in conformity with their individual characteristics. Obviously, they have nothing in common. The best, those who could grow, who try to develop their mental potentialities, are atrophied by the narrowness of their life. In order to promote human progress, it is not enough to hire architects, to buy bricks and steel, and to build schools, universities, laboratories, libraries, art institutes, and churches. It would be far more important to provide those who devote themselves to the things of the mind with the means of developing their personality according to their innate constitution and to their spiritual purpose. Just as, during the Middle Ages, the church created a mode of existence suitable to asceticism, mysticism, and philosophical thinking.

The brutal materialism of our civilization not only opposes the soaring of intelligence, but also crushes the affective, the gentle, the weak, the lonely, those who love beauty, who look for other things than money, whose sensibility does not stand the struggle of modern life. In past centuries, the many who were too refined, or too incomplete, to fight with the rest were allowed the free development of their personality. Some lived within themselves. Others took refuge in monasteries, in charitable or contemplative orders, where they found poverty and hard work, but also dignity, beauty, and peace. Individuals of this type should be given, instead of the inimical conditions of modern society, an environment more appropriate to the growth and utilization of their specific qualities.

There remains the unsolved problem of the immense number of defectives and criminals. They are an enormous burden for the part of the population that has remained normal. As already pointed out, gigantic sums are now required to maintain prisons and insane asylums and protect the public against gangsters and lunatics. Why do we preserve these useless and harmful beings? The abnormal prevent the development of the normal. This fact must be squarely faced. Why should society not dispose of the criminals and the insane in a more economical manner? We cannot go on trying to separate the responsible from the irresponsible, punish the guilty, spare those who, although having committed a crime, are thought to be morally innocent. We are not capable of judging men. However, the community must be protected against troublesome and dangerous elements. How can this be done? Certainly not by building larger and more comfortable prisons, just as real health will not be promoted by larger and more scientific hospitals. Criminality and insanity can be prevented only by a better knowledge of man, by eugenics, by changes in education and in social conditions. Meanwhile, criminals have to be dealt with effectively. Perhaps prisons should be abolished. They could be replaced by smaller and less expensive institutions. The conditioning of petty criminals with the whip, or some more scientific procedure, followed by a short stay in hospital, would probably suffice to insure order. Those who have murdered, robbed while armed with automatic pistol or machine gun, kidnapped children, despoiled the poor of their savings, misled the public in important matters, should be humanely and economically disposed of in small euthanasic institutions supplied with proper gases. A similar treatment could be advantageously applied to the insane, guilty of criminal acts. Modern society should not hesitate to organize itself with reference to the normal individual. Philosophical systems and sentimental prejudices must give way before such a necessity. The development of human personality is the ultimate purpose of civilization.

13

The restoration of man to the harmony of his physiological and mental self will transform his universe. We should not forget that the universe modifies its aspects according to the conditions of our body. That it is nothing but the response of our nervous system, our sensory organs, and our techniques to an unknown and probably unknowable reality. That all our states of consciousness, all our dreams, those of the mathematicians as well as those of the lovers, are equally true. The electromagnetic waves, which express a sunset to the physicist, are no more objective than the brilliant colors perceived by the painter. The esthetic feeling engendered by those colors, and the measurement of the length of their component light-waves, are two aspects of ourselves and have the same right to existence. Joy and sorrow are as important as planets and suns. But the world of Dante, Emerson, Bergson, or G. E. Hale is larger than that of Mr. Babbitt.

The beauty of the universe will necessarily grow with the strength of our organic and psychological activities.

We must liberate man from the cosmos created by the genius of physicists and astronomers, that cosmos in which, since the Renaissance, he has been imprisoned. Despite its stupendous immensity, the world of matter is too narrow for him. Like his economic and social environment, it does not fit him. We cannot adhere to the faith in its exclusive reality. We know that we are not altogether comprised within its dimensions, that we extend somewhere else, outside the physical continuum. Man is simultaneously a material object, a living being, a focus of mental activities. His presence in the prodigious void of the intersidereal spaces is totally negligible. But he is not a stranger in the realm of inanimate matter. With the aid of mathematical abstractions his mind apprehends the electrons as well as the stars. He is made on the scale of the terrestrial mountains, oceans, and rivers. He appertains to the surface of the earth, exactly as trees, plants, and animals do. He feels at ease in their company. He is more intimately bound to the works of art, the monuments, the mechanical marvels of the new city, the small group of his friends, those whom he loves. But he also belongs to another world. A world which, although enclosed within himself, stretches beyond space and time. And of this world, if his will is indomitable, he may travel over the infinite cycles. The cycle of Beauty, contemplated by scientists, artists, and poets. The cycle of Love, that inspires heroism and renunciation. The cycle of Grace, ultimate reward of those who passionately seek the principle of all things. Such is our universe.

14

The day has come to begin the work of our renovation. We will not establish any program. For a program would stifle living reality in a rigid armor. It would prevent the bursting forth of the unpredictable, and imprison the future within the limits of our mind.

We must arise and move on. We must liberate ourselves from blind technology and grasp the complexity and the wealth of our own nature. The sciences of life have shown to humanity its goal and placed at its disposal the means of reaching it. But we are still immersed in the world created by the sciences of inert matter without any respect for the laws of our development. In a world that is not made for us, because it is born from an error of our reason and from the ignorance of our true self. To such a world we cannot become adapted. We will, then, revolt against it. We will transform its values and organize it with reference to our true needs. Today, the science of man gives us the power to develop all the potentialities of our body. We know the secret mechanisms of our physiological and mental activities and the causes of our weakness. We know how we have transgressed natural laws. We know why we are punished, why we are lost in darkness. Nevertheless, we faintly perceive through the mists of dawn a path which may lead to our salvation.

For the first time in the history of humanity, a crumbling civilization is capable of discerning the causes of its decay. For the first time, it has at its disposal the gigantic strength of science. Will we utilize this knowledge and this power? It is our only hope of escaping the fate common to all great civilizations of the past. Our destiny is in our hands. On the new road, we must now go forward.

THE END

INDEX

INDEX

INDEX

INDEX

INDEX

INDEX

INDEX

INDEX

INDEX

INDEX

INDEX